CONTENTS AT A GLANCE

NO LONGER
SEAT
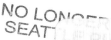

D0400052

Identity Shift

Identity Shift

Where Identity Meets Technology in the Networked-Community Age

Allison Cerra
Christina James

John Wiley & Sons, Inc.

Identity Shift: Where Identity Meets Technology in the Networked-Community Age

Published by
John Wiley & Sons, Inc.
10475 Crosspoint Boulevard
Indianapolis, IN 46256
www.wiley.com

Copyright © 2012 by Alcatel-Lucent

Published by John Wiley & Sons, Inc., Indianapolis, Indiana

Published simultaneously in Canada

ISBN: 978-1-118-18113-3
ISBN: 978-1-118-22721-3 (ebk)
ISBN: 978-1-118-22898-2 (ebk)
ISBN: 978-1-118-22881-4 (ebk)

Manufactured in the United States of America

10 9 8 7 6 5 4 3 2 1

No part of this publication may be reproduced, stored in a retrieval system or transmitted in any form or by any means, electronic, mechanical, photocopying, recording, scanning or otherwise, except as permitted under Sections 107 or 108 of the 1976 United States Copyright Act, without either the prior written permission of the Publisher, or authorization through payment of the appropriate per-copy fee to the Copyright Clearance Center, 222 Rosewood Drive, Danvers, MA 01923, (978) 750-8400, fax (978) 646-8600. Requests to the Publisher for permission should be addressed to the Permissions Department, John Wiley & Sons, Inc., 111 River Street, Hoboken, NJ 07030, (201) 748-6011, fax (201) 748-6008, or online at http://www.wiley.com/go/permissions.

Limit of Liability/Disclaimer of Warranty: The publisher and the author make no representations or warranties with respect to the accuracy or completeness of the contents of this work and specifically disclaim all warranties, including without limitation warranties of fitness for a particular purpose. No warranty may be created or extended by sales or promotional materials. The advice and strategies contained herein may not be suitable for every situation. This work is sold with the understanding that the publisher is not engaged in rendering legal, accounting, or other professional services. If professional assistance is required, the services of a competent professional person should be sought. Neither the publisher nor the author shall be liable for damages arising herefrom. The fact that an organization or Web site is referred to in this work as a citation and/or a potential source of further information does not mean that the author or the publisher endorses the information the organization or website may provide or recommendations it may make. Further, readers should be aware that Internet websites listed in this work may have changed or disappeared between when this work was written and when it is read.

For general information on our other products and services please contact our Customer Care Department within the United States at (877) 762-2974, outside the United States at (317) 572-3993 or fax (317) 572-4002.

Wiley also publishes its books in a variety of electronic formats and by print-on-demand. Not all content that is available in standard print versions of this book may appear or be packaged in all book formats. If you have purchased a version of this book that did not include media that is referenced by or accompanies a standard print version, you may request this media by visiting http://booksupport.wiley.com. For more information about Wiley products, visit us at www.wiley.com.

Library of Congress Control Number: 2011939638

Trademarks: Wiley and the Wiley logo are trademarks or registered trademarks of John Wiley & Sons, Inc. and/or its affiliates, in the United States and other countries, and may not be used without written permission. All other trademarks are the property of their respective owners. John Wiley & Sons, Inc. is not associated with any product or vendor mentioned in this book.

ABOUT THE AUTHORS

ALLISON CERRA has more than 15 years experience in the telecommunications industry, working in both the service provider and equipment vendor categories. She has led the marketing, sales, and product strategy efforts for several new technologies, including broadband, mobile, and video services. She holds two bachelor's degrees from the University of South Florida and Masters of Business Administration and Telecommunications degrees from Southern Methodist University. In addition to *Identity Shift*, Allison is also the co-author of *The Shift: The Evolving Market, Players and Business Models in a 2.0 World* and has published several whitepapers and articles about emerging end-user broadband trends and market potential for next-generation services. She has served on multiple industry and non-profit boards, including the World Affairs Council of Dallas/Fort Worth and the Telecommunications Industry Association.

CHRISTINA JAMES has 15 years experience in marketing and communications in the technology sector. She has helped define, launch, and support strategic communications solutions for service providers and for enterprises, particularly in the education and healthcare markets. She has also worked as a marketing consultant and freelance writer. Christina has Bachelor of Arts degrees in journalism and English from Southern Methodist University and a Master of Arts degree in American literature from the University of Texas at Austin. In addition to *Identity Shift*, Christina is also the co-author of *The Shift: The Evolving Market, Players and Business Models in a 2.0 World*. Christina enjoys travel in the United States and abroad and, in 2008, added adventure travel to her repertoire when she climbed Mount Kilimanjaro.

CREDITS

Executive Editor
Carol Long

Project Editor
Tom Dinse

Production Editor
Daniel Scribner

Copy Editor
Cate Caffrey

Editorial Manager
Mary Beth Wakefield

Freelancer Editorial Manager
Rosemarie Graham

Associate Director of Marketing
David Mayhew

Marketing Manager
Ashley Zurcher

Business Manager
Amy Knies

Production Manager
Tim Tate

Vice President and Executive Group Publisher
Richard Swadley

Vice President and Executive Publisher
Neil Edde

Associate Publisher
Jim Minatel

Project Coordinator, Cover
Katie Crocker

Compositor
Kate Kaminski, Happenstance Type-O-Rama

Proofreader
Jen Larsen, Word One

Indexer
Robert Swanson

Cover Designer
Ryan Sneed

Cover Image
Wiley In-house Design

ACKNOWLEDGMENTS

This book is based upon extensive research into the hearts, minds, and wallets of consumers. It is the culmination of a 12-month journey that endeavored to understand the complexities consumers face at the intersection where identity meets technology. At the same time, it aspired to comprehend the implications for a variety of stakeholders in the ecosystem—from service providers to advertisers to private companies to governmental authorities—as the ways in which we perceive ourselves and those around us fundamentally shift in a networked-community age.

While the authors had the privilege of documenting the study's findings through the pages in this book, the end result simply could not have been attained without the efforts of a highly focused team of experts reaching for the goal. In particular, the authors acknowledge:

- Kevin Easterwood, who drove the conceptualization of the issues and the thinking behind the results at each stage of the study. Without Kevin's insight and understanding, we would probably still be lost in the complexity of the initial question.
- Jerry Power, the key architect behind the research design and process. Jerry was instrumental from the first definitional statements to the final review of the research.
- Derek Richer, who drove the quantitative analysis process from beginning to end. Derek's effort evolved hypothesis into statistically validated fact.

Rarely does one have the honor of working with such an esteemed group of people, unafraid in pushing one another to unimaginable heights. The authors humbly thank our team for making this project possible.

CONTENTS

Who Are You?

It's not easy being green.

—KERMIT THE FROG

In 1976, the show that *Time* would ultimately declare "the most popular television entertainment on earth" hit the airwaves. The premise behind *The Muppet Show* was quite absurd: a variety show consisting of hundreds of puppets in commonplace and ridiculous scenarios. The genius behind the creation was Jim Henson, a man of humble beginnings who happened to come of age during the golden era of television. Inspired by the fantasy of Disney films and the wit of popular comedians, Henson concocted a world at the intersection of whimsy and comedy.

Henson's Muppets are indelibly blazoned on our cultural memory. As children, we remember learning the essentials of life from the fantastical creatures on our screen. As adults, we still identify with one or more of the puppets as reflections of our own selves or community. Henson did so much more than create a fresh approach to children's programming. Indeed, he invented a new world where we could all lose ourselves, even if for only 30 minutes a week.

Before Henson entered the scene, puppets were limited to the confines of a *real* world—their expressionless bodies bound by the physical constraints surrounding them. Henson created an entirely new world void of these natural limitations and, in so doing, breathed new life into his art. Gone were the one-dimensional, one-hand puppets confined to the stage inherent in any theatrical production. In Henson's world, the television itself was the stage and his famous Muppets came to life with a full range of motion to take advantage of the fanciful environments born of Henson's imagination. If Henson was the architect of the mayhem that ensued, his quintessential creation was Kermit the Frog.

Kermit entered our living rooms every week to entertain and educate. Perhaps his most lasting impression predates even the show he would ultimately *host*. In 1970, the now famous "Bein' Green" song debuted on the first season of another entertainment landmark, *Sesame Street*.[1] In it, Kermit laments about the challenges of being green, not the least of which is the monotony of just blending in, while he admires the notion of being something else:

> *It's not that easy being green;*
>
> *Having to spend each day the color of the leaves.*
>
> *When I think it could be nicer being red, or yellow, or gold …*
>
> *or something much more colorful like that.*[2]

Ask just about anyone—child or adult—if he has ever identified with Kermit's plight. Chances are, he has. You may recall a time when you wanted to be something more than you were or, like Kermit, something different. You may remember multiple times in your journey when you were more confused than clear about your own self-worth. You may find yourself struggling with how to pop your unique individuality against the landscape that surrounds you. Perhaps this internal war that many of us fight multiple times in our lives helps explain why the topic of identity is such an emotionally charged and bitterly contested subject in itself. In Kermit's case, there have been no less than 30 artists so moved by his message of finding value in one's self to record their own rendition of the now-famous "Bein' Green." The song belongs to more than just Kermit or these musicians. It could just be the anthem of a society wrestling with one of life's most profound questions: Who are we?

This question has led masses to the therapeutic couches of skilled therapists, spawned a market of self-help merchandise, and stimulated debate between scholarly thinkers through the ages. Although it has lurked in our collective subconscious as a species since we took our first steps on the planet, the question of who we are has only been exacerbated in its complexity in recent years.

Why? It would be trite to suggest that the world has changed, thereby redefining our identities in the process. After all, isn't this the conclusion of every generation as it laments how things were different in the good ol' days? But, just as Henson successfully re-created the possibilities of his craft with a world free of boundaries, our very own stage has transformed radically in just the past decade. And it's not just a change in our physical day-to-day lives that is at the source, but a creation of a new virtual world that has generated with it an expanded view of individual and collective identity.

To better understand just how profound this shift is, consider that human beings have been "wired" for a physical world. We have relied on physical objects, such as mirrors, to cast a reflection with which we identify, an image unique to ourselves. We have lived in a world where it has been easy for us to separate who we are at home from how we are perceived in the workplace. We have been equipped with sophisticated mind–body connections to automatically sense and detect threats and provoke the appropriate physical response to prolong our survival. We have equally advanced capabilities to filter out irrelevant stimuli in our environment to favor our success in exercising sound judgment.

These connections have stood the test of time to preserve our survival as a species in a physical world—a world where these very connections are most appropriate. But, what happens when we enter a world uninhibited by physical constraints but equally able to render our physical mind–body connections powerless? One might just be able to live out being red, yellow, or gold.

To answer the question of how our identity shifts on the global stage that now surrounds us, we must first understand how the notion of self has been enabled or threatened by some of the most transformational trends in the past few years. Among them are the following:

- Social networking has provided individuals with new ways of connecting, engaging, and partitioning their lifestyles based on social and professional pursuits.
- A virtual world void of physical constraints is a beacon of opportunity for those seeking to stimulate their passions and connect with like-minded individuals, while it simultaneously is home to faceless predators trolling for their next victim.
- The thousands of choices we make each day in the physical world pale in comparison to the billions of options available to us in cyberspace—each vying for a piece of our time, attention, or wallet.

Indeed, this *virtual world*, still nascent in its own right, has seen profound transformation in the past decade. Although the 1990s were characterized by the advent of the "digital age," the decade when computers saw their first ubiquitous connections to each other and servers in cyberspace, such connectedness soon gave rise to the "information age." For the first time, consumers were empowered with answers to the most mundane or profound questions and access to a global marketplace with the click of a mouse. Today, those same connections go much further than simply linking us with information. They have ushered in a new "networked-community age," one in which we are joined to one another in a pervasive virtual world that is integrated into our daily lives. Although many can admire how this age has transformed our lives based on its pervasiveness and influence on just about everything we do, few stop to consciously think of its effect on who we are becoming. Technology has played a pivotal role in enabling this new era, but it has also served to disarm our capabilities in navigating a world foreign to our natural senses.

In Search of Identity

Pick up any publication, and you will likely find one or more debates surrounding the contentious topic of identity. Indeed, some of the more emotionally charged stories in the "technology" section of reputable journals have little to do with technology at all but, rather, its role in protecting or exposing our sense of self. Whether journalists are panning the latest consumer privacy infringement, reporting the most recent cyberthreat, or bemoaning the most extreme youthful indiscretions plastered across social-networking sites, there seems to be no shortage of fodder for compelling news in this area.

Despite the proliferation of journalistic evidence, there is something conspicuously absent in the collective narrative. That is, how does a user view his identity? Not just his real identity, but how does that identity manifest itself in a virtual world? We're not suggesting that many brilliant researchers haven't risen to the enormous challenge of viewing an aspect of a user's identity. We've benefited from the fruits of their labor in understanding the nuances of privacy, the impact of social networking on our lifestyles, and the devastating wreckage cybercrime leaves behind for its victims. But there doesn't seem to be a view of identity that examines not just the psychological and anthropological contexts, but also the role of technology in bridging the gap to further self-preservation in a virtual world.

The critical intersection where identity meets technology is the core of this book. Its foundation is built on evidence from an exhaustive primary research study commissioned by Alcatel-Lucent, a global communications leader. The objectives were clear, if not ambitious: How does one's view of identity shift in a hyperconnected world? And what role does technology play in augmenting our relationships with others and perception of ourselves?

As part of the journey, we canvassed more than 5,000 consumers across the United States—with representation across geographic boundaries (rural, urban, suburban), generational cohort (Millennial, Gen X, Boomer), and life stage (teenagers, college students, couples, parents, and midlifers)—to measure the degree to which identity is influenced by generational or geographic factors versus maturational development as one essentially "grows up." As you can imagine, this was no easy task. We had to ensure that the baseline we were measuring was in itself understood before we could draw any meaningful conclusions. We had to understand the extent to which one's thoughts and actions are incongruent and the cause of the misalignment. For example, why are so many security-conscious individuals actively engaging in behaviors that are non-secure by their very definition? Are these folks unaware of the chasm and actually believe that they are protecting themselves? Have they hopelessly written off their ability to sufficiently defend themselves? Are there simply no better alternatives available today? Before we could address technology's role in creating and ultimately bridging the gap, we had to understand the essence of the disparity in the first place.

To do this, we preceded the quantitative study with an exploratory phase designed to view exactly how consumers behave when they forget others are watching. We visited 30 homes across the United States, coast to coast and in the heartland, from young college students to older empty nesters. We watched and filmed respondents for hours at a time doing what they normally do in their daily routine ... washing dishes, getting ready for work or school, and—that's right—connecting to the dozens of devices and technologies that surround them every second of their lives. We probed to understand why they do what they do when it comes to revealing or concealing intimate details about themselves or their loved ones. We sought for the emotional triggers that confound and perplex them as they attempt to maneuver in a virtual world. We documented the experience with hundreds of hours of behavioral and interview footage to support our conclusions. You will find the verbatim responses from some of these respondents throughout the pages of this book. For further context of the respondent's unique back story, turn to the Appendix for a brief profile of each.

By grasping the difference between what people think, what they say, what they do, and what they value, we can evaluate technology-based services that align thoughts, emotions, and actions—and eliminate the uneasiness we naturally find when these forces are out-of-sync (a phenomenon known in psychology as *cognitive dissonance*, which is discussed in Chapter 8).

The 3-P Model of Identity

We would never be so bold as to suggest that we are the authorities on self-identity. Look no further than the masterminds of scientific history, including Freud, Jung, and Erikson, for overwhelming evidence of how our identities are formed—in the *real* world. But, how does one's view of identity shift as we look to the virtual world within which so many of us dwell every day?

Being marketers at heart, we acknowledge our tendency to oversimplify a complex notion. But it is often this very simplicity that allows us to magnify the issues of most critical importance. After interviewing and studying our subjects, we submit that there is a construct for identity that captures our sense of self in a networked-community age. We call it *the 3-P Model*, for obvious reasons:

- **Presentation**—This refers to how an individual projects his image. Now, in the real world, this is fairly straightforward. I appear a certain way at work that is likely different from the image I project at home or church. I engage in appropriate behaviors in each of these environments based on established social norms. In short, my image is largely within my control within the real world. If I happen to make a fool of myself in a social setting, I can only hope that memories fade, gossip mills reach a saturation point, and that I "live" to see another day.

  But the virtual world is far more complex. It is no longer simply I who is in control of my identity, but any other person with a salacious photo or provocative opinion of me who can influence the same. Now, if I make a fool of myself in a social setting, the rumor mill becomes far more sustainable as propelled by texting fingers, cameraphone shots, and a well-trod virtual highway where memories persist. Whether I choose to identify with this *image* of myself or not, it exists as created by others, spawning an interesting tension point because I live in both real and virtual worlds. My image is no longer exclusively my own when opinions, images, and videos of me can travel across the world in a fraction of second.

- **Protection**—This pertains to how I address threats to my person, valuables, or loved ones. These threats can range from benign infractions on my privacy to more serious attempts of malicious harm. Although our mind–body connection is well established in the real world to handle threat (you no doubt remember learning about the "fight-or-flight" response in one of your early physiology classes), these weapons are rendered useless in a virtual world. When our hardwired danger nodes misfire in a virtual world, our ability to measure the extent of possible harm is compromised. My natural defense mechanisms are no match for virtual dangers.

- **Preference**—This relates to how the billions of choices offered in a virtual world can be simplified through profiling capabilities to deliver goods and services on our terms. In the real world, we have been programmed to quickly assimilate stimuli and make nearly immediate judgments as to their merit. Things that interest us naturally catch our attention. But, in an online world with choices lurking around every corner, how can we possibly discover options that could fall within our sweet spot without committing to rigorous search-and-retrieval efforts? Even for those of us able to dedicate the time perusing search engines or tapping our own social network for the perfect discovery, there is a wide range of untapped opportunities entering the virtual retail shelf every day. How can we possibly keep up without being consumed by the choices in the process? Many companies have responded by profiling our behaviors and proactively making suggestions for similar goods. Indeed, we have grown accustomed to these recommendation engines to support our daily shopping and surfing efforts at many sites.

  But, what if these profiling capabilities could go much further? It is not just the transaction history that we leave on a particular site that is useful, but also the thousands of clicks, texts, calls, and channel changes across every connected pursuit in our daily lives that become even more so. In a world where just about any ordinary item—from pill bottles to dog collars to washing machines—can be connected to the network, more will be known about us through the connected things we own than we could possibly share via irregular social-networking status updates. Whether we realize it or not, the trace we leave behind us today becomes more indelible in the future as more objects are connected. My digital footprint reveals who I am, whether I am conscious of the trail left behind me or not.

These three components—presentation, protection, and preference—intersect and influence one another to create a construct of identity that captures the thinking shared by respondents across our study. Because our virtual and physical worlds are becoming increasingly intertwined, this construct is not merely a view of virtual identity, but also relates to how shifts in any of these domains have a profound effect on our physical selves. Do you think that dangers in the virtual world are impotent in the physical sense? Just ask the latest victim of identity theft if the consequences faced online had irreparable effects on his physical life as well. At the risk of taking the alliterative mnemonic too far, all three Ps serve the "Master P"—that of *preservation* of our virtual and real-world identities. When preservation is attained, we have a new construct to support the traditional 4-P Model of Marketing—one in which marketers endeavor to promote their product in the right place at an optimal price. At the intersection of identity and technology, marketers are served by considering the consumer's presentation, protection, and preferences to preserve himself in a networked-community age.

This book is neither exclusively psychological nor technical. We cannot discuss identity without an appreciation of the multitude of scientific evidence that explains how we think, behave, emote, and socialize as human beings. At the same time, we cannot examine the identity crisis perpetuated by a virtual world without a grasp of how technology can serve to remedy the problems it helped create in the first place. As such, we draw from evidence across multiple scientific disciplines, including psychology, neurology, and sociology, to help us understand what makes us tick as human beings and how our sense of self plays a part in fundamentally defining who we are. At the same time, we provide insights from our significant body of primary research to reveal how technology providers can deliver greater market value and restore consumer confidence and control.

Our journey begins with a deeper look at the 3-P Model, with scientific and research evidence to define each of the Ps and examine the level of conflict within and between each domain. We then move to the universal laws uncovered through our ethnography work and substantiated by thousands of consumers in our quantitative study. Although you may find yourself disagreeing in some cases with what these laws suggest, we found them to be so universal in their application that their very existence lays the foundation of behavior and perceptions that unites consumers, no matter their age, socioeconomic status, or gender. Finally, we dive into the differences that emerge in how consumers view their identity, particularly as they mature through critical life stages from childhood to adulthood. Throughout the book, you'll find short stories reflecting current debates in the public discourse, unusual technologies yet to come, or general commentary relating to a chapter's topic. We call these bite-size narratives *Shift Shorts*, and they provide further color to the complexities of our subject. By the conclusion, you should expect a deeper understanding of the conflicts, aspirations, and realities that consumers face in attempting to properly define and sustainably preserve themselves as their real and virtual worlds become one.

Throughout these chapters, you will find implications to various stakeholders in a networked-community age. For technology players, there is overwhelming evidence provided by real respondents as to how they view identity in this new era and how new solutions or policies could augment the existing landscape. For regulators attempting to govern in this emerging space, there are attitudes expressed by these same subjects as to how or where government has a role to play. Last, but not least, every person reading these pages will likely see a glimpse of himself as a consumer struggling with many of the same issues plaguing our research participants. In any case, you will likely find yourself asking more questions by the end of each chapter, reflective of the complexity of this topic and the human nature behind it.

We may not answer the existential question of who you are (we'll leave that one to skilled and licensed therapists), but we give you a better understanding of who you could be in this hyperconnected world in which we now find ourselves—whether as a consumer struggling to control his identity or as a company or regulator attempting to empower him. In the end, you may find yourself wondering how your own identity could evolve once the physical tethers limiting your own range of motion are removed in a world without boundaries. Perhaps there is hope, even for those struggling to be so much more, like our hero Kermit. In the end, he finds that "Bein' Green"—or himself—is just right:

> *When green is all there is to be*
>
> *It could make you wonder why, but why wonder why?*
>
> *Wonder, I am green and it'll do fine, it's beautiful!*
>
> *And I think it's what I want to be.*[3]

Let's begin our journey into the mysteriously enigmatic, perennially fascinating, and uniquely beautiful world of ourselves.

The 3-P Model of Identity

In This Part

In this part, we explore how consumers view the construct of identity in a networked-community age. This introspective position considers how one's image is manifested between online and offline worlds (presentation); how one protects privacy, valuables, and loved ones (protection); and how one navigates the countless options available online (preference). The intersection of these three realms is where consumers offer their most valuable currency in a hyperconnected world—their trust.

Presentation: The Mirror Image

Our self image, strongly held, essentially determines what we become.

—Dr. Maxwell Maltz, author of *Psycho-Cybernetics: A New Way to Get More Living out of Life*

The myth of Narcissus, the story of the youth who fell in love with his own image and, unable to stop gazing at it, died as a result, has endured through the ages. Although the story varies slightly—with at least one version telling of a man who physically wasted away because of his mesmerization with his own reflection and others speaking of an equally macabre tale of suicide—the outcome remains the same: Narcissus's self-adulation led to his gruesome and untimely death. Is his story simply a masterpiece of Greek fiction? Possibly. But, you most likely have invoked his name pejoratively when describing someone you know (not yourself, of course) whose blinding conceit is simply intolerable.

Likely very few possess the maturity or self-awareness to identify with Narcissus's story directly, let alone see the perils of his unfortunate tale as red flags in their own lives. If you believe that his legend is relegated to the halls of fiction or merely serves as a colorful moniker for "other" self-obsessed human beings, this ominous narrative hits closer to home than you may think. Turn your attention from Greek mythology to human psychology and to the name Jacques Marie Émile Lacan. True, his name is not embedded in the fabric of our cultural vocabulary like that of Narcissus, nor does it conjure the same vivid imagery from a famed fable, but Lacan's contribution to psychology in framing our understanding of early identity gives him an equal immortality.

Lacan's contribution to psychology is what he coined the *mirror phase*, which is the critical phase of human development when an infant recognizes his or her reflected image. It occurs somewhere between the ages of six and 18 months, and its parallels to the Narcissus legend are astounding (perhaps explaining how this developmental period corresponds to Sigmund Freud's stage of primary *narcissism*). Lacan argued that it is during this time of our lives when we literally fall in love with our own image, as Narcissus did. Before this critical period, an infant has no understanding of his or her form in the world. The brain cannot comprehend the whole of the body, therefore one's self-understanding is fragmented. When the infant sees himself in the mirror, he realizes that the body forms a continuous whole. As the child realizes that he can manipulate and control the image staring back at him, he finds that this sense of mastery and control is pleasurable. However, it also stands in stark contrast to the child's limited motor control, which creates a fragmented body that lacks the unity and cohesion of the holistic form of the reflected image.[1]

Here's where things get really interesting. There are two simultaneous reactions to the mirror phase. The infant understands that he occupies space in this world. It is the first time, according to Lacan, that one identifies with the mirror image and perceives oneself as a complete entity, separate from others. But, at the same time that the image creates identification, it also causes alienation, as it confuses the infant who begins to associate the reflection with the self. The resulting offspring of this conflict is the ego. Because the reflection at this stage of life offers a more compelling vision of unity than the reality of the infant's own fragmentation, it is superior to the real and improves on it. In addition, the role of the ego is to protect the illusion of completeness and mastery. The infant sees something that is better than actuality. Because the image fills in the gaps of alienation and fragmentation, it is superior to reality, and the ego is born to delude the child from the truth.[2] This theory has found its way into pop culture to explain why we often identify with characters on the screen—a more perfect reflection of ourselves.[3]

Like Narcissus, we become enthralled with our image at a formative age. Like Narcissus, we are duped by that image into believing it is a superior view of reality. And, like Narcissus, this conflict within us can contribute to our own undoing (not as tragically, we hope), an undoing caused when a fantasized view of ourselves collides and often conflicts with reality.

Lacan's theory predates the birth of reality television by more than 40 years. It precedes the Internet's rise of social networking by some 55 years. Ask yourself this: If a simple mirror can have such a seismic impact on self-identification and perception, how much more is this effect exacerbated when one's image now encompasses a compilation of photos, videos, and self-expression strewn across the virtual highway? This *presentation* is an essential component of identity in a virtual world and refers to the image spawned by one's own deliberate efforts and the intended or fortuitous doings of others to create a reflection of self in a dimension where mirrors do not exist.

Worlds Colliding

Before the days when information traveled at the speed of light, life was simpler. We went about our day projecting an image consistent with our contextual and temporal view of our surroundings. For example, work environments, particularly those in a professional setting, demanded conformity—an expectation of image and behavior in harmony with the cultural mores of the company. This often unspoken requirement for a particular physical appearance manifested itself, among other ways, in the acceptable attire for the workgroup, leading to cultural colloquialisms to define a profession based on the color of one's "uniform"—white-collar versus blue-collar.

The networked-community age has broken down the barriers between our work and personal lives. The virtual world knows no time of day and no geographic boundaries or other constraints typical in our physical environment. If managing multiple roles (parent, spouse, employee, friend, and the like) was challenging even when the physical demarcation between these archetypes was at least fairly well understood, then the collision of physical and virtual planes creates more personas with dividing lines that are fuzzy at best. The resulting conflict that arises is not unlike the tension that creates the ego in our formative years, with individuals struggling to create a holistic image that is at least reflective, if not superior, to their actual selves.

Beth, one of our ethnography subjects and a white-collar professional, expresses the sentiment shared by millions like her:

> How do you manage multiple personalities—right? Because you've got kind of your work personality, your home personality and Facebook is kind of forcing them to kind of settle into one personality. I've got some friends from high school that will post stuff on Facebook on my wall that I'm almost kind of mortified because my coworkers, who may perceive me in a different way, would never expect that.

Beth's choice of words speaks volumes. There's a *perception* shared by her coworkers. That perception is based on an *expectation* of her image. And, when someone outside of her control posts something about Beth that contradicts the image she has worked so tirelessly to establish in her professional setting, her emotional response is one of humiliation, or as she puts it, *mortification*. This deeply emotional response is not scarce when speaking about something as fundamental as one's identity. And, in the case of presentation, it is the respondent's emotional trigger of embarrassment, or self-consciousness, that wields the most power.

The challenge of managing multiple online and offline personas is not unique to Beth. Consumers in a networked-community age must balance the opportunity to engage with a seemingly infinite universe of potential friends with the need to preserve one's image as those relationships evolve. In our study of more than 5,000 consumers in the United States, more than 80 percent have sent New Friend Requests to connect with new people. Interestingly, roughly the same number admit to ignoring Friend Requests to limit who sees their postings. Therein lies the conundrum as real and virtual worlds collide: how to enrich relationships otherwise impossible while maintaining an image consistent with one's self-perceived identity.

Look Away, Look Over Here

Perhaps the emotional pull of self-consciousness is so influential in our lives because of its early instantiation during our formative toddler years. Its first appearance coincides with when the ever-important mirror enters the scene once again. The critical stage when that uncomfortable feeling of embarrassment first stirs up anxiety within us is around two years of age. Prior to the age of two, an infant placed in front of a mirror will typically exhibit signs of pleasure—smiling, cooing, and the like—as he wields control over the movements of the reflection in front of him (consistent with Lacan's analysis of the mirror phase). However, at two years, radical new behaviors begin to emerge. Toddlers will sometimes freeze in front of their image or manifest behaviors of shyness, such as tucking their head in their shoulders or hiding their face behind their hands. According to Philippe Rochat of Emory University:

> It appears indeed that by 2–3 years young children do start to have others in mind when they behave. The expression of embarrassment that children often begin to display in front of mirrors at around this age is the expression of such "self-consciousness." They behave not unlike criminals hiding their face to the cameras. Their behavior indicates a drive to vanish from the public eyes, as if they came to grip via the experience of their own specular image of how they present

themselves to the world. Not only do they discover in the mirror that it is themselves, they also realize that it is themselves as perceived by others.[4]

The *mirror* in a virtual world is the representation of our own image, as communicated by ourselves through photos, videos, and other self-governed posts and as expressed by others through the lens in which they see us translated through these same forms of expression. In the real world, the ego protects the ideal of who we are through the mirror image as we see it. My reflection staring back at me is the more ideal version of myself and is colored by my own self-perception. However, in the virtual world, it is no longer simply *I* who is in control of my image. Others can post an unflattering photo or comment about me, and that has an equal, if not greater, impact on how my holistic image is represented online. In fact, these updates as posted by others are more credible in creating my image, ostensibly because they do not suffer the same bias that I am likely to impose to ensure the image represented is a more ideal version of myself. The irony is that the virtual world does not require substantive knowledge or even deliberate malice to potentially distort, if not disrupt, an image one has worked diligently to create. Consider the frustration of Amy, a mother and salesperson, and another of our ethnography respondents:

It bugged me. I ran a race this weekend with a girlfriend of mine who is on Facebook and then I got an email from another friend of mine saying, "Hey, I saw you ran a race with Joan this weekend. Nice job." And, I was so irritated about it because Joan did not ask me to put my picture up of the race on Facebook. And, that bugged me.

In this situation, Joan most likely meant no irritation, yet alone insult, to Amy by posting what may have seemed like an innocuous photo of a life experience on her Facebook page. But such an action clearly stirred up self-consciousness within her friend, who would prefer to dictate if and how to share that side of her image in her own way.

If self-consciousness is not in question, the mere lack of control over how one's image is represented becomes in itself disturbing. One-third of those in our quantitative study admit that it is difficult to control information or pictures about themselves as posted by others. As in the case of Andrew, a 20-something *digital native* in our study (one born and raised in a digital world) some are taking cautionary measures to choose not only what they share online, but with whom they associate based on the same.

> **Andrew:** *I don't like getting tagged in photos at all.*
>
> **Interviewer:** *What do you do about it?*
>
> **Andrew:** *I'll untag myself and if it's something that happens a lot, I'll just unfriend the person on Facebook, which is where it happens. I'm still real-life friends with people that I won't be friends with on Facebook just because of the way they share information.*

In our study, almost half of the respondents have admitted to untagging themselves in a photo online, possibly because of a self-consciousness that creeps in when they lose control over their image. But, self-consciousness has an alter ego—pride—that is equally rooted in the self-awareness developed through our formative years. Just as a child is likely to be strongly governed by feelings of embarrassment that first manifest themselves during his or her toddler years, the child is equally likely to be compelled to action based on the recognition by others for the first time during this developmental phase. The following literary quote, sourced by Mr. Rochat in his dissertation on self-awareness, describes the notion brilliantly:

> *There is a thing that happens with children: If no one is watching them, nothing is really happening to them. It is not some philosophical conundrum like the one about the tree falling in the forest and no one hearing it: that is a puzzler for college freshman. No. If you are very small, you actually understand that there is no point in jumping into the swimming pool unless they see you do it. The child crying, "Watch me, watch me," is not begging for attention; he is pleading for existence itself.[5]*

Although Amy reacts quite negatively to her image being posted without her approval, another natural, albeit completely opposite, response may entail flattery from the same stimulus. Brian, a young city worker and another of our ethnography respondents, offers a startlingly different response to discovering a photo of himself online:

> *It's fun to kind of be recognized. I think in a sense that it's nice to see pictures of you.*

As evidenced by the opposite reactions from Brian and Amy, what is seen as rewarding for one may be perceived as punitive to another. Whereas Amy may prefer to remain anonymous in her recreational pursuits, Brian enjoys the attention of being recognized by others. The polarizing viewpoints are corroborated in our quantitative study when it comes to the aspect of anonymity between real and virtual worlds. Although half of the respondents agree that there is less privacy online than in the real world, the other half state the opposite.

Polarizing opinions and charged emotional reactions reflect the inherent complexity of presentation. From the time we discover ourselves as unique entities in this world—a discovery that occurs very early in our development—human beings strive for security and significance, two primal needs that remain with us through our lives. We discuss security in a later chapter, but the quest for significance is at least partly influenced by our ability to project an attractive image to others. When this significance is attained or threatened, our conditioned emotional response is pride (Brian) or self-consciousness (Amy), respectively.

Mirror, Mirror

In a virtual world born from search-and-retrieval tactics, it is only natural that consumers turn to searching about themselves to reveal the blemishes in their reputation. According to a Microsoft study, 42 percent of Americans have admitted to Googling themselves, with 59 percent, 56 percent, and 36 percent of those in Germany, France, and the United Kingdom indicating the same.[6] For those quick to label this significant portion of adults as narcissists or paranoids, don't conflate self-awareness with self-conceit. Whether you choose to be self-aware or not, that doesn't prevent others from forming a perception about you based on the information acquired through today's traditional online search retrieval tools. And, human resource professionals are among the key groups willing to use such tools to form an opinion about you as a candidate, with 79 percent of U.S. hiring personnel saying that they review online information about job applicants and an astonishing 70 percent admitting to rejecting candidates based on what they have found.[7]

In addition, rather than just Googling themselves when curiosity or need strikes, more than 10 percent in our study have gone so far as to establish a Google Alert to avoid potentially missing information posted about themselves. Although these search capabilities can get one closer to answering the question of how one is perceived online, the answer is limited to the cleanliness, or accuracy, of the data about the individual. Just ask Amy, our runner from above. Joan may never have tagged her in that photo, but that wouldn't stop one of their mutual friends from recognizing Amy's image just the same. A simple Google search or alert would have failed to notify Amy of the photo's existence if her full name did not accompany it through a tag. And, with a smartphone on virtually every hip, the chances of your image being recorded and posted online by anyone—friend, family member, or random stranger—without your consent are more real every day. Today's popular search alternatives fall short in addressing this unclean, non-tagged content, a problem further compounded by the loads of "dirty" data that litter the virtual highways. Perhaps this void helps explain why a service that monitors one's image (not just name) across cyberspace (not just limited to tagging) is among the most popular tested in our study.

Despite the fact that self-monitoring behaviors are increasingly part of our social fabric in an online world, there is still the stigma of being labeled or misunderstood as a narcissist. In the case of Rebecca, a 40-something mother and aerobics instructor, there is one piece of information about her in cyberspace that she wishes didn't exist—her date of birth. Oddly, the concern is not one of protection (which one might assume because a date of birth is one personal bit of information potentially useful to identity thieves). Instead, it's one of presentation. And, even stranger, this is an image problem easily correctable by Rebecca herself. After all, she only need remove the information from her social networking page. Yet, she doesn't. And the reason she leaves this one piece of herself exposed is the perception of conceit that may accompany its removal.

> *Interviewer: Has anything appeared about you that you wish hadn't?*
>
> *Rebecca: My age. My year of birth. Somebody said, "Oh I was sniffing around on your Facebook page and I saw you were born in '63. Whoa, you look hot." And I thought to myself, "I don't remember putting that down." But then I thought, "Well, I'm not going to take it away because that's really vain."*

Rebecca has an image to protect. Part of that image involves appearing nonchalant about something that really irks her (her age), even to the extent that she willingly keeps this information exposed for others to see. But what Rebecca labels vanity is commonplace necessity in a virtual world. Nearly half of our respondents identified with presentation-oriented concerns, dwarfing those who psychologically align with protection- or preference-related psychometrics. Even more telling, these presentation-oriented consumers are also the most likely to purchase services to manage their identities in an online world. In the case of cyberspace, presentation, or image, matters. For many, it matters more than safer protection or smarter preference services. That's hardly a finding relegated to the extreme fringes of the self-obsessed. It's actually far more pervasive than you (or they) may think.

Narcissus is more than a Greek mythological victim. He lives, to a certain extent, in all of us who seek to project the right image at the right time to the right audience. Such an impulse is hard enough to manage in a physical world, where contextual boundaries exist. It is nearly impossible in a virtual world that knows no boundaries or universal mores. Although the buzz in the headlines gravitates to a culture consumed by narcissism—and it may be true that younger generations are more self-aware and savvy about how to project themselves in an online world that has been their domain since birth—we submit that the more accurate reality is that the compulsion to depict an attractive presentation naturally exists, to a degree, in each of us.

Still, that doesn't stop the stigma of being labeled narcissistic from creeping into our social consciousness. As Jack, a 20-something college student, sagely advises, "You don't want to be too, uh—what's it called?—narcissistic about yourself." Although narcissism may be criticized, its reality is commonplace, perhaps helping to explain why the American Psychiatric Association is considering classifying the disorder along a continuum, which recognizes there is a bit of narcissism in all of us.[8] It is not merely "narcissists" who seek to protect a fragile ego developed in childhood, but an army of masses struggling to find their "mirror" in a networked-community era.

SHIFT SHORT: THE CIVILIAN PAPARAZZI

Even though we may not admit it publicly, most of us have at some point indulged in the culture of celebrity obsession. Tabloid media and celebrity "news" are in some ways so pervasive that we seem to absorb the latest goings-on of Lindsay Lohan and her ilk almost by osmosis. From the perspective of the Deadspins, TMZs, and Access Hollywoods of the world, public figures like actors and athletes choose to be famous, and in doing so, they are accepting a measure of media intrusion and ceding some ownership of their image to the world at large. It goes with the territory.

One man, however, is blurring the line between public and private even further. Nik Richie runs a website called TheDirty.com, where you can post pictures and comments about everyday people the same way Perez Hilton does for celebrities. Richie calls posters *The Dirty Army* and refers to his site as a home for *civilian paparazzi*. Some post pictures of exes or rivals to slam them with wild accusations. Some post pictures of themselves or others so that Nik and TheDirty.com visitors can judge their attractiveness. One poster put up a picture of an attractive young woman in a bikini, commenting that she is the "sweetest girl you'll ever meet" and a "total babe." The poster says, "I can't really find anything bad about her, so I figured she'd be perfect for a 'would you?'" Richie responds that he wouldn't, "She is my type, but I am going to pass because of her elongated chin."[9]

Whether the young woman in question knows she has been served up for Richie's hypercritical commentary is—as far as TheDirty.com is concerned—a non-issue. Appearing on an episode of *Dr. Phil*, Richie faced one young woman whose picture was lifted from her MySpace page and submitted to the site. Richie posted a comment that she looked like a man, and visitors added even more harsh critiques, including saying that she had herpes. Sitting across from the crying young woman, Richie distanced himself from the comments while defending the site by saying that she was entering into the public sphere by posting her picture on MySpace.[10] The site does have a Post Removal request form if you are in the picture, you own the copyright to a photo, or your contact information is included in a post or comment. However, the site disclaimer states:

> TheDirty.com, the world's first ever reality blogger, is all about gossip and satire. The content that is published contains rumors, speculation, assumptions, opinions, and factual information. Postings may contain erroneous or inaccurate information. All images are credited to their original location. The owner of this site does not ensure the accuracy of any content presented on TheDirty.com.

Richie's lawyer told Dr. Phil that Richie isn't legally responsible for the posts of others or their impact—even when the talk show host specifically brought up the possibility of someone harming themselves as a result of harsh critiques. Apparently, however someone may react to having their image co-opted and whatever the result, in Richie's view, it just goes with the territory. On TheDirty.com, we're all public figures as soon as someone else decides we are by snapping our photo and posting it online.

2

Protection: Exposing the Blind Spots

People protect what they love.

—Jacques Yves Cousteau, explorer

When you first meet her, this 44-year-old mother of three seems like a normal person. However, there is something quite abnormal lying beneath the surface. She laughs in the face of what would cause many to recoil in terror. She pets snakes as though they were playful kittens. She experiences horror movies with delight. And, by her own diary admissions, she engages in behavior that some would find unusual if not outright dangerous. While walking through a park one night, a man threatened her with a knife to the throat. A church choir practicing could be heard nearby. She calmly replied to the knife-wielding druggie, "If you're going to kill me, you're gonna have to go through my God's angels first." Apparently, even the drug-addled can sense abnormality, as this odd response was enough to send the perpetrator running in the other direction. The next night, she continued about her routine and walked through the same dark park, business as usual.[1]

This is not the product of a fiction author's imaginative musings. She is a real 44-year-old mother of three, known to the scientific community as simply "SM." The cause of her abnormality lies in a gland shaped like a pair of almonds and located in what is referred to as the *emotional brain*, inward from the temples. Though relatively small in size, the amygdala gland can propel our entire body into immediate action based on its ability to detect danger within milliseconds. SM possesses a rare congenital disorder that began to destroy her amygdala in early childhood, rendering this part of her brain completely dysfunctional by the time she was a pre-teen.[2]

The amygdala is just one example illustrating how complex our brains are with patterns and workflows designed to incorporate full sensory perception and activate the body with the appropriate response. The brain has three major components, each with a different purpose:

- **Brain stem**—The brain stem handles basic survival skills in all animals and is commonly known as the *reptilian*, or in more casual vernacular, "lizard" brain.
- **Emotional brain**—In mammals, the emotional or limbic brain is wrapped around the brain stem.
- **Prefrontal brain**—In humans, the higher prefrontal brain is developed to handle logical thought, language, and problem-solving.[3]

Multiple mappings exist between each of these three functional areas of the brain to govern our thoughts, emotions, and body responses. But the highly traveled pathways going from the emotional brain to the brain stem are most interesting in analyzing the mind–body connection engineered for our most primal protection.

Continuing with the case of SM, consider how one blind spot in the brain's complex inner workings can create such unusual and reckless behavior. The *amygdala* is the brain's opportunity and danger detector. Within fractions of a second, it reads emotions from others and activates our own for fight, flight, or approach behavior. It is so sophisticated in its design that it is able to sense and detect the slightest nuance in the dozens of facial muscles whose only purpose is to signal a person's emotional state. It can do the same simply by assessing a person's tone of voice. It has been defined as the gateway to trust by determining if someone is safe or dangerous. It can even spot cues of subtle inconsistency in someone's words and behavior to determine if the person is trustworthy or deceptive. Although the strength of this capability differs in each of us, some have been reported to be able to separate truth from deception with nearly 100 percent accuracy.[4]

That's just one gland in one component of the brain. You don't have to imagine the exponential mappings of the brain's advanced design in reading cues from the physical environment to engender the right response from the body. There are scores of scientific experiments proving that the connections exist. Consider the development of these mappings over the generations of humankind since our first existence—an existence in the physical world. But, because many of these connections rely on the brain's ability to map sensory perceptions of our physical environment, how do they succeed in a virtual world that can limit, if not deliberately confuse, the same? How can the mind–body connection prevail in an artificial world to protect the real human being on the other end of the device?

The Blind Spots

Our primal protection responses are literally programmed into our DNA. At the same time, when just one misfire occurs, the results can be profound, as in the case of SM, but also as evidenced in the host of psychological disorders identified by the scientific community up to this point. When the threat can be seen, our body is primed to respond. But, what if the threat is invisible? Or, even more confounding, what if it exists in some machine, or *bot*, in the virtual sky?

Science fiction novelists have conjured a world dominated by machines for decades. It appears that the imagination of fiction authors is not as farfetched in a virtual world sustained by machinery, and the threat detected by Bob, an ethnography subject, is all too real:

> I think the information is ending up in supercomputers and it's like any other society—if the information falls into the wrong hands, that's when it becomes a problem. So, that's probably a fear that a lot of Americans have when they think of the supercomputers keeping track of everything.

Although some may consider Bob's rant to be paranoid, the fear factor in a virtual world is shared by other respondents. Even if others don't share Bob's concern of "supercomputers" in the sky, they still question the wisdom of putting their trust in those with the most power to violate it. Consider Todd, another of our ethnography respondents and one much younger than Bob:

> The thing I'm thinking is, if we have all these people that know how to go in and make all these programs, then we also have all these people that could just go in and access our accounts. I would imagine that if they can write a program or build a program or anything like that for us to use, that they can just do the same kind of thing and just bypass the password and go in and look at your stuff.

And the problem extends beyond the misuse of a typical program. Others are perplexed about how to trust nameless, faceless individuals able to camouflage the nuances of facial expression, tone of voice, mannerisms, and actual identity behind the veil of an anonymous keyboard. Consider Julie, a 30-something soccer mom, as she envisions a new type of service, one that could render truthful information about the anonymous person on the other end of the connection:

> You know when it's a fake driver's license, right? So, you can't fake this certain person is this age—you know—this information on them.... All that information needs to come out. And it would be their identity—their real identity.

Whether the threat comes from a bot, programmer, hacker, or casual acquaintance, sensory deprivation in a virtual world creates new blind spots that confound our automatic abilities to protect ourselves and discern deception. The opportunity is not for technology to fully inoculate the innocent from the predatory. After all, technology cannot substitute for the sophisticated judgment capabilities resident in the higher-order emotional and prefrontal brain structures mentioned earlier. However, just as technology has allowed for the creation of a world where others can mask their identities—either for harmless or malicious intent—it can also serve to remedy the blind spots that naturally occur as a result. Much of this prescription is possible simply by augmenting the landscape with tools that allow users to manage the dangers online. We're not simply speaking of anti-virus and firewall solutions that have existed for some time. These valuable elements serve an important purpose—to protect the device and information contained therein from dangerous attack, an essential shield for any terminal connected to a broad network. The capabilities we refer to are conspicuous by their absence in a world that connects not only machines but also the human beings behind them, each with a real capacity to be harmed.

The Extent of Violation

Not all dangers are created equal. In the physical world, a threat can be as relatively harmless as an affront, up to a more dangerous assault. The virtual world is no different, although the threats are more complex to discern. The concern shared by Bob above of supercomputers tracking our every move may seem extreme to some, but the digital footprint we consciously or unconsciously leave behind us with every click, call, or channel change adds up to a wealth of information. When used positively, the tracking of our habits and behaviors can help shape our virtual and physical worlds to pinpoint the targeted content, people, or offers tailored and practically guaranteed to meet our unique needs, especially as more information is revealed and collected.

But, when used negatively, these same habits and behaviors are weapons used against us by annoying solicitors or more insidious predators.

In the case of advertising, this nuisance factor is not a problem best solved by technology, but by company policy. As consumers, we are literally bombarded with thousands of impressions every day by solicitors attempting to woo our hearts such that we are compelled to open our wallets. This market has allowed us to enjoy many services we love for "free," including television, radio, and the majority of Internet sites, simply in exchange for the ability to deliver an advertiser's message. We expect this. After all, how could most media subsist if not with the revenues derived from advertisers? The alternative would result in higher prices for many of the services we enjoy, and most would likely find this outcome less attractive.

However, when our own behaviors are tracked without our knowledge, as buried within obfuscated privacy policies that are far too common in the virtual world, the resulting offense is more obvious. Worse yet, because consumers may not realize that their desire for privacy is in conflict with their online behaviors or perhaps have no alternative recourse to align the two, the need for clear and conspicuous policies becomes more pronounced. Although privacy was a hot topic among many ethnography subjects, we also witnessed behavior of these same respondents blindly accepting arduous policy statements to get to a site or content desired. Is this a case in which consumers should take responsibility for not thoroughly reading a policy before impulsively continuing about their online pursuits? Perhaps. But we submit that many of these onerous policies are clearly written by lawyers for lawyers (a necessary evil born of a litigious society). As such, they unintentionally create an additional blind spot, indeed as many respondents blindly click by the technical legalese, given its overwhelming presence in these "authorizations." And, even if consumers attempt to remedy this blind spot by changing their privacy settings, 20 percent of those in our study admit difficulty in doing so. Perhaps this point helps explain why nearly 60 percent of respondents prefer simpler, as opposed to more comprehensive, privacy settings.

For these consumers, it is not technology they crave, but respect. Several companies have made significant profits providing consumers with valuable services for "free" by monetizing the clicks made by the user to serve up targeted advertising. In fact, this has been a key differentiator of Internet advertising, which has made it such an attractive media for advertisers and users alike (a key topic that we explore in the next chapter). However, when such information is proffered to the highest third-party bidder without the user's explicit, opt-in consent, the questionable blind spot once again enters the picture to diminish the consumer's defense mechanisms. In addition, the blind spot in this case does more than simply disarm consumers—it also has an impact on the image of companies attempting to serve them.

As we cover throughout this book, consumers are complex. They have become accustomed to "free" services made possible through advertising, yet their expectations about how their information is collected and used gives them pause. In a networked-community age, the "price" they pay for said services is information that identifies them as users, such as through the unique address assigned to their computers, IPTV set-top boxes, or mobile devices. In our study, more than 40 percent identify with the statement that, to get the most out of online services, one must provide a certain amount of information. Among the most heavily network-engaged consumers in the study, the figure jumps to more than 50 percent. Furthermore, nearly 90 percent of those in our study agree that all technology players—service providers, social networking sites, and search companies—should be governed by the same laws and regulations regarding the collecting, analyzing, and sharing of online data. Yet, despite these findings, our data also conclude that consumers will and do hold companies to measurably different standards when it comes to privacy permissions. In fact, the consumer's perception of the company has a significant impact on the degree to which he allows his digital footprint to be monetized, marking an interesting collision where company and consumer identities intersect.

As such, one point of competitive differentiation in a networked-community age will be the degree of respect afforded to the consumer. For some companies, that respect will be measured in practical terms, with fair, conspicuous, and understandable policies governed by the same mechanisms that allow users to easily control and adapt their privacy settings at any time. In our quantitative study, consumers gravitate toward options that place their privacy within their direct control. In fact, among the most favorable company policy positions to engender consumer trust is a provider's requirement for opt-in consent before sharing any information about the user with other interested third parties; among the most damaging inhibitors to trust was sharing the same information with affiliates unless the consumer advises otherwise (the opt-out approach). Here again we have the interesting contradiction that is the U.S. consumer. Most services rely on the opt-out approach today, and several well-known companies have established viable business models with it as their foundation. Despite this, other companies looking to do the same may discover a market less tolerant of their right to play. An opt-in approach appeals to consumers who are becoming increasingly aware that their information is up for grabs, and who are more comfortable deciding when and to whom this veritable gold mine is offered. The potential reward to companies that understand this respect boundary is significant according to our study. More than 80 percent of consumers say that they are very or somewhat comfortable sharing information if they have control over when personal preferences, location, or availability is revealed to others.

In contrast to the annoying nuisances created by unwelcomed spammers hiding behind company policies, there are far more serious threats lurking online. Although technology is never a substitute for common sense, it can support consumers in a virtual world where primal defense mechanisms are ill-suited. In these extremes, it is not a case of respecting consumers' privacy (a relatively tame endeavor, by comparison), but an issue of protecting them and their loved ones from those seeking to do them irreparable harm. As we discuss in a future chapter, parents, in particular, are lacking in their means to protect their children, who are far more adept in navigating a virtual world. Some parents, like our ethnography respondent Susan, resort to ineffective, prehistoric Band-Aids to compensate. Susan is the mother of a teenage son who is immersed in the world of online console gaming. While attempting to balance her son's desire for fun and social interaction with her role as a parent to protect him, she takes matters into her own hands (literally) when he engages with others using his gaming headset:

> **Susan:** *I'll just come down and put my hand out and he kinda knows. He's got to take it [the headset] off and let me listen. So I kinda sneak in and listen to make sure.*
>
> **Interviewer:** *And what are you checking for when you listen?*
>
> **Susan:** *Mostly older adult people.*

Although one would be misguided to judge Susan's sincere attempts to protect her child from harmful strangers, there is no doubt that her approach leaves much to be desired. Susan is using her sensory defense mechanisms acquired in a real world—such as listening for tone of voice or profane content (another concern expressed by her during the interview)—to assess danger in a virtual environment. In fact, nearly 40 percent of parents in our study admit difficulty in protecting their children from inappropriate content and offensive language online. Unfortunately, physical mechanisms like those used by Susan are of meager effectiveness in a pervasive virtual world waiting 24 hours a day, seven days a week to attract curious teenagers. What if technology could reveal the danger in a more sustainable and effective way and alert Susan to the possible threats to her child, similar to the way she relies on her brain's mappings to do the same in the physical world?

This actually is not an impossible endeavor. Since the dawn of media and live broadcasts, we have used slight transmission delays to allow manual removal—or muting out–of offensive content spewed over the public airwaves. The technology used to support live broadcast content seems dated, in comparison, to today's highly evolved, intelligent IP-based networks that are light-years from yesterday's manual intervention techniques. Look no further than IPTV-based services, such as AT&T's U-verse, for an example. Using one connection to the home, AT&T is able to deliver voice, data, and video traffic. The network adjusts to the user's behavior in the household to offer the desired service at the right performance. When the network detects that more bandwidth is needed for a particular service—such as when the consumer changes channels to a bandwidth-hungry HDTV show—it automatically gives the HD stream a higher priority to allocate network resources accordingly. In technology circles, this quality of service (QoS, as it is known in industry parlance) is typically seen as an enabler to deliver higher bandwidth speeds dynamically and reprioritize voice, video, or data traffic accordingly. It certainly does so, but what if we turn QoS on its head to address Susan's concern for her child?

What if QoS could be used to slightly delay voice traffic coming through an audio headset connected to a gaming console? What if those voice packets could be systematically recognized and compared with a database of offensive words to determine appropriateness and "mute" the questionable content, similar to the way we have slightly delayed live broadcast transmissions for years? The network is also smart enough to impose no delay on the actual game play, ensuring that the teenage gamer on the other end of the console is not penalized with additional latency where it matters most—such as in high-twitch games, like first-person shooter varieties.

Skeptics will offer many reasons why this is not possible or desirable. Some will argue that even a slight voice delay compromises the gamer's ability to interact in real time with others online to organize their efforts, a critical social element of gaming that makes it such a communal activity. Although this is true, why not let the parent weigh the benefits and consequences of unencumbered game-play versus a more controlled environment for his or her children? Others will say that regulators will intervene. After all, how is it fair that a particular game be the subject of packet reprioritization, and a different user experience as a result, simply because it draws an audience that engages in more colorful verbal expression? As a counterpoint, video games have been the subject of parental ratings for some time, precisely because of the concern of parents attempting to protect their children from this content. If others interacting in the game environment use profanity or other offensive language that distort a game's PG rating to something more distasteful, shouldn't the same rules of parental notification apply? Finally, some will take issue with the attempt to censor the content of free speech in the first place. They may say that it is the parent's job to do the parenting, not anyone else's, least of all a technology player. But we would turn their attention back to Susan, a parent attempting to do the right thing for her child but unable to defend him fully in a virtual world. Is using a technological approach to remedy a situation enabled by technology in the first place really that objectionable?

This isn't an issue to be solved in the pages of a book. Yet it illuminates the possibility of using technology as an additional defense mechanism in a world where our physical danger detection wirings can be blinded. As measured by willingness to pay, such a service is not only necessary but desired by parents in our study.

No White Knight

The civilized world is accustomed to law and order. Break the law and suffer the consequences. There are systems established to impose justice on miscreants. And there are reputable law enforcement officials—the proverbial white knights—to serve and protect the public. All of this exists in a world where we also have our primal defense mechanisms in play to protect us from or alert us to danger in the first place. In comparison, such a system is relatively nonexistent in a virtual world, where threats can come from any direction and where our physical senses and danger mechanisms are already compromised. The virtual world has no police jurisdictions, no universal system of governance. Going back to Bob, he expresses the frustration shared by many:

> You know all of the hackers that are going on. It's like a game for these people to see what they can steal and destroy. That's kind of real annoying that every time you've got to hear about all of this identity theft and all of the—just a lot, a lot of fraud—and they [companies] say, "Oh we can't trace it because it's in another country."

To whom does the consumer turn when he finds himself the victim of a cyber-crime or less threatening online nuisance? The Wild Wild West of the World Wide Web still exists, and consumers believe that, when it comes to protection, the buck stops with them. Nearly two-thirds of consumers in our study agree that it is impossible for the government or any one company to police the Internet. Instead, it is an accountability they ultimately own for keeping themselves and their families safe from online predators. This should be welcome news to technology companies, who already understand that technology alone will never substitute for sound judgment. It should be sobering guidance to well-intentioned regulators that consumers do not expect or welcome government intervention, despite the inherent online threats that persist in a virtual world. At the same time, there are practical prescriptions in the way of conspicuous company policies and new technology solutions that will not absolve one's responsibility for protecting oneself but will offer the individual additional tools with which to do so. We tested 20 of these possible solutions in our quantitative study. Throughout this book, we continue to offer which services are most appealing as measured by respondents' willingness to pay for them.

The Mind–Body–Technology Connection

Our mind–body connection has been hardwired through the ages but has significant limitations outside of our real world. Although the virtual world allows us to be anyone we choose to be, it also exposes us to dangers from the nefarious cloaked in virtual anonymity and seeking to inflict harm. A world governed only by technology can rely on the same to mitigate these risks. Just as our amygdala senses our real environment for danger or opportunity and alerts us accordingly, the role of technology in doing the same in a virtual world is apparent. Whether such capabilities manifest themselves in the authentication of online acquaintances to validate that they are who they say they are (an idea inspired by Julie), enhanced QoS parameters to censor potentially objectionable content from our children (thereby relieving Susan and others like her from resorting to more primitive tactics), or reporting tools to alert users of the digital footprint consciously or unconsciously left by them in cyberspace (a resource that would most likely be welcomed by Bob), technology has a role to play in correcting the blind spots it helped create in the first place.

Recall SM from the beginning of this chapter, who is a case of a real person afflicted with a real blind spot in the real world. Her ability to sense danger and respond appropriately as a result is irreparably compromised. Unfortunately, there are millions of SMs with their own blind spots in a virtual world who are unable to properly discern the difference between a threatening and non-threatening encounter. Although most consumers agree that the final accountability for triggering the appropriate defense response rests with them, many are simply unable to avert danger accordingly. Companies who understand this fundamental need and respond with transparent policies and intuitive solutions will find a significant market ready to respond. With the corresponding mind–body–technology connection that results, one can imagine a virtual world with far fewer SMs obliviously wandering the remote corridors of cyberspace simply waiting to meet their own perpetrators.

SHIFT SHORT: HACKING THE PERSON

Phishing, the unsavory mechanism used by hackers to lure unsuspecting victims into providing sensitive password or account information, has been around for some time. Here's generally how it works: The target receives an e-mail from a "trusted" organization, say, her bank or other company with whom she does business. Of course, the e-mail is not really from said organization. It just appears that way from the e-mail address and the link that directs the target to a seemingly official website where such sensitive information can be populated. The website is actually a fraud, perpetrated by the hacker to appear legitimate, although designed to dupe unsuspecting victims—*easy bait* in fishing parlance—to surrender their sensitive information.

If the target is to take the bait, research suggests that she is likely to do so within the first hour of receiving the phony e-mail. A study by secure browsing solutions provider Trusteer revealed that 50 percent of people who fall victim to a phishing attack do so within the first 60 minutes. Hence, there has been considerable focus in the industry on spotting the attacks much more quickly, such that the site may be blocked or disabled. On the positive side, because phishing has become one of the nastier side effects of a virtual world where primal defense mechanisms are compromised, it has also entered the public discourse. As such, the number of phishing attacks as reported at the end of 2010 had declined considerably in recent months.[5]

SHIFT SHORT: **HACKING THE PERSON** (*continued*)

But hackers are not easily deterred in their pursuit and come with no shortage of creativity in their arsenal. A new flavor of phishing is a bit more insidious in its approach. Using information assembled through social media and other sites, hackers are now evolving from spraying millions of e-mail addresses with the same fraudulent e-mail to targeting specific victims and masquerading as someone much closer to home. You may delete outright an e-mail requesting your Social Security number from your bank or other company. At a minimum, your spider senses may compel you to contact the organization to confirm that such an e-mail is legitimate. But what if the same e-mail purportedly came from your mother through her e-mail address? What if the veiled threat appeared to come from someone who actually knows you—someone you intimately trust?

Known as *spear phishing*, this is one of the newer threats to hit the cyber scene. "It's a really nasty tactic because it's so personalized," says Bruce Schneier, the chief security technology officer of the British company BT Group. "This is hacking the person. It's not hacking the computer."[6] In June 2011, Google reported its discovery and deflection of such an attempt to compromise hundreds of Gmail passwords to monitor the accounts of prominent people, including government officials. The threat is not limited to consumers. Increasingly, enterprises find themselves the target as unsuspecting employees innocently respond to e-mails designed to compromise the firm's security perimeter.

Bots, faceless predators, hackers. We can now add a new category of threat to the online waters—those who dig deep enough to apparently know us and cloak themselves in the disguise of a friendly face to con us.

3

Preference: The (Un)Conscious Filter of (In)Finite Choice

Every man builds his world in his own image. He has the power to choose,
but no power to escape the necessity of choice.

AYN RAND, AUTHOR

Elliott was a 30-something successful man with a wife and children when he encountered what many would consider their worst nightmare—a tumor: more specifically, a brain tumor. But Elliott's case did not end in the premature death of a vibrant young man, at least not in the physical sense. Doctors were able to remove the benign tumor from the prefrontal cortex of his brain, and, by all indications of post-operative tests that followed, Elliott was back to "normal." Doctors found minimal impact on his neurological and psychological function. The location of the tumor meant that Elliot's language and motor skills were unaffected. He scored at or above average levels in numerous tests, over and over again. Yet, despite the negligible impact on his cognitive skills, it soon became apparent that something did die with that tumor. This was not the same Elliott.

Although Elliott retained his short- and long-term memory, his expertise and knowledge base, and his ability to analyze data in great detail, he could no longer hold a job because he couldn't prioritize his work, manage his time, or complete needed tasks. Without steady employment, he entered into several foolish business ventures, losing his life savings in dealings with disreputable people. Soon he was divorced and then remarried to a woman that his family warned him against. Then he was divorced again. Although he was still an intelligent, knowledgeable, and capable person, Elliot was jobless and dependent on friends, family, and disability payments, which were about to be stopped because, by all medical accounts, he was fine. After yet another round of psychological testing, he was referred to neuroscientist Antonio

Damasio, expert on the interdependency of mind and brain, mind and body, and the evolutionary purposes served by the mind and our emotions.

Damasio conducted another battery of tests designed to identify known problems in Elliot's processes of decision making and moral judgment. Many of the tests involved remembering and manipulating numbers, images, objects, and concepts in a variety of scenarios designed to simulate real life. For example, he was given a task to develop alternative choices in social situations and list the positives and negatives of each, explaining why each had certain likely outcomes. Elliot performed extremely well, but at the end of the task said, "And after all this, I still don't know what to do!"

This response and other observations throughout the examination led Damasio to determine that Elliot's issue wasn't that he couldn't reason or that he didn't have a grasp of social conventions or societal principles. His problems began at the end of the reasoning process when it came to closing the deal and making a choice. In addition, some of the tasks that he could talk through and decide on in a laboratory setting, he couldn't do successfully in real life, as his track record showed. Something was inhibiting his ability to prioritize the values of his options and act accordingly. So what was different about Elliot in the real world?

> More often than not, real life faces us with a greater mix of pictorial and linguistic material. We are confronted with people and objects; with sights, sounds, smells, and so on; with scenes of varying intensities; and with whatever narratives, verbal and or pictorial, we create to accompany them.[1]

Elliot was overwhelmed by the *volume* of choices, which, ironically, his intellect helped him to be beyond proficient at devising. Plus, in the real world, once he had assessed a situation and arrived at a response to his environment, the environment presented him with new data. Imagine you are in a discussion with someone. The conversation isn't over just because the other person says "A" and then you say "B." Saying "B" elicits another response from the person with further considerations, further input, and perhaps new conditions and goals for decision making. In a laboratory, the experiments occur within a fixed amount of time. In real life, the iterative process can go on and on.

Observation of Elliot's behavior yielded another clue about what was wrong. All the time that the doctor and patient were discussing this dilemma, Elliot remained dispassionate, calm, and relaxed. At times, Damasio notes, he the doctor became more emotionally disturbed and frustrated than the patient. Therefore, Damasio had a colleague conduct another test, showing Elliot a series of emotionally charged images, such as cities damaged by earthquakes, houses burning, and people being injured in gory accidents or near drowning. Although pre-tumor Elliot would have been upset, post-tumor Elliot had no emotional response—positive or negative. The location of the tumor and the resulting surgical damage were in one of many sectors of the brain linked to emotional processes. Damasio concluded:

> [T]he cold-bloodedness made his mental landscape hopelessly flat. It might also be that the same cold-bloodedness made his mental landscape too shifty and unsustained for the time required to make response selections, in other words, a subtle rather than basic defect in working memory which might alter the remainder of the reasoning process required for a decision to emerge.[2]

Elliot's case highlights two key areas of decision making that are important to our discussion of the formation and execution of preferences. First, the heart of the process involves the ability to sift through options, organize them, and attach value. Second, how we as humans do that is a complex brain process that relies not only on reason and thinking, but also to a substantial degree on emotion and feeling. We have a dual-process method of knowing and information processing, and emotions are essential to the assignment of value and prioritization, which are needed to make final decisions.

Why is this? For Damasio and many other scientists and doctors who view our mental processes through the lens of evolutionary biology, the mind exists because its processes help regulate and preserve our lives. Some of those life-regulating functions are completely automatic: one's heart beating, breathing, balancing biochemistry. If we had to make an active, deliberate decision on those basic life-regulating functions, we'd never survive. Our brains are structured to exchange messages with the body to moderate a host of operations and maintain homeostasis without intervention of a conscious mental supervisor. Our conscious supervisor is the director in our mind who deliberately recalls images, makes observations via our senses, and pulls all the information together to make a plan of action in what appears to be a logical fashion.

Other life-regulating operations require the supervisor's active decision making. Some are still more basic and primal: Back away from the mountain lion and map a path of escape to avoid being its dinner. However, some are more subtle as our sense of homeostasis becomes more sophisticated, because human lives and choices are more complex: Eat healthy to keep the mind and body in top working order and avoid disease. Or, in Elliot's case: Give weight to the forewarnings of caring friends and relatives. Avoid investing your money with questionable business partners. Don't marry a problematic spouse if you want peace. Underlying these conscious decisions are still unconscious drives pushing us to act in favor of our survival—saving our lives directly, creating advantageous conditions, or reducing the influence of potentially harmful ones. Our experience of those drives is through feeling states in the body and emotional states in the mind, which are often linked together.

In any case, we have developed ways to make life-regulating decisions more efficiently by automating all or part of the process. Emotions are mental processing shortcuts that arise from assessing the environment and mapping connections in our mental log of experiences and information. Some assessments are conscious and some unconscious. As we move through life and obtain more experiences, our minds map more and more shortcuts to help us, moving greater portions of some decision making down the continuum from conscious to unconscious, from deliberate to automatic. These elements and more form a working network in which you make your decision—consciously, unconsciously, or somewhere in between. Your auto-piloted, homeward-bound route is a well-worn groove that has become the path of least resistance to homeostasis and life regulation—your sense of normality. Psychologists have outlined the role that routines play in what they call the "theory of preference."[3] Within this framework, a person is confronted with a "decision problem." The mind's first response is to look for a shortcut, a *routine*—a quickly executable pattern of mental and physical processes that can serve as a solution. In evaluating which routine to follow, a person considers both cognitive (thinking) and affective (feeling) components—matching the current situation with situations he has experienced or heard about in the past. Our preferences are our personalized set of go-to routines. Although the virtual world opens the doors to a seemingly infinite set of choices previously unavailable to us, technology also creates new shortcuts that enable our navigation of these decisions, assuming that those shortcuts are valid and reliable. To make these virtual shortcuts more relevant, consumers are willing to share information about themselves. In our study, nearly 70 percent agree that they are very or somewhat comfortable sharing information online if it helps them find items of interest. Consider the viewpoint expressed by Christine, one of our ethnography respondents, as she reflects on how technology allows her to wade through a sea of choices and discover new information or content:

> I enjoy the easy access—like things at my fingertips. The looking things up to get answers on the spot. Or having the dictionary in the palm of my hands when I want a thesaurus. Or the convenience of when you're on iPhoto, you just hit the Facebook [icon], and it'll export the whole thing. The interconnectedness of how life meets technology and how you can surround yourself with things that make that blend very easy and opportune.

The Power of Experience

As we go about our lives building a working network of routines, we integrate them with a corresponding web of emotional associations. These associations help us evaluate the environment and context of a decision and choose the optimal routine. These are *whispers* of emotion that psychologists call *affect* and describe as the "goodness" or "badness" that we experience as a feeling to indicate the positive or negative quality of a given stimulus or choice.[4] Feelings create a strong tie into your intuitive, more instinctual responses and are more easily mapped to your mental routines and information-processing shortcuts. "Goodness" and "badness" are evaluated in the context of survival—again, escaping immediate life threats, creating advantageous conditions, and mitigating negative ones.

Consider the difference between having direct versus indirect experience—either positive or negative. Direct experience yields stronger associations because the affective association is made directly from the emotion you personally experienced: for example, the pleasure of enjoying a meal at a restaurant or, conversely, the anxiety felt when arguing with the manager over an incorrect bill. The resulting association of "good" or "bad" with that particular restaurant will always be stronger. At the mention of that restaurant in the future, your mind will reconnect with a feeling tied to "Mmmm, the food was fantastic!" or "Oh, my gosh, the service was bad." These thoughts may not even be consciously expressed. This connection is more than just a rational filing away of facts to be weighed regarding your meal. You could read a survey in which 1,000 people conclude the opposite of your experience. When someone mentions the restaurant, you'll always remember the taste of the chocolate mousse you loved (*pleasure*) or the constriction in your chest as you confronted the manager over the bill (*pain*).

You remember the feelings and associated emotions. Affective reasoning based on experience is powerful. Even if considering the experiences of others, you are more likely to contemplate the opinions and experiences of someone with whom you have an emotional connection. Depending on the intensity of the experience and the closeness of the relationship to the person affected, you may take on their associations as your own. We discuss this further in our chapter on the "Law of Recall."

For respondents in our study, personal experience goes a long way in determining loyalty (or lack thereof) to service providers vying for sustained customer relationships. In fact, according to our study, providing extraordinary customer service is the attribute most correlated with trusting a provider, whereas offering personalized products and services to meet the consumer's unique needs is a close second. As Brian, a 20-something recent college graduate, considers the relationships he has with various companies, he provides a glowing endorsement for his mobile provider.

> *I've had no problems with them [the mobile operator]. Which is surprising, because I've heard horror stories about other mobile carriers. I love my provider. They have service everywhere I go—whether it be in a tunnel or in an elevator. They always seem to have service. Plus, there aren't a lot of hidden charges.*

Reflect on Brian's choice of words to hear the emotion that binds him to his provider. He "loves" them. In fact, he is "surprised" at his own enthusiasm given the "horror" stories he has personally heard from others about their own experiences with other operators. It is both his direct experience with his provider and the close association with others who have experienced quite the opposite that serve as powerful emotional connectors solidifying Brian's loyalty.

Service providers connect us to the virtual world that has become so essential in our daily lives. In addition, that virtual world has taught us that unlimited choice and customization are possible, albeit overwhelming, pursuits in an online domain where shelf space comes cheap. No longer are consumers relegated to popular fare within a restricted local area. No longer are they confined to content on a particular timetable dictated by television programming schedules or box office show times. Time and again, we heard consumers express gratitude (as in Christine's case) for the "fingertip access" common in a networked-community age. However, what is appreciated by some becomes an expectation for others. Although service providers are indispensable in connecting consumers to the online world they crave, consumer expectations are now shifting to require that these same providers deliver customizable options themselves.

In the case of Brian, he "loves" his mobile operator but calls his cable provider "persnickety." Why? As Brian's roommate explains:

> *I think the problem with most places [providers] is they don't give you a plan that just fits your needs. Why not come up with a plan for college students? If you're in college, you're going to be going from place to place year by year. Why do we need to pay for a setup fee and all these charges and try to figure out the best plan when they should just have certain plans for certain people?*

This direct experience of being frustrated (or at a minimum, confused) with what appear to be onerous charges creates a perception that the company in question is unwilling to adapt to its consumers' unique needs. Of course, in a physical world, there are tangible costs associated with turning up services, for example, a cable operator who must dispatch a technician to install service. However, becoming accustomed to an Internet experience where "unlimited" choice is remotely achievable, consumers come to expect the same level of customization for other services in their lives—no matter the difference in economics that persists between the physical and virtual worlds. This increasing level of expectation may be partly to blame for the growing incidence of video cord cutters—those consumers who forego paid television services entirely or in part in favor of online options offered by Netflix, Hulu, YouTube, and others. In our study, approximately eight percent of network-engaged consumers have canceled their paid television subscription in the past two years; another 23 percent have cut back.

Are You Paying Attention?

Advertising has been the domain of creative geniuses. So much so, in fact, that those in the field work tirelessly to break through the clutter that surrounds consumers each day. Their industry rewards achievers for attaining the goal—both in dollars and recognition. The Clios, advertising's nod to creative professionals in the field, have long been the benchmark for measuring excellence, even marked by an annual awards ceremony. Although the Clio is deeply coveted among several advertisers as validation of their work, it seems that there is more to the Clio than just pomp and circumstance. Indeed, evidence suggests that creative ads are more successful in capturing the elusive attention of consumers in an increasingly cluttered market.[5]

Advertising has made big business of capturing and keeping consumers' attention and helping create consumer preferences for client brands. In the days marked by print, radio, television, direct mail, and every other form of media in the "real" world, the way to ensure doing so meant creating the memorable. The Clios became one way of distinguishing the ordinary from extraordinary among advertising agencies. They also helped winners command a premium for their creative work among desperate clients looking to break through the proverbial clutter.

In the "real" world, clients are left with few choices to make an impression. They can hire an agency with a reputation for creating the memorable, select outrageously expensive media events (such as the Super Bowl) where air time is the scarce resource, or tirelessly endeavor to optimize messages and media with garden-variety tactics. This conundrum led many companies to engage in desperate "spray-and-pray" approaches, so termed because clients would "spray" their messages across multiple media formats and then "pray" that something actually worked. It also led to the most oft-quoted statements in advertising to express the natural frustration that followed. In the late nineteenth century, John Wanamaker, a department store mogul, quipped that half the money he spent on advertising was wasted, but that he didn't know which half.[6]

The online world changes the paradigm. Click-through rates can be tracked. Even if they don't get your money, advertisers are assured they've at least grabbed your attention—and they can measure how effective specific ads on targeted sites are at doing so. But there's a problem with Internet advertising. It's become so commonplace that many consumers have learned to tune out obnoxious banner advertisements or block annoying pop-ups all together. In addition, given that some with nefarious intentions have exploited banner advertisements and pop-ups to infect devices with malware, consumers are guarded in just how carefree they can afford to be when one click can lead to unintended consequences. In the words of Bruce, a 22-year-old subject in our study:

> *I never get pop-ups on my computer. Banner ads? Every once in a while I may click on one to see what's going on.… But I'm more cautious as to what I do click on because I hate dealing with issues with the computer. It's frustrating.*

So, what's an advertiser to do in a world where *traditional* media like television, radio, and print are difficult to measure and *new* media like the Internet are experiencing clutter and other nuisances of their own? Many are turning to targeted advertising as the new darling to outperform even the most creative of advertisements. Of course, targeting is nothing new to advertisers. For decades, advertisers have targeted where to run advertisements in the media that serves a coveted demographic, such as within popular primetime shows that cater to a particular cohort. However, there's still a bit of "spraying and praying" in the approach, in that advertisers are relying on generalizations to target the message. For example, an ad on the Disney Channel deliberately directed at moms (the demographic most represented in the audience) ignores stay-at-home dads, who may feel excluded, if not offended, because they are not represented. When advertisers have but one spot to run in a particular time slot, they must play to the averages—and the averages ignore critical niches that surround the edges.

The virtual world changes the economics of advertising, just as it changes those of physical goods. If creativity is the idol of traditional media, revered by advertising executives in glamorous awards ceremonies, targeting is the differentiator of new media that just may finally answer which part of the advertising budget is wasted. Although pop-up ads never reach Bruce's radar and banner ads are met with caution, he offers an interesting observation for other types of ads he notices, and they just so happen to be targeted to his interests:

> *I do notice ads on Facebook every once in a while on the right hand side. You can tell that they know what you're surfing for or what you've been surfing for. I was looking for stuff for my motorcycle and then there's an ad on Facebook about motorcycles.*

In a virtual world, our clicks are tracked, and our time spent on sites is measurable. Eventually, what we search for, where we visit, and how long we stay represent a collage of behaviors that begins to define us as a human being—not some generic demographic cohort. In some cases, we actively raise our virtual hand to indicate our preferences such that technology can do the work for us in discovering the content tuned to our needs. Brian, our recent college graduate, extols the virtues of Pandora, an online streaming music service, in filtering his preferences:

> *Pandora gives you a music choice tailored to a specific song. So say it's Def Leppard.... It will select songs for the next 3–4 hours that are similar to those music qualities.*

In this case, Brian knows that Pandora is aware of his preferences, because he has actively raised his virtual hand as a fan of Def Leppard to receive music tailored as such. However, as we covered in Chapter 2 on protection, consumers also leave behind a visible trail of footsteps in a virtual world—whether or not they voluntarily choose to do so. The sensitivities to this reality are palpable among some respondents as they ominously foretell an Orwellian existence. As Todd, another of our 20-somethings, laments while visiting his favorite search engine:

> *The only thing I see on here [at the search engine portal] is just stuff for searching on different things. In a way, I feel like there should be something on the page that is going to let me know that what I'm searching for—that no one is watching over, like a Big Brother type of a thing that's watching everything that I do. You'd like to know that you're secure....*

If security is not the prime concern, there are less lofty ambitions online consumers ask of companies—like just knowing who they are in the first place. Indeed, in a virtual world where targeting is expected, if not feared, there is more frustration when the invisible filters just get it wrong. Andrew, a viewer of online video sites like Hulu, relays his experience:

> *Hulu is free. It's ad-supported. [The ads] are annoying. A lot of them are for cat food, which has always been very distressing to me. I don't know what in my profile makes them think that cats are my thing but [shakes his head]. It doesn't matter how many times I click thumbs-down to indicate the ad is not relevant to me, just more cat food keeps coming.*

Consumers are aware of the tracking capabilities in a virtual world. In our study, 80 percent indicate their belief that notable technology players track personal preferences across a variety of network activities. Yet, here's the fascinating part: The knowledge of being tracked, and in some cases of being victimized by fraudulent companies, does not deter consumers from jumping, head first, into the virtual swimming pool. Despite no change in behavior, there is a definite difference in trust. In our study, brands that are seen as being more trustworthy in protecting one's sensitive information are also those more likely to command a premium for a tested service, all else being equal. Also, in a world where shelf space comes cheap, trust certainly does not.

That brings us back to Elliott. In his case, the mind–body filters to affect reasoning and choice misfired. He was unable to assess risks accurately. He could no longer *feel* the difference between right and wrong. He could not pull the trigger when it came to making a choice. In a world unconstrained by physical boundaries and overwhelmed by choices, our own natural mind–body filters are faulty. We must rely on technology to do the work for us. We must trust in companies to know us without exploiting us. Although our cognitive filters may be insufficient, our affective reasoning is not. Companies that connect positively with us, show that they understand us, and respond to us are preferred. Companies that are not able to walk the line between trust and exploitation will find themselves just as commoditized as the endless virtual shelf space that surrounds them.

SHIFT SHORT: THE ULTIMATE CLIFFHANGER

Four times she bought a new dress. Four times she bought champagne. Alas, the wedding she anxiously anticipated attending was not to be—literally. It wasn't a real wedding at all but one conjured by the imagination of writers trading in daytime drama. The bride and groom were fictitious characters Alice Matthews and Steve Frame in the imaginary Bay City—home to long-time soap opera *Another World*. The eager attendee? None other than a die-hard fan so frustrated by the on-again, off-again romance of the couple that she was compelled to write a letter to the show. That was back in 1976.[7] *Another World* was canceled in 1999. It was replaced 10 days later by another soap, *Passions*, which would find its demise in 2008. In 2011, ABC announced that long-time favorites *All My Children* and *One Life to Live* would soon be added to the long list of canceled soaps. A genre that counted nearly 20 shows in its heyday is on the verge of just four survivors at the time of this writing.[8]

Soap operas were the long-time bastion of advertisers seeking a fairly defined target—women (and some men) confined to the house during the daytime hours. Advertisers were enthusiastic supporters of a genre known for keeping its audience on the edge of their seats. In the case of Proctor & Gamble, the consumer packaged-goods giant actually produced several of the popular series. In the 1970s, soaps were so popular that the traditional 30-minute format began seeing its first extension to hour-long episodes. These episodes, capable of attracting and keeping eyeballs and advertisers, were the cash cow engine to fuel less profitable primetime series. Back in the 1970s, a show like *Kojak* cost $250,000 to produce and delivered just $200,000 in revenues. In contrast, the cost of one week's worth of episodes for *Days of Our Lives* cost NBC $170,000 back in the day. With just one episode, the network collected $120,000 in advertising revenues.[9]

SHIFT SHORT: **THE ULTIMATE CLIFFHANGER (continued)**

But something happened along the way to fragment the once fiercely loyal audience of the daytime drama. Some blame it on the droves of women who selected the workforce or university as their daytime dwelling. Others suggest that cable network television was to blame—the increasing number of choices on the dial gave viewers other options. Some have gone so far as to blame OJ Simpson—his trial preempted daytime dramas for weeks back in the 1990s, and the shows were never able to recoup their ratings after its cessation.[10]

Whatever the reason—or combination of reasons—a genre that once drew a daily audience of tens of millions of viewers now finds itself attracting just three million, on average, to each of the six daily soaps still on television.[11] The audience changed. Advertisers adapted. And a growing crop of new entertainment increasingly lures the eyeballs once dedicated to soaps, including social gaming and reality television.

The formulaic soap opera is known for an essential ingredient—the *cliffhanger*—the jaw-dropping moment at the end of each week that grips the viewer, leaving her desperate to tune in again after the weekend for its resolution. True to its roots, this story may have its own cliffhanger as die-hard soap fans across the nation protest the upcoming demise of two longtime favorites. Consumer campaign efforts have been successful in reviving canceled shows before (such as *Father Knows Best* in the 1950s). But resuscitating an entire genre is a much taller order. The next few months will tell how this cliffhanger ends—whether *All My Children* and *One Life to Live* are spared. As Agnes Nixon, the shows' creator, foreshadows about the imminent final episodes, "We're not going to have everybody be happy and fade into the sunset. It's going to be very satisfying, but there are some things that one would want to watch in the following weeks, if anybody wants to pick us up."[12] Someone may just pick up the series if convinced the audience will follow. If not, we can only blame the changing preferences of U.S. consumers for the death of Erica Kane.

4 Trust: Meeting at the Crossroads of Identity

You may be deceived if you trust too much, but you will live in torment unless you trust enough.

—Dr. Frank Crane, minister and author

He was the former chairman of the NASDAQ stock market and vice-chairman of the National Association of Securities Dealers. He lived the life many only dream of—multiple homes, extravagant cars, private jets, and yachts. Now, he is simply prisoner 61727-054.

You may know him better as Bernard ("Bernie") Madoff, the mastermind behind one of the largest financial frauds ever perpetrated on the public. Over 16 years, he bilked investors out of billions of dollars, orchestrating one of the most sophisticated Ponzi schemes in history—a financial bait-and-switch in which the assets of new investors are used to pay off failed investments from older investors. Once an outsider to the financial pedigree of Wall Street he so admired, Madoff soon skyrocketed to fame and fortune with his proven, though thoroughly misunderstood, black-box techniques. While other investment firms relied on human brokers, Madoff used computers with advanced algorithms to secure his client's next bet. But when those investments turned sour, Madoff turned to unscrupulous tactics, now his infamous Ponzi scheme, to cover his missteps and lure naive investors into his web of lies. His house of cards came crashing down when the market crashed in 2008 and federal agents arrested him upon confession of his $65 billion Ponzi scheme.

Madoff's "black box" was mysterious even to expert investors, those who should have been on to his con well before they were victimized themselves. As he recounts from behind prison walls, his home for the rest of his life thanks to a 150-year sentence:

> *I had, through the funds, some of the heads of the biggest trading desks on Wall Street who had access to all the data. I had senior partners at Goldman Sachs. These guys didn't think that I was running a scam. So how do you expect Mrs. Green of Fort Lauderdale, Florida to be spotting the red flag?*[1]

Indeed, Mrs. Green, along with the rest of Madoff's victims, was duped. Many placed their life fortunes in the hands of a manipulative crook. But this crook did not sneak up under the cloak of darkness, weapon in hand, to assault his victims. No, this crook came with a distinguished reputation, clad in expensive business suits, fraternizer to industry regulators and armed with a proven track record of success. It was much more than financial wealth that Madoff shamelessly stole from his victims. He robbed them of something far more difficult to replace. He bankrupted their *trust*.

Our trust bank account begins accepting deposits during infanthood. When infants are less than a year old, they begin exhibiting signs of trust and its alter ego, wariness. At about the third quarter of the first year of life, the smiling response begins to be restricted to familiar individuals. At the same time, proximity-seeking responses tend to be confined to caretakers, and fear responses to strangers begin to emerge.[2] These wariness behaviors arise as the child begins to adapt his or her responses to people or things in the world based on familiarity.

Wariness is related to the fear response but distinct from it. The fear response is more about fight-or-flight and basic survival. *Wariness* is "a period of immobility during which a stimulus is appraised in relation to stored experience and a response deemed suitable in the light of the appraisal process selected."[3] A moment of wariness puts a person at a crossroads—with or without actual sensations of fear. Wariness can entail curiosity as much as suspicion. It can be about interest and excitement as well as uncertainty and caution. Babies at this life stage may be wary of a new person or toy but still crawl forward and approach. In that moment, we would argue that a person's presentation, protection, and preference form the basis for the evaluation of what is ultimately a question of trust. Each individual will call upon the decision-making processes we discussed in earlier chapters of this book to decide on the trustworthiness and suitability of a new entrant into the environment.

Living in the Intersections

Presentation, protection, and preference are coexistent, codependent aspects of our identity in a networked-community age. Our *presentation* is a reflection of our image and is subject to control. Sometimes, we are in control of how we are perceived. In other cases, we are at the mercy of friends, family, or random strangers, who can present us in an image as they see us, whether or not we agree with that reflection. *Protection* deals with how safe we feel in a world of faceless predators. The extent of violation can range from annoying spammers attempting to grab something as innocuous as our attention to nefarious miscreants out for our wallets, loved ones, or lives. And, in a world of overwhelming choices, *preference* relies on the invisible filters to refine our decision-making processes. In some cases, we are conscious of the choices we make. At other times, we unconsciously leave a digital footprint behind us. The composite of our choices reveals preference, which can be leveraged to offer us better alternatives or leave us exploited to questionable parties.

Yet, within each of these domains, there are intersections that reflect new behaviors where the crossroads meet. Where presentation meets protection, a person displays revelation or concealment behaviors, deciding what to share and what to hide. For example, people make an effort to keep their Social Security numbers, addresses, pictures of their children, and the like private in the physical and online world to ward off varied threats. Where preference meets protection, a person displays approach or avoidance behaviors, being drawn toward or running away from the stimulus. Think about getting an e-mail with a ZIP file attachment from a strange e-mail address. No matter how sufficiently the e-mail content appears to match your preferences or interests, it likely takes about a nanosecond for you to avoid and delete it. Where preference meets presentation, a person displays affiliation or disassociation behaviors, deciding which people or things are in alignment with a person's self-image and which ones are not. For example, some of our ethnography participants choose to disassociate from social media because they don't want to be one of "those people" who feel the need to share every minute detail of their lives. Others fear missing out and are highly attached to their social media, gathering hundreds of friends or followers as a badge of honor. The separate parts of identity are interconnected, motivating different actions in the real and virtual worlds.

Let's look at Julie, a victim of identity theft. Three years ago, she opened a retail account and began receiving two statements for the same account—one with her name and one with another name. She inquired with the store, and they initially suspected her of using another woman's Social Security number to open the account.

> *They told me I wasn't me. That I got this lady's Social Security number*
> *and opened a credit card with her Social Security number. And I was,*
> *like, "No, no, no, because I'm looking at my Social Security card. It's*
> *in front of me. I know who I am. What are you talking about?"*

She checked her credit report and received a list of creditors with whom her Social Security number was used. After communicating with the Social Security Administration and the FBI, she discovered that 17 people had been using her number—some since she was seven years old. As part of her response to the identity theft, Julie avoided applying for credit at all for a while. A breach of trust puts people back into a state of wariness, having to reassess the environment and make new decisions.

> *I fear for my kids' information the same way. I have that locked up....*
> *And I know it by heart, so if I need it, I can just write it down.*

Julie's past experience has made her hesitant to share any information—to the point of only trusting the security of her mind when it comes to storing her children's information. Although she enjoys the convenience of online bill payment and is willing to share her banking information with a variety of merchants—including AT&T and her local utility company—she has established a personal policy of only using sites whose encryption status is clearly indicated by the lock symbol in her browser. Recently, she was paying a bill for a furniture store and noticed that the site didn't have the symbol, so she now mails her payment instead of using the website. When discussing her decision to start using the mail instead of e-payments, she mentioned that she had an additional concern because, when speaking with the company's customer service desk, the agents were foreign. She expressed a fear that if she used the site anyway, she'd wake up and her money would be gone. One interesting element of Julie's story is that, on one hand, the lack of affiliation—the foreignness—of the agents increases her wariness, making her less certain about completing the online payments. At the same time, when she recounts the tale of discovering the illegal use of her Social Security number, she mentions going back to question her mother about how someone could have gotten access to her information—including asking if her mother had ever sold her information. In discovering that the breach of trust went back so far, Julie was forced to examine all her relationships, including those closest to her. Affiliation alone was insufficient to yield trust.

Like other manifestations of identity, trust has evolved in complexity as human beings have shifted from hunter–gatherer band societies to our modern complex world of interconnected cultures and nations. The primary drivers for the development of trust as a human behavior are the specialization and interdependence inherent to advanced societies. Think of it this way: thousands of years ago, a clan of 30 to 50 people lived and died in relative isolation. Division of labor was minimal—maybe along gender lines—and everyone had to perform multiple roles and jobs to sustain themselves and their small community.

As communities grew larger, division of labor increased, and people began to specialize in particular roles and share or trade their expertise with those around them, dividing and conquering survival tasks. With specialization came a greater dependence on neighbors to handle their business, so that you could handle your own. The ability to trust others and to gauge trust accurately and appropriately gave a person or family a greater survival advantage. Of course, this is why affiliation or identifying someone as "like us" becomes a trigger for trust. The assumption is that the closer the relation, the more like us someone or something may be, the closer our dependency and the greater the mutual risk. Also, the more we know, the better our chances of assessing trustworthiness and competence. Trust in its origin is social and involves extending one's sense of personal survival to a shared communal survival. It also involves more than simple reliance on one another in a series of transactional exchanges. Trust means maintaining a relationship where you deal fairly, honestly, and reasonably with one another and are accountable to one another if you don't. Another of our subjects, John, a 30-something technology director for a small company in Seattle, says he only buys online from large, established retailers or smaller independent companies that are local—examples of how affiliation yields trust in a networked-community age.

> If I'm buying direct from a company, it's like a local online game company I know. They're in Kirkland [Washington]. OK, fine, if they screw me over, I'm going to go knock on their door and scream.

John is in the majority when it comes to engaging with companies he knows. In our study, more than 80 percent say that they are very or somewhat comfortable sharing information when visiting or using a familiar website or application, respectively.

The Price of Distrust

The ability to trust as a survival advantage is also about having an accurate gauge for the appropriateness of trusting certain people and, in some moments of wariness, choosing distrust. As philosophers Robert C. Solomon and Fernando Flores describe it:

> Authentic trust is a judicious combination of trust and distrust, superior to blind trust, which is foolish precisely because it bars distrust from consideration. But to talk about trust is to recognize, first and foremost, that we are (like it or not) in this together, whether "this" is a marriage, a business relationship, a corporation, a community, a continent, or the world.[4]

Distrust isn't the opposite of trust, but an essential part of its practice. Certainly, Julie considers her mother generally trustworthy, but asking the questions about who may have had access to her information is part of her necessary due diligence. Her example speaks to the fragility of trust, which is more than just an abstract concept or feeling. Also, as our own study attests, trust and love are two different things. We asked consumers how much they trusted various technology companies with whom they have a relationship. We also asked them which kinds of providers they loved or hated. When we mapped consumer trust and love against a respondent's willingness to pay for a particular service, the data revealed that trust within a particular brand had a 62 percent correlation with an increased willingness to pay for the service, all else being equal. In contrast, love for a brand only had an 11 percent correlation to revenue. Trust is practiced and performed—manifest in one's actions, which in the business world means buying and delivering revenue. Consumers might have all sorts of positive feelings about a brand, but without trust, the warm fuzzies are meaningless, and willingness to pay falls through the floor. Our research shows that providers gain a price premium for offering trusted services, but for offering services that aren't trusted, there is a price penalty nearly three and one-half times as large. Lack of trust carries a heavy cost.

One aspect of Solomon and Flores's argument about the role of trust in society provides a jumping-off point for how trust has changed in today's world. They assert that, "Business requires well-circumscribed trust," as opposed to a relationship such as marriage, which entails "vast, open-ended trust." In our new, hyperconnected world of permeable boundaries and the breakdown between public and private, this becomes problematic. No matter how well circumscribed that trust is, it cannot be confined to the explicit conditions in any policy document. There is always an implicit component as well, and it is that implicit component that companies have to build on with consumers through their actions. This is an issue that has seen its fair share of media coverage, particularly when a company makes use of its customers' information in an attempt to launch new services or enable third parties to do the same. Some well-established companies have earned a black eye in the court of public opinion when such information is exploited, even when acting in accordance with their stated policies. Regardless of the explicit contract between a provider and its users, if users develop a discomfort with the novel way in which their information will be used, it doesn't matter. It has the same effect as a violation and returns users to a state of wariness with regard to using the company's service. It sends users flooding to their privacy settings, reexamining and tweaking, as they try to maintain control of their information. These incidents may not lead to a decision to terminate the relationship with the company altogether because other priorities may win out, such as cost and availability considerations, but they disrupt the trust relationship. Few services or brands have the resilience to withstand repeated bouts of hysteria brought on by violations of trust—real or perceived.

In addition to living up to explicit, clearly stated agreements, companies must account for the implicit and unknown harms yet to surface as technology rapidly changes. Simply saying, "ABC activity is in accordance with our policies," is insufficient. Looking at trust as delivering on explicit promises (i.e., of a contract) implies that violations can be addressed by the contracts and by laws, such as recovery of actual and punitive damages, jail time, and other typical legal punishments—or that some definable remedy always exists to make the other party whole. Today, that may not be, and often is not, the case. Trust violations in a virtual world have greater impact on the consumer's very identity than in business models, technologies, and sociocultural contexts of the past. To view trust as merely explicit and contractual removes the relationship component of trust. This approach reduces the exchanges between companies and consumers, between companies, and between consumers to simply transactional. If it is true that, "Business requires well-circumscribed trust," then business in the networked-community age is in trouble.

Take the 2011 Sony PlayStation security breach as an example of what happens when trust is violated. Sony is the well-established brand that has delivered innovation to consumers for decades. One of the more popular products offered by the company is its PlayStation gaming console and the connected online service accompanying it that allows millions of gamers the world over to play with one another from the safety and comfort of their own homes. In April 2011, on an otherwise ordinary Tuesday afternoon, Sony engineers were baffled when several servers running the PlayStation network mysteriously and suddenly rebooted. The investigation that ensued over the next several days revealed a security breach by unknown hackers who ripped off the names, passwords, and, in some cases, credit card information of millions of victims worldwide. Adding insult to injury and fuel to the hysteria that followed, Sony did not reveal the details of the breach—or even that a breach had occurred—for several days. Instead, the company abruptly disabled the service to its paying customers without explanation or a timeframe for restoration.[5] At the time of this writing, the corporation faces class-action lawsuits from consumers who trusted the established company to protect their sensitive information. Sony's financial costs to rectify the situation could exceed $1 billion. But, according to at least one analyst, there's something far more valuable at stake. Mizuho Investors Securities analyst Nobuo Kurahashi predicts that restoring trust in online services will be essential if Sony continues to push its network business strategy forward.[6]

So what are some other guidelines for companies looking to build trust with consumers? For one, companies must be watchful of control and the balance of power in their customer relationships. As Solomon and Flores explain, when the balance of power is disproportionate, "talking of trust, even mentioning the subject, can be viewed as an act of manipulation and deception." If you know that some people have near-total control of you or of your information, they can look at you as earnestly as they can, smile, and say, "Trust me." But do you? If it were true that you can trust them, would they have to make the declaration? One of the reasons people express so much distrust of institutions like government or corporate management is a sense of powerlessness, which renders authentic trust impossible because there is a feeling of having no choice in the matter. There's no belief that you and the institution are "in this together," just the belief that the institution is holding all the cards. Trust is about showing, not telling, and it must accompany freedom and control over one's own future and choices.

Of course, as we've already explored, many choices are more unconscious than conscious, which poses a problem in maintaining a trusting relationship. This dilemma isn't something that companies will be able to resolve fully—even with the best of intentions. However, this is something of which companies should be consciously aware and seek to understand. Areas of consumers' decision making that are unconscious or unknown to them are potentially areas of high risk and exposure. Viewing trust as part of an ongoing, consistent relationship with a focus on long-term results is helpful in mitigating this risk.

Another challenge in establishing trust in the virtual world is when technology frustrates our ability to read cues in our environment. The decline in face-to-face communication or even vocal communication over the phone cuts out a key way we are engineered to detect trustworthiness. Amy, a mother of four, also works with a virtual sales team for a technology company. She met some of her coworkers at a company event for the first time after years of working together.

> One gentleman came up, and he said, "Amy, I would recognize your voice across the room." And I knew immediately who it was because he and I have talked to each other for three years on the phone and never had met.… We'd been tied to deals and trusted each other to get work done and had a totally professional relationship.… There's something to be said about the voice—even beyond the IMing and emailing and everything. Being able to pick up on those cues when you're talking on the phone is really important.

The extent to which technology can be created or adapted as an extension of human behaviors and processes to mirror, support, and govern our rules of engagement is a determining factor as to whether technology is a help or hindrance as a tool of trust in the digital world. When we tested specific services with consumers, many of the most popular services involved extending a user's eyes, ears, and risk detection abilities to monitor the ecosystem in a way most people don't have time, energy, or capacity to do. For example, young people and families show a high interest in a service that leverages information across the Web to help verify that someone interacting with them is who he says he is. A service that would monitor profile accounts and devices for unusual activity—much like a credit monitoring service—also scored well across a wide swath of demographics. Many of these services are basically wariness tools. Companies that can monetize not only trust but healthy practices of distrust have a better chance at getting a share of the price premium consumers will pay to have someone in the market who they can believe is in it along with them.

And yet, consumers also have an obligation to trust at some level, else risk a life of suspicion, if not one with fewer rewards. The Madoff scandal inspired economists to study the correlation between trust and reward among financial investors. Although there is a correlation found among those who were too trusting and financial repercussions (as was the case with Madoff's victims), there is also a link between those who are too distrusting and fewer financial rewards. What is more fascinating is that the cost of distrust is actually found to be higher than that of excessive trust. Moreover, although both excessive trust and distrust are both found to be individually costly, distrust is also socially costly because it reduces investment and the creation of surplus.[7] As we learned to trust one another in ancient times to prosper, we must again learn to trust each other in a networked-community era. Of course, the challenges in the latter are far greater because threats can go undetected and innocent bystanders, as in the Sony case, can be caught in a predator's crossfire.

However, the virtual world beckons with a seductive attraction. As one victim of the Sony case laments on the debacle, he does not question the sanctity of his financial information. Instead, he yearns for the gaming service he has come to enjoy, despite the violation from the company that provides it to him. David Hancock, journalist and avid gamer, writes:

> It's been seven days now—or is it 7,000?—since the Sony PlayStation network went down.... I wish I could get riled up over this latest security breach—but honestly it's the third time in three years that I've received notification that my credit information may have been compromised. At this point in the digital age, I've become reconciled to the fact that lots of strangers are rummaging through the underwear drawer of my credit history. What's truly disheartening about Sony's security fumble is how much I miss posting my best scores on the Sony network. And more insidiously, the addictive nature of video games.[8]

Technology is, in many cases, similar to Madoff's black box. No, technology won't fleece consumers out of billions of dollars. Those crimes remain the domain of the disreputable. But, like the algorithms that propelled Madoff's black box, technology is itself mysterious. Consumers must offer a modicum of trust to engage in a virtual world. And, as Hancock's remarks reflect, the lure of temptation is often too great to resist. Those companies who operate within the crossroads of identity will find a market primed to respond—and trust.

SHIFT SHORT: THE PUBLIC TRUST

Arnold Schwarzenegger, John Edwards, Christopher Lee, Anthony Weiner, and more names than we have space to fill. We've seen a parade of politicians caught figuratively—and some literally—with their pants down in a variety of sex scandals including affairs, children with mistresses, and seedy engagements with camera phones. When scandals hit, an issue often raised is whether the politician's behavior constitutes a violation of the public trust that renders him unfit for public office.

Weiner, in particular, is an interesting case. A rising star in the Democratic party, he was wildly popular with his constituency and considered an effective leader ready to run for mayor of New York City. His indiscretion—tweeting a picture of himself in his underwear to a young Twitter follower and having it inadvertently posted publicly—breaks no laws and doesn't appear to have included an actual affair, just creepy cyberspace nonsense. Sexual mores aside, what was Weiner's "crime"? Besides having an unfortunate name that made him easy media fodder, what got Weiner in trouble was the cover-up and the improbability of his defense as it evolved from hacking to a joke that got out of hand. His popularity led many to believe and defend him, including former roommate and political humorist Jon Stewart. But even long-time friend Stewart was looking at Weiner sideways when he proclaimed that he couldn't say with "certitude" whether the picture in question was or was not him. On Stewart's popular mock news program, *The Daily Show*, the comedian said there are three things in life he knows with "certitude": *The Empire Strikes Back* is the best Star Wars movie, OJ Simpson killed two people, and—paraphrasing to avoid vulgarity—what he looks like in his own underwear.[9] As we've discussed, one of the first moments of identity formation for anyone is progression through the mirror phase. Recognizing our own image is a basic human ability. For Weiner to pretend he couldn't do that elicited a visceral groan of disbelief even from his supporters.

SHIFT SHORT: THE PUBLIC TRUST (*continued*)

And that was his biggest violation of the public trust. Weiner's dishonesty was so transparent, yet he expected us to believe him and reacted indignantly when doubted. His repeated denials and their changing nature didn't help—especially as more and more pictures, tweets, and texts came to light. He lied so badly, so stupidly, and with such insistence that he, in effect, begged his constituents to suspend their trust in him and no longer allow him to represent them.

WNYC radio analyst and former political advisor Jami Floyd listed Weiner's mistakes in her blog: not telling the truth, not being honest, not being civil, not being transparent, being cowardly and evasive, and delivering a too little, too late apology. Her distinction between telling the truth (letter of the law) and being honest (spirit of the law) gets to the heart of how trust works:

> *A truth-teller can also be a liar. That is why, when you do tell the public your ultimate truth, every comment must be earnest and from the heart. Because the public can sniff out a liar. And if [you] lie, in whole or in part, you will fall.*[10]

And thus Weiner fell because in failing to be honest and direct, he took what may have been a temporary moment of public shame and turned it into a deep character issue and monumental distraction that made it impossible for him to serve.

2 The Universal Laws

In This Part

The 3P Model of Identity that you read about in Part 1 is about how consumers view identity from an introspective point of view; the universal laws covered in this part of the book are those external forces that shape beliefs and perceptions. Whether consumers believe they have less control over their external environment than they actually do (learned helplessness), assume they have greater control over their surroundings than is actual (illusion) or are easily swayed by environmental noise (recall), they may fall victim to their own misperceptions. The process whereby consumers attempt to harmonize seemingly contradictory beliefs and behaviors is rationalization, and consumers' abilities to self-deceive should not be underestimated by companies attempting to serve them in a networked-community age.

5

The Law of Learned Helplessness: Failure Is the Only Option

Sure you're powerless, sure you are just one person, sure you can't change anything ... but you don't have to be miserable about it as well.

—Lydia Lunch, musician

She had made the walk to her bus stop so many times before. But on June 10, 1991, 11-year-old Jaycee Lee Dugard's life would forever be changed. On that fateful day, Jaycee was kidnapped by convicted sex offender Phillip Craig Garrido and his wife Nancy and entered a world of captivity and rape. For the first several years of her imprisonment, Jaycee was physically restrained by handcuffs in the Garridos' backyard shed. But, eventually, the hubris of her perpetrators compelled them to release her from her physical shackles, even exposing her to others in public under a newly created identity as Garrido's niece. Despite the physical ability to run away, Jaycee never did. She never signaled that she was in distress even when in the presence of others. Sadly, the legal system itself was of no help to her either—as law enforcement officers visited parolee Garrido in his home no less than 60 times during her years of captivity, yet not one bothered to explore the backyard shed that was home to Jaycee and ultimately her two children fathered by the sex offender. Her nightmare ended when astute campus police officers at nearby University of California Berkley witnessed Garrido proselytizing on campus with Jaycee and their children and sensed something unusual about the "family" unit. When investigators finally descended on the case, Jaycee initially remained committed to her cover as Garrido's niece before succumbing to the pressure by persistent interviewers to shed the façade and reveal her true identity. Her rescue would come 18 years after the abduction that stole her childhood.

Why would an able-bodied individual with multiple opportunities to escape a vicious predator over several years fail to do so? It's something not even Jaycee herself fully understands. When interviewed by Diane Sawyer in 2011, two years after being rescued, she reflects on the question:

> *Sawyer: Did you think about taking those two girls [her children fathered by Garrido] and running?*
>
> *Dugard: I'm sure I did, but it wasn't something I felt I could do. The situation felt like it wasn't an option. I don't know how else to explain it. There was no leaving.*
>
> *Sawyer: What would it have taken for you to believe you could leave?*
>
> *Dugard: I've asked myself that question many times.... There was no leaving.*[1]

Although the physical handcuffs confining Jaycee during her initial years of captivity had long been removed, there was something far more powerful paralyzing her ability to escape. Some were quick to label Jaycee a victim of Stockholm syndrome—a condition in which a prisoner develops feelings for her assailant. But in reviewing Jaycee's diary entries over the period of her captivity, experts arrived at a very different conclusion. It's a condition called *learned helplessness*, and, if you think you would somehow react differently than Jaycee if faced with the same horrific circumstances, don't be so sure.

Learned helplessness was first identified back in the 1960s when American psychologist Martin Seligman and his colleagues discovered the role of conditioning in eliciting a behavioral response in animals. In his historic experiment, Seligman placed three groups of dogs in harnesses. Dogs in the first group were simply placed in the harnesses for a random period of time before being released. The second and third groups were placed in harnesses and yoked together. Dogs in both groups were treated with electrical shocks. The dogs in the second group were able to eliminate the shocks by activating a lever. However, the lever was impotent for dogs in the third group, who were completely reliant on the dog in their yoked pair to remove the electric stimulus. As such, dogs in the third group had no effect on their environment, and the relief from the electric shock was perceived to be entirely random, and thereby inescapable, given its dependence on the action of another animal.

Seligman and his associates took the experiment one step further. In its next phase, the team placed the three groups of dogs in an apparatus divided by a low and easily climbable barrier. On one side of the barrier, the floor was treated with electric shocks; the other area was not. Dogs in the first two groups learned quickly to jump over the low barrier to reach the safety of a floor on the opposite side void of electric impulses. For the most part, the dogs in the third group lay helplessly and passively on the electric floor, not attempting to easily climb over the barrier to relieve the pain. Despite the conditions of their environment changing in quite a dramatic way, these dogs had learned that their efforts were futile and did not attempt, yet alone succeed in, escape.[2]

This experiment has been replicated with other animal species with similar conclusions. Place a rat in a maze with a food reward at the other end. Obstruct the rat's path with a transparent divider, whereby it can clearly see the food goal but is unable to climb over the barrier, and it retreats back to its starting point. Now, remove the barrier in its entirety and run the trial again, and the rat is likely to stop, as if hitting an invisible obstacle, precisely where the real one once existed, look curiously at the food goal clearly within reach, and retreat back to its starting position. The rat learns that it cannot control its environment and, despite a meaningful change in its surrounding conditions, fails to attempt to persevere after such conditioning has occurred.

Rats and dogs are simple animals, relatively speaking, when compared with the human species. Surely, our superior cognitive capabilities immunize us from falling victim to the same obstacles. That would be a wrong assumption, as evidenced by a study conducted by Watson and Ramey in 1969. In it, the psychologists divided infants into two groups. One group was provided with a sensory pillow in their crib that could control a hanging mobile. The other group had no control whatsoever. Later, all babies were placed in cribs with the sensory pillow that allowed control over the mobile. Despite all babies now having the ability to control the unit, only the group that had learned to use the sensory pillow attempted to do so.[3]

But, that's in the case of *infants*. They don't possess the cognitive reasoning skills that developed adults do. We certainly have the capacity to learn differently, right? Not exactly. A similar experiment was conducted with people who performed mental tasks in the presence of a distracting noise. Those who could disable the noise by flipping a switch had better mental performance (even though they rarely bothered to activate the lever) than those who could not. Merely knowing that such control over one's environment existed led to better mental performance.[4]

"Learned helplessness" has made its way into our social narrative to help explain chronic psychological illnesses like depression, elucidate how children learn to accept failing performance, and enlighten us on how Jaycee's otherwise inexplicable behavior becomes so much more relatable. And, in the case of consumers struggling to control their environment in a hyperconnected world, we can again turn to learned helplessness for rationalization of otherwise unjustifiable behavior.

Why Bother?

Voting has such a profound impact on the future of democratic societies that it is compulsory in some nations. This isn't the case in the United States, the zealot, if not outright architect, of a free society. In a nation where American flags wave as reminders of the paramount sacrifice made by so many soldiers who fought and died for that very freedom, roughly 40 percent of Americans choose not to exercise their right to vote for the highest office in the land.[5]

Some analysts point to learned helplessness as a possible explanation. In a two-party system in which only 11 percent of Americans have faith in Congress and nearly half favor replacing their elected officials with random names drawn from a phonebook, the skepticism about government is palpable.[6] Just as the animals in the staged experiments before us, so many Americans feel helpless to control their environment, despite a tangible means of doing so at the polls. In this way, learned helplessness can actually paralyze an entire society, not merely an individual. In the case of voting, the consequences are severe as individuals become disenfranchised with the system designed to liberate them. In the case of a virtual world, *netizens* are equally distraught about how to have a meaningful impact on their environment. They turn to apathy as a natural defense mechanism to ignore or deaden any associated discomfort.

Amy, our busy salesperson on the go, voices the sentiment shared by so many like her, where the thought of attempting to control one's environment in a virtual world that is constantly changing is in itself too much to bear.

> *Amy: I plug in my wireless card and I'm on the Internet and I can continue to work on the way home if I need to or on the way in if I am taking the bus in and I have work to do in the morning. So one time, I was talking to a customer while I was doing that and she's like, "That's so bad for your computer to be traveling and on the move." And, I was like, "I can't deal with that. I don't know what you're talking about." So I ignored it. I don't know. Maybe there's a concern but I chose not to*

believe her. I think she was trying to say I could get viruses or corrupt
my computer or something when I am connected and on the move.
Who knows? It could be totally true. I have no idea.

Interviewer: *Do you care?*

Amy: *No.*

Amy certainly has more control over her environment than she is perhaps willing to admit. She could do some basic research on the topic, such as calling her wireless service provider as a starting point, to assess the security risks. She could use basic encryption protocols to secure her data transmission. Or she could opt to not connect on her way to or from work while using a wireless connection, particularly for sensitive transactions, if the threat appears more real than perceived. But Amy chooses none of these viable options. Instead, she opts for denial. Does learned helplessness apply here? We argue that it does. However, there is also likely inertia in play, further paralyzing Amy's motivation to act. Amy enjoys working on the go and isn't tolerant of information that could challenge or rebuke this behavior. Couple this inertia with a learned helplessness that security threats are bigger than her ability to respond and you have a powerful psychological cocktail inhibiting Amy's ability to take necessary precautions.

Amy is not alone. Samantha, a 20-something consultant and part-time entrepreneur in our study, is deaf to identity threat concerns despite the prodding by her boyfriend:

He gets really nervous about throwing away documents even if they're
shredded. Like, he'll be like, "What if somebody gets a hold of that
information? How will I be protected?" I guess maybe I should care
more about it, but I don't.

Reasonable precautions like shredding documents, hardening passwords, or curtailing otherwise risky behaviors are no match for Samantha's apathy. Even among the non-apathetic, learned helplessness is still at work. Consider Amanda, a 30-something mother and wife of a military computer programmer. Being a military wife, Amanda is no stranger to security concerns. In fact, she readily admits that she often thinks about online security, particularly identity theft worries, and is chastised by her tech-savvy husband that her online banking behavior could place her at risk for this devastating crime. Amanda relies on her husband's skills to magically scrub her online profiles and purge her devices of harmful software deposited by hackers, thereby minimizing her own abilities in potentially doing the same:

> He does something every time I go on the computer. He'll come on after me and do his little computer trick. I don't know what he's doing. I guess something to erase it and clean it. I'm not sure how that works.

There's a bit of learned helplessness in attempting to fully protect herself from pervasive security threats:

> Every program that you go to, they are constantly managing it and looking at it and seeing who's on it to monitor every step that a person's making, which, in my opinion, there's no way to do that when there's millions of people. There's a way to break through. There's always a way to break through. For example, the craigslist stalker. You're not supposed to put this [information] on [the site]. They have all these rules and regulations but nobody abides by them so in terms of security, there's never a guarantee.

All those "rules and regulations" that Amanda references are intended, in part, as safeguards to mitigate reckless behaviors. However, as we discussed in Chapter 2 on protection, many guidelines have been obfuscated by complex legalese in onerous privacy policies, thereby thwarting their effectiveness as practical and comprehensible prescriptions for consumers. Given the inertia that keeps Amy happily connected during her morning commute, Samantha unabashed in tempting identity thieves, Amanda engaged in online banking, and millions of others active in whatever online pursuits fulfill them, "there's never a guarantee" when it comes to online security.

The impact of learned helplessness in a networked-community age is far more pervasive than these few ethnography respondents. A study by Norton among 7,000 web users worldwide finds that 65 percent have been victims of cybercrime (which includes computer viruses and malware, online credit card fraud, and identity theft). Although more than half were angry or frustrated with the attack, nearly 80 percent didn't expect that the criminals would be brought to justice. Combine this belief with a propensity to blame oneself for the attack, and you have a classic case of learned helplessness. "We accept cybercrime because of a learned helplessness," says Joseph LaBrie, associate professor of psychology at Loyola Marymount University. "It's like getting ripped off at a garage—if you don't know enough about cars, you don't argue with the mechanic. People just accept the situation, even if it feels bad." And people are not as likely to change behavior as a result. According to the same study, only half indicated that they would *consider* changing online activities if victimized.[7]

A Powerful Antidote

You might be different from our ethnography respondents. In fact, you might be downright proactive when it comes to taking measures to protect yourself online. Most in our quantitative study certainly believe so. Indeed, it appears that many protection-oriented behaviors are ubiquitous across the online population:

- Ninety-three percent clear their browser cache or delete online cookies at least once in a while (with more than 40 percent of respondents indicating they frequently engage in such behavior).
- Eighty-eight percent use security service or applications that protect them online or on mobile devices, such as anti-virus, anti-malware, anti-spyware, or anti-adware options.
- Eighty-six percent password-protect their home wireless connection.

These numbers would suggest quite a different picture, one in which the majority of those online are active in taking measures to protect themselves—hardly an outcome you would expect from a population of learned helpless. We submit that there's something else at play here, and it's a powerful antidote to learned helplessness as evidenced in several behavioral experiments: *control*. To mobilize the masses, control cannot be separated from simplicity. Given that many consumers are perplexed by technology (much like LaBrie's parallel to cars), providers can enable control through simple tools. When consumers are equipped with tools that are easy to implement and adopt, they will do so, as our evidence supports. (Recall the earlier point of more consumers preferring more simplistic, as opposed to more comprehensive, privacy settings.)

Despite nearly universal behaviors by consumers attempting to protect themselves online, today's alternatives are lacking. More than one in three in our study admit difficulty in protecting their privacy by limiting what information is collected and shared by the sites they visit. Many say it is not as easy as they would like it to be when it comes to a range of social networking safety measures—from limiting the information posted online to only those the consumer wants seeing it, to changing privacy settings to meet specific needs, to customizing communications for different types of people.

However, once behaviors become widely adopted thanks, in part, to more intuitive tools, learned helplessness can become *learned empowerment*. To help explain this, consider that there is at least one aspect of learned helplessness that some experts argue is unique to humans—that of vicarious learning (or modeling), the notion that people can learn to be helpless through observing others encountering uncontrollable events.[8] In other words, just the mere observation of others in a helpless situation paralyzes our ability to assess our own environmental conditions or personal abilities accurately. If this is the case, we argue that the opposite may also help explain such high numbers of protection-seeking behaviors in our study. Stated differently, once a technology that is simple to use becomes widely adopted, others who might otherwise be prone to learned helplessness respond in kind. Let's go back to Samantha for a view of how the psychology of the mind works. What would make Samantha more prone to protecting herself?

> *If it was something everyone else did, that might make me more likely to go along with it. Just because I would be like, "This guy and this guy are doing it, it's probably a good idea. I should do it too." I guess if it were easier. It's just such a hassle to have somebody constantly monitoring all your stuff. I don't want to make a purchase and have 10 million bells and whistles go off like, "Oh my gosh, Samantha bought something weird that she normally wouldn't buy. We're going to call her or stop the transaction." That would be annoying.*

Samantha's comments reveal the powerful weapon of simplicity in overcoming learned helpless inertia. If something intrudes with her daily online activities, she is prone to ignore it (the inertia we've referenced with Amy and Amanda as well, and a topic that will be examined at a different angle in the next chapter). But, assuming something was easy—such as the tools that automatically protect one from malware or seamlessly allow one to establish a secured Wi-Fi connection at home, as measured in our quantitative study—she is prone to adopt it. And the adoption by others like her is likely to influence her to engage in the same activities.

What's the answer to propel these protection-oriented behaviors forward? Some might argue that this is a case in which more regulation is necessary. After all, the Internet can be a scary place, one without jurisdiction, and citizens often turn to their governments to protect them from the world's dangers. But, as we covered in Chapter 2, consumers in our study state otherwise. Only nine percent of those surveyed agree that the government is responsible for keeping the Internet safe and for protecting them and their families from cyber attacks and predators. In contrast, nearly two-thirds of respondents indicate that it's impossible for the government or any one company to police the Internet. Instead, these respondents believe that protection is a personal responsibility.

If you are like us when we first saw this data and attempted to reconcile it against the learned helplessness tendencies we witnessed in our ethnography study, you're undoubtedly scratching your temple in bewilderment. How can consumers simultaneously turn a blind eye to security threats while acknowledging their personal responsibility to protect themselves? How can these same consumers reject "help" from government agencies or companies purporting to be a white knight in an uncertain online world? We hypothesize that it's precisely the enormity and complexity of the Internet that lead consumers to believe there is no means for any other to fully protect them. As Amanda ominously stated, *"There's always a way to break through."* If a persistent hacker can break any system, it seems counterintuitive to believe that a faceless governmental agency could protect the victim. Note this does not imply that these consumers wouldn't want punishments for violators. It just acknowledges that the online world we have helped create is simply too vast for any one company or government agency to protect us.

So, where does that leave providers looking to convert consumers from helpless victims to empowered netizens? Is this a case in which the problem is simply too big to tackle? We're not quite so pessimistic. Companies endeavoring to be a white knight in an otherwise lawless kingdom must acknowledge the consumer skepticism they are likely to encounter in attempting to occupy such a role. That said, these same companies can provide unobtrusive, simple solutions that equip consumers with tools that take online safety to another level. Whether this comes in the form of monitoring online activity to detect suspicious events and notify the consumer as such (one of the most popular services we tested across all respondents), monitoring features that report all online and device activity within a household (one of the most attractive services to parents in our study), or authentication capabilities that verify the person on the other side of the connection is who he says he is (one of the most interesting services as rated by teens), these are just a few services yet to be introduced that could afford consumers more control in their online surroundings. We cover these and other capabilities in later chapters, but, for now, understand how they can counteract an otherwise natural tendency for consumers to turn a blind eye to the risks in their online pursuits.

Learned helplessness is a powerful, paralyzing force. We have discussed its effects among animals, infants, crime victims, and adults. But perhaps the antidote of control is best seen among seniors. In a classic experiment conducted by psychologists Judy Rodin and Ellen Langer among nursing home patients, the scientists split the patients into two groups. On the first floor, each patient was given a plant to keep and take care of and offered a choice as to what night he would prefer to see a weekly movie. On the second floor, each patient was given a plant that the nurses would care for and *told* which night he was scheduled to watch the movie. Although they were offered similar things, the patients on the first floor were provided something far more valuable—the ability to control certain aspects of their environment. These residents became more active, had higher morale, and were less depressed. Eighteen months later, they were also more likely to be alive, showing just how influential helplessness or empowerment can be in our lives.[9]

If learned helplessness can seduce us through our lives, we are certainly not immune to it when walking the virtual world. Most of us engage in protection-oriented behaviors that have now become widespread because of the simplicity of tools encouraging the same. Although there may never be a white knight to relieve every danger in one's path (nor do most consumers believe such a fantasy is even possible), there are multiple opportunities for providers to transform consumers from helpless to empowered. Consumers are waiting for more solutions and tools to help control their online environment. They are anxious for providers to step up and remove the invisible barriers that create an otherwise unstoppable inertia preventing their own ability to protect themselves. However, there is a fine line between actual and perceived control. In addition, to the extent that consumers overemphasize their own abilities in influencing their environment, there are other pitfalls that wait, the topic of our next chapter. As for the helpless, although the obstacles in their path may be largely *perceived*, the rewards for their removal are very *real*—not merely for consumers but for providers who answer the call.

SHIFT SHORT: DON'T SEND IN THE CAVALRY!

Consumers may be the learned helpless when it comes to online safety, but that doesn't mean that they are unaware of the potential dangers. Nine in 10 Americans are aware of the recent privacy and security concerns at companies like Sony and Citi. Despite this knowledge, more than half in our study often share information about themselves in exchange for coupons, discounts, and updates. More than 20 percent admit to sharing as much as they can in order to get better, customized online deals. The knowledge of a threat is real, but it does little to deter the behavior of the U.S. consumer. Learned helplessness may be, in part, to blame. If users don't feel any power over their environment, they question the point in trying. Couple this with the power of an instant-gratification society in which the network makes commerce and forming connections easier than ever, and you have a formula that inhibits significant behavioral change.

One would think that consumers would want someone else to look out for them, but most feel that they can look after themselves. Nearly two-thirds of Americans say online protection is their responsibility, not third parties. Well-intentioned legislators are considering the boundaries of this contentious debate. At the time of this writing, the Congress and the Administration are contemplating privacy legislation in the realm of online behavior tracking, consumer data collection, social networking, location-based services, and search. But do consumers want more online protections in the first place? And, if they do, what are the right areas of focus?

Our study reveals that many policy makers may be barking up the wrong tree. Consumers may be worried about being attacked—but the perceived threat revolves much more around hackers fleecing one's bank account than personal details about themselves and their loved ones being exposed. In our study, nearly 90 percent of Americans say they care more about their financial information being jeopardized than about their personal information being exposed. Ninety-five percent say that Congress should do more to address financial security as it relates to Internet and cyber threat, with Republicans, Democrats, and independents in complete agreement.

SHIFT SHORT: DON'T SEND IN THE CAVALRY! *(continued)*

How do we square this circle: a learned helpless mentality; the general belief that individuals are responsible for online protection; and the simultaneous, seemingly contradictory demand for government action? We learned that consumers won't stop pursuing behaviors that gratify but that they also desire better tools to better protect their pocketbooks. Consumers view government as a powerful spur to addressing cyber financial security—but they also view the government as not an effective actor in protecting personal financial security online. Case in point: We tested a secure authentication service that offers greater protection than current password protections. Consumer liked it. But when we asked them who should offer greater cyber protection, they want a private Internet service provider, not the federal government.

This preference for a private Internet provider to provide better tools reflects in part acceptance of personal responsibility for online protection. Preference for private versus public solutions might also reflect that service providers are seen as better able to meet the customized demands and needs of consumers in terms of cybercrime. And it might be that Americans put more faith in the competence of private entities versus the government generally. In any case, we can infer that consumers draw distinctions between how to best fight online theft and burglary versus how to fight these same crimes offline. In the real world, more cops on the beat are provided by the government to fight theft and burglary, and this is popular with the public; online consumers prefer private entities to provide them the night sticks instead.

This issue will only become more complex as our lives online become less virtual and more *real*. Prescribing an antidote to the wrong set of symptoms could produce unintended consequences that online consumers will greatly resent, rather than the desired remedy that all desire. At the very least, our findings suggest that caution is in order from Congress and other policy makers.

The Law
of Illusion:
Lie to Me

A false sense of security is the only kind there is.

—MICHAEL MEADE, AUTHOR

Owen Thomas had his life ahead of him. At 21 years old, his intellectual capabilities earned him enrollment at the prestigious University of Pennsylvania, and his athletic prowess resulted in his election as a captain by his football teammates. The popular junior was a third-generation football player who acquired his taste for the sport when he began playing at the age of nine. The love of the game was shared by his family, who delighted in seeing talented Owen crush the competition with jaw-dropping hits. "He loved to hit people," his mother said. "He loved to go into practice and hit really hard. He loved to intimidate.... We all love football. We all love watching. We all love these great hits."

Yes, Owen Thomas *had* his life ahead of him. That is, until he opted for suicide instead on a fateful Monday afternoon in April of 2010. The news was staggering to those who knew him. He had never shown signs of depression. His cell phone, at the ready for a call that was never to be placed, lay in his pocket as he took his life by hanging. Family and friends had no solace or closure from an explanatory note that was never left behind. Evidence of events preceding and at the horrific scene hardly painted a picture of a distressed young adult with a premeditated appetite for suicide. Instead, the tragedy was as mysterious as it was heartbreaking—until an autopsy of his brain revealed what could be part of the answer to an otherwise inexplicable act. Owen, as it turns out, is the youngest known football player to suffer from a brain disease known as chronic traumatic encephalopathy (or CTE, for short), a deteriorating condition linked to depression and impulse control, one previously largely reserved for NFL players.

Although we cannot know for sure if Owen's brain condition was the sole cause of his suicide, some experts believe that it was a contributing factor. Doctors assert the disease was the result of thousands of subconcussive collisions he withstood in his dozen years of football—those amazing hits he sustained while his brain was still developing. The disease leapt into the headlines in 2006 when Andre Waters, a Philadelphia Eagle and another hard-hitting athlete, also committed suicide. Owen's father still remembers the day when he read about the Waters case and his immediate thoughts that had persisted up until his son's death: "Thank goodness that's only the NFL—it can't happen to Owen."[1]

Why would Owen's father have cause for concern? After all, Owen had taken the necessary safety precautions for the rigor of football; among them, he had faithfully worn his protective helmet. And, by all accounts, that helmet had done its job because Owen had never been diagnosed with a concussion since his start as a youngster playing the game. It is this sad twist of fate that now has some experts questioning if the one piece of apparatus meant to protect Owen from injury may have, instead, played a part in his untimely death. They claim that advances in new high-tech helmets actually serve to give players a false sense of security that encourages more reckless behavior—those jarring hits that fans so love to see.[2] It is these thousands of hits sustained over a hobby or career, undetectable to one's pain sensors thanks to a hardened helmet, that place football players, both professional and amateur, at heightened risk for CTE.

A false sense of security deadened Owen's pain and his parents' concern. Unfortunately, its reach is not limited to the football field. Over the past several decades, studies have shown just how dangerous a false sense of security can be, whether in seducing drivers during the early days of the automobile airbag to believe the new contraption was a sufficient defense mechanism that rendered the seatbelt useless (an erroneous and deadly assumption),[3] compelling citizens to spend millions of dollars lighting public streets to deter crime (no such correlation has been clearly proven),[4] or lulling drivers into a false belief that hands-free communication is safer than holding a cell phone (when in actuality the deterioration in driving accuracy is associated with the distraction of conversation itself, not the means by which the device is used).[5] Given the overwhelming evidence on the topic, it is not surprising, although frightening all the same, that we discovered the illusion of safety as a powerful disarmament to one's practical sensibilities in a virtual world.

The Threat of Illusory Correlation

Brenda is a mother of two adolescent boys and a kindergarten teacher. Like many other parents we spoke with in our study, she struggles with keeping her children safe online. But Brenda has a safeguard that at least in part addresses this concern. She places family computers in shared household areas where parental eyes can monitor the online habits of curious teen boys:

> *I like to see what they're doing, that's why I set up the laptop in the middle of the kitchen. Or, in the study, I can be in and out. Upstairs [where the boys' rooms are] it's hard if I'm downstairs. I mean, they're good kids but still I think it's better not to have that.*

Brenda's assumption seems reasonable. After all, she grew up in a time when parental monitoring of children was paramount to protecting them from potential predators. Take the story of Adam Walsh, which is sadly and indelibly burned in our collective memory. Like Brenda's children, Adam was a good kid. Unfortunately, that didn't stop a monster from abducting him from a Sears department store in 1981 while Adam's mother let him out of her sight, if only for a few minutes. Tragically, Adam's severed head was found a few weeks later. His heartrending murder was not in vain. It inspired the passing of legislation in the young boy's name to help lost children in department stores and the formation of the National Center for Missing & Exploited Children. For anyone who remembers the time of Adam's disappearance or has heard the story since, the ominous warning remains clear: Keep an eye on your children.

This certainly couldn't be truer in the realm of parenting. Brenda is wise to take precautions that limit her children's online activities to places where she and her husband can "see" what they are doing—right? Or is this another case of a false sense of security that may, in fact, be deadening Brenda's senses to the real, yet invisible, dangers that lurk beyond her monitored perimeter?

Cut to Brenda's son, who is upstairs in his bedroom, outside of the controlled boundary of her watchful eye. He willingly shows the interviewer how he often passes his time with the plethora of applications available on his iPhone. Among them is Facebook, a site in particular that has earned Brenda's attention and one she deliberately monitors while her sons are on the family computers within the established border of her visibility. Unfortunately for Brenda, she has neglected the computers that remain persistently in her children's pockets, the smartphones that not only connect them to the safety of home while away but to the potential dangers of the online world while "safely" at home. For Brenda, these computers are all too often outside the protective defense mechanism of the shared computer safeguard she has worked so deliberately to create.

There were many parental subjects in our study like Brenda. You may be like her and find that you have created a safe zone within your home where parental observation is possible. If that is the case, you and Brenda both suffer what is known in psychology parlance as *illusory correlation*. Illusory correlation is simple if not profound. It is the phenomenon of seeing the relationship one expects in a set of data when no such relationship exists. It helps explain why stereotypes persist. For example, say you meet a few nice people and they happen to be from small towns. You may form the conclusion that most people from small towns are pleasant. You may, in fact, ignore the times when you have met people who are not so nice from small towns and reject their origin. You have formed a correlation in your mind that city population is correlated to kindness, when no such correlation actually exists.[6] Illusory correlation is also in play with Brenda. She has formed a linkage between her confinement of technology to shared spaces of the home and a greater likelihood that her children will be safe, if not monitored, online. Remember: *Keep an eye on your children*. What she has ignored in this equation is that the virtual world cannot be contained to a few rooms in the household when her children have computers (smartphones) on their person 24/7. In addition, unlike Adam Walsh's attacker, predators in an online world cannot be "seen" by the naked eye of a watchful parent. As such, Brenda's children are hardly safer simply because the laptop is downstairs. Worse yet, Brenda's assumption of safety—and the illusion or false sense of security she derives from it—may actually serve to deaden her sensibilities and, by her absence in the upstairs dwelling area, enable potentially more reckless behavior by her teenage sons, the one outcome she is most interested in thwarting.

When the System Fails

For years, engineers have studied the unintended consequences that result when safeguards are added to enhance a system. The reputable "Father of Modern Science" Galileo reported one of the first known examples of this occurrence. In Galileo's day, stone columns, popular raw materials for buildings of the time, were often stored prior to use. If the stone came in contact with the ground, the soil would tend to stain and discolor it—not an attractive outcome for the building that would soon be adorned by it. To prevent discoloration, it was common to store the columns off the ground, supported by piles of stone or timber at each end. This sometimes led to a column breaking in the unsupported middle, fractured by its own weight. A well-intentioned worker, seeing the outcome, developed the idea to place another element in the system—a third set of boulders or timber stationed beneath the middle of the column. The intention was to eliminate the potential failure of the system encountered when a column broke under its weight by fortifying the space beneath the center and balancing the load across three equidistant structures. What resulted instead was the introduction of a new point of failure in the system.

You see, as the supports sat outside in the weather beneath the weighty stone column, they would settle—and rarely would they settle at exactly the same progression or level. After some time, the actual support of most of the columns reverted back to just two of the three structures—the piles of stone on either end of the column as in the original system or by one end support and one middle support. Here's the more interesting part: Not only did the original breakage model persist, but because the middle support was an "add-on" to many columns already in storage, its settlement into the soil occurred at a much slower pace than the two end structures already intact. As such, some columns were left sustained only by the middle structure over time, leading to a new breakage, or point of failure, nonexistent in the original system.[7]

Beyond an interesting factoid that may help you impress your friends with your knowledge of Galilean history at your next social gathering, what does this have to do with identity in a virtual world? Remember all those protection-oriented behaviors we referenced in Chapter 2? Nearly 90 percent of respondents in our study indicated that they had taken the safety measure of using anti-malware, anti-spyware, anti-virus, and anti-adware solutions to protect themselves online or on mobile devices. But what if the system that is intended to protect the respondent is actually made impotent by the respondent's own doing or incompetence? Although nearly 90 percent report that they have taken measures to protect themselves, it's difficult to ascertain how many of these respondents actually are shielded versus those who recklessly surf with outdated or disabled software—all the while thinking they are, in fact, protected.

Because this latter group is ignorant of the dangers, they may be engaging in online behaviors that are riskier simply because of their illusion of safety. The system that was intended to protect—as was the case with the third set of load-balancing weights in Galilean times—actually creates another fault (more reckless behavior) that was likely not present before these individuals thought they were protected.

If you're finding it difficult to process how individuals could engage in riskier behavior simply by being under the misguided premise that they are more protected, look to yourself for the evidence. As human beings, we are accustomed to substituting one risk for another. It's the same reason we speed up when we put our seatbelts on. It explains why insurers in the United Kingdom, once accustomed to offering driver discounts to those who purchased cars with safer brakes, no longer do so. Why? According to John Adams, a risk analyst and emeritus professor of geography at University College London, "There weren't fewer accidents, just different accidents." Buoyed by a false sense of control that comes with enhanced automobile safety systems, these drivers were found to take more risks, such as going faster even when the roads were slippery.[8] In addition, when our virtual seatbelts are improperly fastened in an online world, we are much more likely to engage in riskier behavior by taking faith in an impervious safety harness that exists only in our imagination.

Caroline is a single mother and aspiring entrepreneur with her own personal stylist business she operates online. Caroline is not someone who is particularly tech-savvy. By her own admission, she struggles with how to reflect the best possible image of her business online given her lack of computer prowess. However, she was certainly savvy enough to incorporate safety measures to secure (and thereby encourage) financial transactions. These tools should protect Caroline and her customers, right? Well, things got a bit interesting when we probed Caroline about her use of Wi-Fi:

> **Caroline:** *I have to go to a place that I know for a fact has Wi-Fi [like Starbucks and McDonalds]. Now if someone was purchasing something from me, I have a secure site so I don't know that would be an issue. When I'm out, it's unsecure. So, I wouldn't take care of banking information or anything like that. I don't worry about it that much. I probably should have.*
>
> **Interviewer:** *If somebody's purchasing something from you?*
>
> **Caroline:** *I probably wouldn't use the Internet there.*
>
> **Interviewer:** *But you do?*

Caroline: *But I have.*

Interviewer: *What gives you the sense that it might not be as secure when you're out and about?*

Caroline: *Because people can hack into your computer anywhere. I think they can even do it at my house. But, it's a secure site though, so I don't know. I never even thought about that. Now you all are telling me this so now I'm thinking about it.*

It's fascinating. Caroline is a responsible entrepreneur who has presumably secured her site with the necessary e-commerce precautions. She's not sure if that security protects her over a public Wi-Fi connection (back to our point about her not being the most tech-savvy), but that doesn't stop her from reluctantly admitting she has engaged in those transactions just the same. The fact that her site is secure leaves her questioning if that applies to a public hotspot. But, whether or not her virtual seatbelt is properly fastened, she conducts business using the public airwaves. Despite not knowing for sure if she is putting her customers at risk, she assumes that the software on her site is sufficient and engages in even more precarious behavior. To justify her otherwise irresponsible actions, she turns to our old friend learned helplessness to explain away what she doesn't believe she can influence about her environment in the first place ("Because people can hack into your computer anywhere. I think they can even do it at my house.").

There are many delusional netizens engaging in risky behavior online, like Caroline, yet believing they are somehow safer than they are. In our study, more than one in three fall into this category, believing that their online activity is confined to familiar sites and people that would not put them at risk. Despite this belief, these seemingly unaware individuals are equally likely to admit to engaging in a range of risky behaviors like the rest of the population, including shopping online while using public Wi-Fi hotspots, interacting with people online whom they have never met in person, giving credit card information to a site just discovered, or making a purchase from an unknown seller via an online classified ad.

For another example of seemingly irrational behavior, consider Vickie, a protective mother of three girls, and another of our study's respondents. Vickie and her husband take every reasonable precaution to protect their children. Their girls do not sleep over at friends' homes. They are not allowed out with a friend whom their parents do not know or whose parents they have not met. In addition, like any responsible parent raising children in a virtual world, Vickie has installed parental software to protect her children from inappropriate content. As with Brenda, the family computer is downstairs, adjacent to the kitchen, where loving eyes are a few feet away.

Yet a fascinating occurrence happened while we were in the home. Vickie's teenage daughter was happily surfing on that family computer when a strange security warning blocked her passage to an otherwise familiar site. Perplexed, the girl didn't know what to do. Should she ignore the warning and continue about her surfing? Instead, she did what any "good kid" would do: She called to mom for help. What happened next may not exactly stun you. Vickie reviewed the security warning, indicated puzzlement as to what it meant, and then haphazardly clicked to ignore it, thereby giving her daughter "safe" passage to continue.

It seems inexplicable. Why would such a protective parent willfully ignore a security block that, by her own admission, she did not understand? We assert it could have something to do with the frequency of security alerts that have become so common and all the while annoying. In real life, these false alarms, meant to protect us, have actually been shown to create a false sense of security themselves. A fire at a Philadelphia Housing Authority high-rise apartment building surprised its residents not by the alarm that was triggered, but by the fact that the fire was *real*. According to tenants, false alarms at the building are all too common. Moe Jones, a lifelong occupant, had grown accustomed to frequent false alarms at the building. But, when he saw smoke, his basic survival instinct kicked into gear and he fled the building, "I'm gonna leave out, cause I'd rather be safe than sorry. Everything happens for a reason, that was like a sign. 'Cause a lot of people never came out and now they will, 'cause they know it's for real."[9]

Perhaps Vickie is accustomed to one too many casual security warnings that are hardly warnings at all. In our study, nearly two in three are like Vickie and admit they have proceeded with what they were doing online despite a browser warning of a security threat. It would appear that the bypassing of these alerts has yet to result in an unfortunate consequence. Similarly, the repeated dismissal of false alarms by residents in that Philadelphia apartment building had never resulted in a consequence—that is, until the day the fire was real. Unfortunately for Vickie and others like her, the detection of that threat may not be as easy as it was for Moe—pesky online attacks do not bring with them familiar signals, such as smoke that can literally be seen and smelled when it accompanies the fire. The fires burning online are undetectable by our primitive senses in comparison.

Ignorance Is Not Bliss

As individuals become more entangled in a virtual world, the imperative to shatter illusions of safety becomes more critical. How can anyone ever completely safeguard themselves online? As we have stated, technology will never be a substitute for common sense, nor will it be a fail-safe remedy for the foolhardy. However, it can serve to increase the visibility of threats that unsuspecting victims don't even have on their radar. In the case of outdated or unintentionally disabled anti-malware software, the network can detect such security breaches and notify the user as such. Of course, it remains up to the user to take action (or mistakenly assume that the alert is an inconsequential false alarm), but at least the threat is now within his field of vision. In the case of Brenda, who relies on her physical presence to thwart online attackers, the network can provide a report of all sites visited by any technology source in the home, including those ever-present smartphones in her sons' pockets. Note that this raises an interesting question of parental control versus childhood empowerment, which is covered in Chapter 12, but for the purposes of rectifying Brenda's illusion of control, such a tool may be a welcome solution in her home. Again, how she chooses to use such information in her parenting style is at her discretion, but at least the false sense of security created by a laptop contained within a shared familial area is removed from the equation.

In Chapter 5, we postulated that an alleviating factor to combat learned helplessness behavior is simplicity. If you make tools simpler for consumers to incorporate (such as the anti-malware solutions that have become so popular), they are more likely to be adopted. This seems fairly rational and not altogether groundbreaking. However, consider the damage that can result when the very presence of these safety mechanisms encourages riskier behavior and spawns new threats as a result. Furthermore, contemplate for a moment how a consumer would even know he was at greater risk when the new threat is not even detectable. In Owen's case, his helmet was simple to use. In fact, he used it faithfully. That same helmet arguably did its job—it protected Owen from ever experiencing a concussion during his lifelong love of football. But the thousands of hits, innocuous as independent occurrences but collectively debilitating during his formative years, remained undetectable to Owen's threat sensors and his parents' known concerns. It's the metaphorical thousands of hits we take as online enthusiasts each day, sustained by a false sense of security and control, that produce new threats with the riskier behavior that often accompanies the safety systems intended to protect us.

In the case of false safeguards and the erroneous sense of security they perpetuate, ignorance is clearly not bliss. However, we're not suggesting that practical safeguards are bad. Despite Owen's untimely demise, there is overwhelming evidence (if not common sense) proving that helmets measurably reduce injury. Likewise, anti-malware options that have become a staple in the overwhelming majority of connected homes are not inherently bad. After all, they serve a viable role in protecting millions of consumers every day from the threat of hackers trolling for an easy target. But when the presence of these defense mechanisms serves to deaden the sense of threats beyond their perimeter, the result can be a blindsiding attack on the victim. Worse yet, when the actual system of protection itself is compromised, as was the case with a helmet that protected against concussions but facilitated a far more serious and sustainable brain injury for Owen, individuals are rendered both powerless and naive to threats that aren't even in their realm of visibility, yet alone control. Although technology is not a panacea to cure all ills, it certainly can reveal when one's sense of security is unfounded. In Owen's case, the mere awareness of his vulnerability to those mistakenly assumed impenetrable hits could have meant the difference between life and death. For online citizens, including innocent parents under a false notion that their watchful eye alone can protect children in a world of faceless predators, the extreme cases could mean the same.

SHIFT SHORT: SECURITY THEATER

If you fly enough, you have the airport routine down. Boarding pass, ID, shoes off, bag of liquids and laptop out. Coins, belts, and metal in the basket. Walk through whatever machine the airport has deemed fit. Maybe get wanded or patted down. Then, reassemble everything you just disassembled. Keep moving. We may gripe and complain, but in the end, the memory of 9/11 compels compliance. The inconvenience is a small price to pay to make us safer.

But what if most of the measures introduced post-9/11 are ineffective at reducing our risk of attack? What if they're mostly for show? Security expert and author Bruce Schneier says that many of the TSA processes are more *security theater*—a term he coined in his book *Beyond Fear: Thinking Sensibly about Security in an Uncertain World*—than effective countermeasures. Security theater is a production designed to give the illusion that the authorities are in control, which allays fears and reduces challenges. In one sense, security theater is effective. Put up a camera, and we assume we're being watched and act accordingly. But that doesn't change the fact that underneath this placebo effect, there may be little real security.

Take the liquids the TSA tosses out. They don't test those bottles, Schneier says, "They're not even scared of it. They put it in a trash can right next to them.... So because it's not treated as dangerous, there's no point in taking it away."[10] In an interview with *Popular Mechanics* on the controversial new body imaging machines, Schneier said they won't actually catch things like the underwear bomber, whose failed attempt helped prompt more invasive screening.

Popular Mechanics: *So what kind of attack will this prevent, that otherwise might be successful?*

Schneier: *There are two kinds of hijackers. There's the lone nut-case, like someone who will bring a gun onto a plane because, dammit, they're going to take the whole plane down with them. Any pre-9-11 airport security would catch a person like that.*

The second kind is the well-planned, well-financed Al Qaeda–like plot. And nothing can be done to stop someone like that.[11]

Defense expert Ben Wallace, who consulted for one company developing scanner technology, said the new image scanners wouldn't likely detect the attacks in recent memory—including the Christmas 2009 plot aboard a plane to Detroit. He says they give greater visibility and speed to screening, but adds a large caveat: "There is a big *but*, and the but was in all the testing that we undertook, it was unlikely that it would have picked up the current explosive devices being used by al-Qaeda."[12]

Obviously, that's not what anyone wants to hear, and in the wake of each attempted attack, all of which, Schneier points out, have been thwarted or unsuccessful, people expect the government to do *something*, so they did. "It's politics. You have to be seen as doing something, even if nothing is the smart thing to do. You can't be seen as doing nothing," Schneier says. Hence, adding new acts to airport security theater.

The Law of Recall: Taking It from the Top

Memory itself is an internal rumor.

—George Santayana, philosopher

Think of summer and what comes to mind? Beaches, sunshine, vacationing, and … sharks? If you were reading this back in the summer of 2001, these carnivorous predators would likely have been at the top of your list. It all started in July of that year when eight-year-old Jessie Arbogast was swimming with cousins off the Pensacola coast one evening around sunset. Suddenly, a six and one-half foot, 200-pound bull shark engulfed Jessie in its mouth, biting the child's thigh before clamping onto his right arm above the elbow. Jessie's uncle rushed to action, grabbing the shark's tail and giving it a determined tug to release Jessie from the deadly grip. Jessie was let loose and so was his arm, which remained in the shark's mouth. A National Park Service Ranger dealt three deadly gunshots to the carnivore's head, and the boy's extremity was ultimately retrieved, where it was later reattached to his body.[1] The horrific, unbelievable story seemed plucked from the silver screen, and the ensuing drama that unfolded was fodder for the evening news and morning paper. Reporters followed the story 24/7 as Jessie battled for his life, escaping the jowls of death only to find himself in a coma struggling for survival.

Just as Jessie's story was capturing headlines and less than two weeks after the incident, two more found themselves victims of shark attacks on separate occasions. The feeding—and media—frenzy had kicked into full gear. On July 30, *Time* released a cover story of the recent events and ominously dubbed the season, "The Summer of the Shark."[2]

For the next two months, the media circled the story with network footage of sharks schooling around the coastlines of Florida and warnings of a shark epidemic that seemed clearly in play.[3] Then, just as suddenly as sharks leapt into the public narrative, they were given a quick (and quiet) exit on September 11, 2001. The date needs no explanation. The media juggernaut that had defined a summer and paralyzed beachgoers with terror turned its attention to a very different attack and predator—the terrorists who killed thousands of innocent victims on that fateful day in history. The shark was no longer the story. But the damage in the court of public opinion had been done nonetheless.

So, was 2001 indeed the Summer of the Shark? Not so much. It turns out that there were 13 fewer shark attacks worldwide than the year before. Although sharks accounted for 13 human deaths in 2000, they only amounted to four deaths in 2001, by comparison. Yet, although attacks and deaths were down, media exposure and public fear were up exponentially. As George Burgess, head of the International Shark Attack File, reflected in 2003, "Prior to 2001, the public was becoming more aware of the need for shark conservation. But the 'Summer of the Shark' changed all that.... Public perception took several steps backwards to the 'Jaws' mentality." Burgess's excoriation seems founded. In 2003, a survey of 1,010 Americans revealed that 70 percent believed sharks were dangerous, and roughly the same number thought that shark populations were just right or too high. The latter perception, ostensibly the remnants of a media whirlwind two years before, was wrong. Evidence suggested that (with the exception of one) all 400 species of sharks had declined at least 50 percent in the previous eight to 15 years—the result of overfishing and pollution.[4] Therefore, in an ironic twist, human actions were far more severe in crushing the shark population than the other way around. Yet people remembered the Summer of the Shark and the horrific attacks on Jessie and the others. Public opinion had been swayed.

In his 1999 book, *The Culture of Fear: Why Americans Are Afraid of the Wrong Things*, Barry Glassner lists numerous examples of how heavy media coverage of dramatic diseases, crimes, or social problems generates a level of fear out of proportion with the actual probability and harmful impact of those events. He mentions school shootings, strangers kidnapping children, flesh-eating bacteria, and the famous urban legend of razor blades in Halloween apples and candy. On the flip side, more mundane, but more prevalent dangers such as childhood poverty or the decline of blue-collar jobs went relatively under-reported, and, as a result, public fear or interest in more real social issues remained low—at least in 1999. Social scientists measured the public's risk assessments, and those issues that received more coverage routinely rated higher fear factors than stories covered less in the media—despite occurring much less frequently or, in the case of razor-bladed candy, not at all.

Of course, part of the issue is that a news teaser screaming, "The everyday item in your house that just might kill you," is much more attention-grabbing and intellectually manageable than, "The complexities of income inequality and its impact on our social fabric. News at 11." But other forces are also at work in the minds of people receiving and processing information and estimating risk probability. Risk–benefit assessments are affected by your own personal experience and/or the personal experiences of people you know. People generalize from these relatively small, but personally relevant, samples. As discussed in Chapter 3 (on preference), the more direct an experience, the more relevant it seems to be in our decision making. However, we do this not only because of the emotional connections we make, but also because that information is at the top of our mind.

Whether it's the media or our own experience hammering information into our decision-making patterns, some ideas, facts, and examples are more easily recalled, and we give them greater weight. What's *top of mind* is given top priority. Psychologists call this reasoning shortcut the *availability heuristic*.[5] If you can recall an example of an event more quickly, you judge it as more likely to occur and more likely to have an impact on you. In one simple demonstration of this, researchers read off a list of names and later asked subjects if there were more male names or female names on the list. Each list included a mix of famous and non-famous names. Participants overestimated the number of male names when more famous male names were listed, even when there were actually more female names in the list. People give greater weight to information and events that have greater meaning and connection to them because those events are top of mind.

In the study, researchers found six areas that contribute to the availability bias in reasoning. Among them were the familiarity of the incident (such as the media frenzy that captured the shark attacks in 2001), the salience of the topic (with more striking events having greater emotional impact, such as Jessie's story, carrying higher recall), the recentness of the event (we no longer discuss the Summer of the Shark, although it was certainly top of mind in 2001 with residual damage in the court of public opinion as late as 2003), and *imaginability* (which speaks to how well one can generate imagined contingencies when evaluating an encounter, leading to several media outlets in 2001 publishing facts about shark attacks and what to do if victimized).[6] These variables influence how easily a person can recall an example in their judgment process. Easier recall yields a greater feeling of affinity with the dangers or benefits of a situation. We will simply refer to this tendency as the *Law of Recall*, and it is evident across cohorts in our own study.

Emma is a Boomer-aged grandmother and former pharmaceuticals worker, living in North Carolina. She is unemployed and concerned with cutting expenses. During our interview, she reveals that she once had her purse stolen along with her Social Security card, checkbook, and credit cards. As a former theft victim and current unemployed single female struggling to make ends meet, the need for protection of sensitive financial information is a must for Emma. When asked to name companies that she believes are doing a good job in this pursuit, she references PayPal:

> *I think that they're taking certain security steps. I don't know how they do it, but I've been using PayPal for a while, and I haven't heard anybody else that uses PayPal come across the same problem.*

Although she doesn't understand what they do, Emma assumes PayPal must be taking necessary steps to protect users because she knows how frequently she uses the service, and her information has never been stolen or misappropriated via PayPal. Her limited technical understanding of online security coupled with the lack of available examples of PayPal's failures yields a kind of trust, which is, to a certain extent, blind.

Because Emma is a former employee of the healthcare industry, we were also curious to measure her concern regarding electronic health records. Those following the public debate surrounding healthcare are familiar with the role these digital records will play in optimizing patient care and reducing administrative costs. However, one's personal medical data is sensitive and subject to intense security measures. Despite this, Emma isn't concerned at all about having her medical information stored online or in the "cloud" to deliver health services. She stops to ponder the question as she contemplates what issues might arise but can't think of a reason for (or example of) anyone using medical information for an inappropriate purpose. Again, because she can't conceive of how this might be a bad thing, she simply believes it to be okay.

This lack of imaginability is a pitfall that technology providers must consider when attempting to build trusting relationships with some consumers. In our quantitative research, we asked study participants a series of questions about their interest in different services. Participants were presented with the benefits of a service and then, through a series of choices, were asked to reveal their interest. Afterward, some participants were also shown a video clip styled like a news story, which presented risks associated with the service (think of this as simulating the media hype effect). In some cases, the unknown technical realities of how the services work and the inability to understand the implications of a service yielded dramatically different results for those who were given a service's potential risk. For example, we tested a service in which connected appliances and devices automate some household operations and allow for connectivity and notifications, remote operation of appliances, and the like—all as part of the *smart* digital home. Participants who were only presented with the positives had nearly four times the willingness to pay than those who were also exposed to the potential negatives, such as how the service might affect them and whether it's worth the money. What sounded like a great idea in the abstract had some concrete downsides that weren't imagined if they weren't presented.

Overall, the top five services we tested out of 20 were those most resilient to the exposure of potential downsides, preserving consumers' willingness to pay. For those services outside the top five, surveyed consumers who saw only the positives had an average willingness to pay nearly three times higher than consumers who saw the negative "news" clips. There was an imaginability gap, which over the long term could threaten the trust between consumer and provider. Although consumers may not understand risks up front, if they sign up for a service and then are exposed to its negative impacts—through experience, word of mouth, or media coverage—their trust in the service provider could be diminished. Services that can withstand a media onslaught concerning risks, privacy, and the like have greater potential for long-term profitability and pose the least threat to consumer trust.

And, overwhelmingly, this lack of imaginability is in effect in our everyday lives, with everyday services we have come to depend on—not just among future-oriented services tested in the confines of a research instrument. If the topic isn't the headline of the day, the water cooler conversation of the afternoon, or the result of direct personal experience, it isn't likely to draw a second thought among consumers, nor is it likely to trigger the imagination of what dangers could be lurking on the periphery. Consider Samantha, our 27-year-old event planner and avid mobile user. In particular, Samantha admits to using location-based services, like Google Latitude, on a continuous basis. When asked if she is concerned about security threats on her phone, she honestly answers:

> *No. I guess I won't ever worry about it until something happens to me and then I'll be like, "Oh, sh*t, I guess I should have been more concerned about that."*

We suspect Samantha may submit a different viewpoint if we were to speak with her today, amidst the headlines that are proliferating around mobile security. Several months after our interview with Samantha, *The Wall Street Journal* reported that federal prosecutors are investigating whether numerous smartphone applications illegally obtained or transmitted information about their users—including location data—without the consumers' permission.[7] Given that the story has inspired a flurry of media activity on the topic, Samantha's proclivity to use free smartphone applications (including location-based services) and the fact that her event planning work is with a consulting firm to the military, we can't help but wonder if Samantha's fear sensors are a bit heightened since our initial interview based on her proximity to, and the recent availability of, these mobile security stories.

In other cases, the Law of Recall acts as a protection mechanism to influence behaviors based on perception of the risks. Melinda, a 53-year-old retired teacher, uses Facebook to keep in touch with family and friends. Melinda is guarded about what to share online after hearing warnings from a boss and other teachers. One teacher, she says, lost her job after kids posted a video of her teaching ineffectively on YouTube. Another teacher got in trouble when students found pictures of him showing his nipple rings. Melinda believes teachers to be especially vulnerable to the potential troubles of a networked-community age. These stories of teachers in conflict over social media stick with her, and her proximity to some of those affected only deepens her perception of the risk.

The media extends word of mouth, selectively creating more availability of recall for risks that might otherwise not occur to us. Melinda mentions "hearing on the news" that visiting unsecured sites can give you viruses, which she's sure is what happened when her own computer was infected, believing her sons went to sites they shouldn't have. One of her sons also had a credit card number stolen, which they discovered when purchases from all over the country showed up on the bill. Melinda is now careful about where she uses her credit card.

> *They say it can happen if you use your card in a restaurant. Someone can copy up your number or they can really get it off the Internet.*

Reports and personal experiences have created a list of potential risks in Melinda's mind: using her credit card, visiting unfamiliar websites, and, even riskier, connecting the two practices together by using a credit card online. When she says that "they" can "really" get your information off the Internet, she's multiplying the potential harm of using credit and shopping online. For her, the nebulous online world actually creates extra imaginability of associated risks.

Melinda has other concerns as well. Her husband has health problems, and she is surrounded in her neighborhood by women who have outlived their husbands. She ran through a list of these women off the top of her head and then talked about being an empty nester whose children are extremely busy and don't always return her calls. Throughout the interview, it became clear that the thought of being older and alone adds to Melinda's sense of vulnerability and keeps more of the risks she hears at the forefront of her mind. In some ways, the invincibility of youth is a great example of the lack of imaginability. Younger people may think of some dangers but believe themselves to be more capable of dealing with potential situations than they rightfully are. Youth raises the threshold for familiarity, salience, and recentness. The older we get, the less invincible we feel and the more likely we are to associate others' distant misfortunes with the probability of our own. Not surprisingly, this helps explain a direct correlation to the age of the respondent and his perceived fear of online threats in our study. The question remains, however, as to whether this feeling of invincibility is related to the naïveté of youthful exuberance or the realization that there is far more to lose as one gets older. When asked why his concerns for privacy and security online are relatively minor, Jack, a 24-year-old college student in our study, answers with a matter-of-factness that is obvious:

> *Because I have no money now. If I had money and property and stuff like that, I would like to protect it. I would pay for protection when I have something to protect.*

Gender also affects how some assess their vulnerability to online risks. Whether it's because women are generally at a physical disadvantage, because women are targeted more because there is this perception, or because stories about female victimization are more reported, women are generally considered to be at greater risk when it comes to safety. This association of female with "at risk" in the online world is, to an extent, an illusion that can result in greater recall for the dangers faced by women and a disproportionate view of online dangers along gender lines. Some of our ethnography participants expressed greater concern for their female children online, and one participant rated his risks as a man lower. Jack says:

> *Girls get a lot of crazy guys. They get a lot of stalkers. I don't think a guy could be stalked by a girl.*

Jack then quickly recalls examples of girls who ran into trouble online, including a girl he knew who lost her virginity to a man she met in a chat room and a local woman who dumped her online boyfriend and then was murdered by him. Women, he says, have to keep a good head on their shoulders. This association that he and others make in their minds helps these examples of women in danger stick.

As with any of the laws we discuss in this book, the Law of Recall is observable across gender lines, age groups, and parental status. Rachel, a mother of three from Minnesota, admits to being more concerned about her daughter than her sons, saying, "I don't know if it's correct, but we are." Her older son is a wrestler and a football player, and she says his physical advantages lead her to be less worried—even online. In addition to the association of danger with girls over boys, there is also the association of the online world with sexual activity and sexual predators, both of which raise higher concerns for girls versus boys in the minds of parents. Rachel's 13-year-old daughter mentions that her policeman father worries about her online because of "boyfriends and stuff." Rachel says her husband's job and the cases he sees also contribute to the worries they have about their children.

Beyond creating concerns, the Law of Recall can work to allay fears and provide information. When we spoke with Bruce, a 22-year-old, full-time college student living near Dallas, he relayed his suspicions of the paid advertising links that show up on a Google search—that is, until he spoke to a friend. The friend is an entrepreneur who uses paid search as a key part of marketing his own business. Knowing a person who not only uses the service but benefits from it helps legitimize the ads in Bruce's mind and creates a willingness to click.

In a virtual world, "news" is no longer relegated to professional media outlets. Indeed, everyone is given a voice, and the advent of *crowdsourcing*—an online occurrence whereby people share user-generated video or comments about a particular topic, company, or person—takes the Law of Recall to another level. For those looking to avoid buyer's remorse, sites like AngiesList.com feature customer reviews on contractors and service companies. For women seeking to duck questionable dating prospects, the site DontDateHimGirl.com allows women (and also, technically, men) to post profiles on hated exes; network to share stories; and help each other detect cheating, lying, and jerky behavior. Of course, no one was verifying the truth of anything posted, and the site also became an outlet for vindictive behavior. After media exposure and a few lawsuits from men who felt libeled, the site began allowing those profiled to respond. Interestingly, the founder of the site has also started a communications consulting company with a practice in social media and image management. The role of new media shrinks the world, providing greater reach for our information-gathering and recall abilities. This phenomenon raises the stakes when controlling presentation and image for both individuals and companies.

Although the Summer of the Shark seems like ages ago, the lessons of that fear-induced season remain. We are susceptible to those perceptions most accessible in our memory banks—either through personal experience or inflated media exposure. This is just one of the many invisible filters our mind uses to process the volumes of data inundating us each day. However, when that filter leads to a distorted view of the dangers that truly exist, the result can be a paralyzing fear not unlike what beachgoers remember from that fateful summer. In addition, given the mind's limited ability to process dangers not yet imaginable, the implications for providers attempting to win our trust while simultaneously protecting us from ourselves become significant. Although shark attacks are relatively few and far between, the threats online are far more pervasive, if not so dramatic. Managing the believability gap between actual and perceived threats is both the challenge and opportunity for providers in a virtual world—whether or not the story steals the headline of the day.

SHIFT SHORT: THE UNENDING DEBATE

It happens every few years or so. A report is released to question the effect of cell phones in causing cancer. The event usually triggers a swarm of evidence to support or refute the claim. The headline captures the attention and imagination of millions.

There's no question why the debate is heated. If you are like the majority of those in the United States, you have a cell phone on your person right now. If you are like the average person, you check that cell phone between 100 and 200 times per day. More people worldwide have access to mobile technology than they do running water.[8] To suggest that mobile phones are indispensable and pervasive would be an understatement.

The debate reemerged in 2011 as the World Health Organization (WHO) concluded that cell phone devices are "possibly carcinogenic." Overnight, the media seized the story and fanned the debate's smoldering embers. Headline after headline asked the provocative, scary question—could that indispensable device residing in your pocket cause you harm, if not cost you your life?

SHIFT SHORT: THE UNENDING DEBATE (*continued*)

Although interesting fodder for capturing attention and selling media, this debate is far more nuanced than a headline, two-minute news story, or even this *Short* can allow. The WHO's conclusion is not based on new research but, rather, a review of numerous existing studies. The panel's decision to classify cell phones as "possibly carcinogenic" was based largely on epidemiological data showing an increased risk of a rare type of brain tumor (called a *glioma*) among heavy cell phone users.[9]

Roughly 30 older studies have tried and failed to find a linkage between cell phones and cancer. One study even found that those who use cell phones had a lower risk of cancer than those using old-fashioned landline phones. Some question why there has not been a significant worldwide increase in brain cancers given the rise of cell phones, if such a linkage does, in fact, exist.[10]

But it all depends on how you define "possibly carcinogenic." According to Dr. Meir Stampfer, a professor of epidemiology at the Harvard School of Public Health and a paid advisor to the cell phone industry:

> ...the important thing is putting it into the perspective of what 'possible' means, and the likelihood that this is really something to be concerned about. The evidence doesn't support that. Comparing this to going out in the sun or any number of normal everyday activities that we're not really concerned about, I would put cell phones in the lower part of that category.[11]

Of course, a paid advisor to the cell phone industry may be accused of bias, thus it might be best to let the distinguished panel that formed the conclusion speak for itself. In its finding, the WHO ruled only that cell phone risk be reclassified to a category deemed possibly carcinogenic to humans—a category that includes 240 other agents, including engine exhaust, pickled vegetables, and coffee. Its findings stopped short of assessing the risk that the technology may pose to human health. As the leader of the distinguished panel Dr. Jonathan M. Samet states, "Our task was not to quantify risk."[12]

The debate won't stop anytime soon. And, it's a meaningful one to have, given our reliance on the devices that increasingly connect us. Perhaps the most sage advice comes from the operating manuals of those devices, many of which provide guidelines for using a headset and keeping the phone a certain distance from the head. Of course, texting fingers can also do the trick. If nothing else, we can thank the recent headlines for reminding health-conscious consumers of the practical safeguards one can take, regardless of whether risks have yet to be quantified.

8 Rationalization: Finding Harmony in the Discord

When you rationalize, you do just that. You make rational lies.

—Author Unknown

Dorothy Martin talked to aliens. They told her of the cataclysm that would destroy much of the civilized world. On a fateful Tuesday, water was to engulf much of the land between the Arctic Circle and the Gulf of Mexico, destroying cities on the West Coast from Seattle to Chile in its wake. Earthquakes would rock the Midwest, devastating Chicago, among other cities. That would be just the beginning. Within the next year, the entire world would see its doom. The Tuesday when the world would see the first prelude to its horrific final act was December 21, 1954. That day came and went. The highly anticipated cataclysm did not.

Although Dorothy received her messages directly from *aliens* on the undiscovered planet Clarion, she was not the only one to believe the prophecy. Indeed, she amassed a cult following of 13 disciples, who had forsaken their material lives in anticipation of being rescued by spaceships on the eve of the predicted disaster. Among them was Dr. Charles Laughead, whose proselytizing of Dorothy's prophecies to his students at Michigan State College led to his untimely dismissal from his prestigious job—and $10,000 annual salary that accompanied it (equivalent to approximately $82,000 in today's dollars).[1]

In the months leading up to the prophesied catastrophe, Dorothy and her followers, particularly Charles, begrudgingly indulged curious journalists fascinated by the group's unorthodox predictions and otherworldly messengers. One article caught the attention of social psychologist Leon Festinger and his associates. The psychologists successfully infiltrated the group, under the pretense of being believers themselves, to record the sociological phenomenon as it unfolded. The scientists ultimately documented the inner workings of the group in the now historic *When Prophecy Fails*. The book outlines the sequence of events on December 21, 1954, the same day that would see the beginning of the world's demise and the rescue of Dorothy and her followers by a spaceship at the stroke of midnight.

> *The time is midnight. The same time the spaceship is to arrive. As instructed, the group has taken great measures to remove all things metallic from their persons, including zippers and bra straps. The group waits, but no spaceship arrives.*
>
> *It's now 12:05 AM. Someone notices another clock shows the time as 11:55 PM. The group agrees it's not yet midnight.*
>
> *At 12:10 AM, the second clock strikes midnight. There's still no sign of a spaceship. The predicted cataclysm itself is no more than seven hours away.*
>
> *It's 4:00 AM and the group remains in stunned silence. Explanations are hollow. Dorothy begins to cry.*
>
> *At 4:45 AM, Dorothy receives another message from her "space brothers." The cataclysm has been called off. Presumably, the small group's undying faith has reflected like a beacon of hope for the rest of the world. God has given the world its reprieve. The human race has been spared.*
>
> *On the afternoon of December 21, the followers mount a publicity campaign to spread the news far and wide as to how and why destruction was averted.*[2]

Beyond offering interesting journalistic fodder in 1954, Dorothy and her cult provided something far greater to the scientific community. Festinger's observations of the group led to the discovery of *cognitive dissonance*, a natural feeling of psychological discomfort that arises when one's behaviors are out-of-sync with one's beliefs. However, contrary to conventional wisdom, Festinger and his associates concluded that, when such dissonance surfaces, the tendency is for people to change their beliefs to fit their actual behavior, rather than the other way around.

Dorothy may have fancied her purpose in life to be the doomsayer of the world's ending. Instead, she and her cult followers became the poster children that gave cognitive dissonance its face. Rather than admit that the prophecies were wrong, the group continued unabated in its resolve. The prophecies *had* to be right. After all, the followers had already put everything—material possessions, livelihoods, relationships—on the line. The spaceship's failure to rescue was not a failure at all, yet alone a sign that the predictions themselves were in question. Rather, the group's unwavering faith caused a higher power to rethink a tragic ending to humankind. Thus, in fact, the prophecies *were* right. The group *had* succeeded. The sacrifice of all things lost was *not* in vain. The group recommitted behaviors to match irrational thoughts, taking its new message of hope to citizens across the land. To do otherwise would be inconsistent with dogma. To change those beliefs would be more painful still because the reality of the sacrifice might be too much to bear.

Cognitive dissonance is not banished to the fantasy world of cult followers or the clinically insane. It causes psychological discomfort for each of us when it surfaces. Thus, like Dorothy and her followers, we *rationalize* to bridge the gap between behaviors and our belief system. *Rationalization* helps us explain the otherwise inexplicable and gives meaning to the complicated mosaic of behavioral inconsistencies that emerge in a networked-community era.

Rationalizing the Laws

The Laws of Learned Helplessness, Illusion, and Recall are prevalent across generations and life stages in our study. They can also coexist within the same individual. Amy, our 30-something career mom, nonchalantly dismisses a friend's warning of the potential dangers of using a laptop while wirelessly connected. Learned helplessness has taught her that determined hackers will find a way in, and rationalization takes over from there. If I have little impact in preventing a hacker from victimizing me and I already derive productivity gains from working wirelessly on my commute to work, why bother with precautions that are both unnecessary and inconvenient? Amy quickly rationalizes away why she avoids investigating the subject further. When probed further on if such investigation is prudent, Amy's response is candid:

> **Amy:** *I don't know. Maybe there's a concern but I chose not to believe her [the friend who warned her about the dangers of surfing wirelessly].*
>
> **Interviewer:** *Do you care?*
>
> **Amy:** *No.*

Amy chooses not to believe information that is inconsistent with her current behaviors, thereby avoiding cognitive dissonance and its associated discomfort. At the same time, recall has heightened her sensitivities to potential threats online, particularly those from hackers.

> *Recently, I've been reading the Stieg Larsson series on* The Girl with the Dragon Tattoo. *She's this little computer hacker. She gets her information from digging around in other people's computers. It's been super eye-opening. I mean, it's total fiction ... but it's so eye-opening to see how hackers can get into your computer and access information.*

Despite the "eye-opening" experience, rationalization again takes root, allowing Amy to write off the book—and its main character, who specializes in hacking—as nothing more than the creative musings of a talented "fiction" author. "Fiction" strikes close to home as Amy reveals that her household computer has been recently infected with a virus. Despite being victimized herself, she conveniently defers to illusion to rationalize away a persistent threat. That is, she doesn't manage a Facebook or LinkedIn account and, given that those are the sites where these attacks occur (at least in her mind), she is confident that the virus is the result of the carefree social networking pursuits of her nanny.

> *Oh my gosh, our computer crashed. I do not manage a Facebook or LinkedIn account ...but my nanny does. I think we ended up with some sort of virus. I'm going to blame Facebook on it because it's an easy scapegoat.*

How can the same individual, one who is successful at managing a busy career and bustling family, be the subject of such contradiction? She simultaneously dismisses the potential threat of wirelessly connecting her laptop while in commute, admits she has been enlightened by the treasure trove available to savvy hackers through her fictional reading pursuits, and has been personally victimized by a virus that led to a computer crash. When examined through the lens of rationalization, Amy's behaviors become understandable, if not relatable.

Rationalization allows us to minimize the dissonance associated with contradictory beliefs and actions. If we believe our environment is unchangeable (learned helplessness), we forego protective behaviors that we perceive to be futile, if not inconvenient. Actions match beliefs and cognitive dissonance disappears. If we believe our actions are sufficient in protecting us (illusion), we may dismiss compelling evidence to the contrary and strengthen our initial beliefs. Again, actions and beliefs are in sync. Finally, if we succumb to external hype that may or may not be founded (recall), we may adopt those beliefs and adapt behavior accordingly. New behaviors now coincide with a new set of beliefs. In each of these cases, actions and thoughts are correlated. The disharmony associated with cognitive dissonance is minimized, if not eliminated. And, we continue to behave in ways that are not always as *rational* as they are *rationalized.*

Do as I Say or as I Do?

In 1934, Richard LaPiere embarked on a 10,000-mile social experiment. Set against the backdrop of pervasive racial prejudice in America, LaPiere traveled the country with a Chinese couple seeking service in hotels and restaurants. In each case, LaPiere remained out of sight as the couple negotiated the price of a room for the evening (hotel) or asked to be served (restaurant). In some cases, the couple was presentable. In others, they appeared disheveled. The experiment would take the researchers to more than 250 establishments, and only one time was the couple denied service.

Six months later (and with no mention of any previous encounter with the establishment), LaPiere followed up with a questionnaire to each location with a pivotal question, "Will you accept members of the Chinese race as guests in your establishment?" He received responses from 50 percent of the venues. Of those, more than 90 percent of respondents answered the question with an unequivocal "No."[3] Thus marked one of the initial forays in social psychology to assess the bridge between what we say and what we actually do.

LaPiere's research has met its fair share of critics. Some challenge the timing of the study, in the midst of the Great Depression, as justification for why attitudes and behaviors were out-of-sync. After all, establishments were hard-pressed to turn away any paying customer during the toughest economic time of our history. Others challenge the methodology. The only conclusive way to prove that a disconnect between attitudes and behaviors existed was to ensure that the same individual who serviced the Chinese couple completed the survey six months later. No such controls were in place to verify that this was the case. Finally, not all establishments responded, leading some to question if the 50 percent completion rate was sufficient in proving LaPiere's conclusions.

Still, LaPiere triggered an interesting social conversation that inspired additional research on attitudinal and behavioral consistency (or lack thereof). In 1937, Stephen Corey conducted his own test to measure the correlation between the two. In his seminal study on cheating, Corey observed 67 educational psychology students over a five-week period. Each Friday, students were given an exam to measure the aptitude of the week's curriculum. The following week, the papers were returned to the students for self-grading. Unbeknownst to the subjects, the tests had already been graded, although unmarked, and recorded. Students were unaware of any checks-and-balances to verify the accuracy or integrity of their grades. In essence, the purported self-grading arrangement relied on the honor system.

Additionally, Corey measured the students' attitudes toward cheating using a questionnaire. When correlating the students' attitudes (either sympathy or antipathy) toward cheating with their actual tendency to inflate their self-graded exams, there was no correlation found. In essence, one's attitude toward cheating had no predictive value for one's propensity to commit the deed.[4]

When combining the LaPiere/Corey findings with those of cognitive dissonance, a complex portrait of human psychology emerges. From a cognitive dissonance perspective, it is uncomfortable for thoughts and actions to be out-of-sync, and rationalization fills the void between the two. From a research point of view, it is common for expressed thoughts to be in conflict with actual behaviors. The latter has nothing to do with cognitive dissonance. Rather, it is a combination of social expectations, self-monitoring, and/or poor questionnaire design that may lead researchers to conclusions based on what people say, not what they actually do.

Muddy the waters further with a complicated topic like technology, where attitudes, beliefs, and behaviors are influenced by one's savviness on the matter, and the picture becomes even more complex. According to our study of more than 5,000 online consumers in the United States:

- 18 percent psychologically identify as "private" people, carefully managing what they share and where they are with others. Yet more than half in this segment also admit to regularly updating their social networking page with details of where they are or where they plan to be. Furthermore, less than one-third frequently change privacy settings on their profile to adjust what is shared with others.
- 11 percent see the world as a "scary" place—requiring care to avoid placing themselves or their family in harm's way. Yet nearly 30 percent of this group admit to exposing their full date of birth online. Additionally, more than two-thirds confess to having offered their credit card information to a newly discovered site to make a purchase.

- 15 percent psychometrically align as bargain shoppers, those who get "excited" when finding a good deal on the things they want or need. Yet less than half in this group frequently check multiple sites to ensure that they are getting a good deal when purchasing something online. Less than 15 percent admit to frequently using mobile applications that scan barcodes in the "real" world for easy comparison shopping.

Although we didn't physically travel 10,000 miles as LaPiere did to find these contradictions, we discovered them nonetheless. In addition, these inconsistencies measured the same respondent's attitude versus his reported behavior in answering questions within the same questionnaire. Imagine how much greater the variability is when observing individuals in their habitats. You have already seen some of these inherent contradictions among our ethnography respondents. There are more to come in the remaining pages of this book.

The Laws in Practice

As we continue to profile consumers across life stages in subsequent chapters, the familiar Laws of Learned Helplessness, Illusion, and Recall will rear their heads. Additionally, the blatant rationalization of respondents to mitigate cognitive dissonance will also be evident. At a macro level, understanding where one fits in the larger market reveals a truer understanding of how and why behaviors are not always aligned to beliefs. For providers and marketers attempting to win the hearts, minds, and/or wallets of these consumers, the optimal go-to-market approach differs depending on the magnitude of and reason for the dissonance. As an example, take the following taxonomy to reflect the interesting market landscape that is revealed when contemplating online privacy and security, a metaphorical lightning rod in the virtual identity debate.

The Determined

In our study, 38 percent of respondents categorized themselves as security-conscious when it comes to online pursuits. According to these consumers, they do everything within their power to ensure that they are protected. However, if behavioral evidence is any indicator, their best may not be good enough. Conspicuous opt-in policies and security controls empower this market to take necessary precautions.

The Unaware

If illusion is in play, consumers may not even realize they are in harm's way. In our study, 37 percent of respondents fall into the category of believing they are sufficiently safe online given the familiarity of websites visited and people engaged. Interestingly, there are almost as many *unaware* as there are *determined*. These delusional individuals overestimate their own defense mechanisms. Many will benefit from education on the potential dangers, but it will likely take an act of recall (either significant media hype or a situation that hits closer to home) before behavior is altered.

The Helpless

If learned helplessness is to blame, consumers may simply give up. Continuing with our security example, 12 percent of respondents fall into the category of admitting that it's simply too complicated to fully protect privacy and security while online. What's fascinating about this segment is that the helpless may actually be the savviest. The more likely the user is to regularly engage with technology, the more likely she is to agree with this mind-set. These individuals may understand the inherent complexity of a virtual world and will seek greater controls, not a white knight, to put them back in the virtual driver's seat.

The Apathetic

There are always those who simply don't care, and this topic is no exception. Twelve percent of respondents agree that online privacy and security are just not worth the time or effort. If something were to happen, they would simply deal with the repercussions. There may be learned helplessness in play for some in this segment, as witnessed with Amy's response to potential dangers of wirelessly commuting with her laptop (why bother when a hacker will always find a way in?). The challenge for this segment is the imaginability problem we covered in Chapter 7, on recall. Often, respondents cannot even visualize what the extent of a potential problem could be. Like the *unaware*, these individuals will likely not change behavior until recall enters the scene.

This is just one categorization for one aspect of the virtual identity dilemma. Although one may be *unaware* when it comes to online privacy and security, he or she may be *helpless* as it pertains to presenting an idealized version of self in a virtual world. Although one may be *apathetic* when it comes to finding content, goods, or people unique to his interests, he may be *determined* in protecting himself online. There is no cookie-cutter approach to this segmentation. The power of rationalization and confluence of disparate laws create a market as complex as the individuals representing it. However, there are nuances that coalesce around identity as one matures through compelling life events. These commonalities represent the entry point for understanding individuals in a hyperconnected world—whether as ourselves or as consumers we attempt to serve.

The topic of identity is fraught with inconsistencies. As human beings, we struggle with our own contradictions. However, through complexity comes opportunity. And, technology has a role to play in enlightening the deceived, arming the helpless, and fortifying the determined. However, it is no panacea and cannot compare with our own means to rationalize the seemingly inexplicable, nor can it disrupt the truth we hold in our own belief system.

Dorothy and her converts waited a lifetime for an apocalypse that would never come. Up until her death in 1988, she preached of a new age, one when Atlantis would be raised from the deep. Despite a spaceship rescue that never occurred, her followers kept their faith and attempted to convert others accordingly. On the day before the highly anticipated cataclysm, the followers accepted calls from individuals curious about the predictions. As Charles, the formerly successful professor who sacrificed his career and material possessions, told a newspaper about the callers, "Some of them were genuinely concerned, but most of the calls were just a nuisance. We've been bothered by a lot of crackpots."[5] For the record, Charles himself was not a "crackpot," at least not according to experts. After the much ballyhooed event that never was to occur, he was evaluated by a medical team and ultimately cleared from being diagnosed clinically insane. Indeed, it was not insanity in play, but something that lives at one time or another within each of us—cognitive dissonance. One can only imagine how rationalization will restore psychological harmony in a time when thoughts and actions may not always align, yet alone coincide across real and virtual worlds.

SHIFT SHORT: DEFINING OBSCENITY — SEX VERSUS VIOLENCE

In June 2011, a court case before the U.S. Supreme court pitted the State of California's restrictions on the sale of violent video games to children against the video gaming industry's desire for self-regulated content creation and distribution. In its decision, the Supreme Court sided with gaming companies, granting video games First Amendment protections as cultural artifacts and ruling restrictions on sales to minors unconstitutional.

In writing the majority opinion on *Brown v. Entertainment Merchants Association*, Justice Antonin Scalia had this to say, "Speech about violence is not obscene," ruling that unlike sexual content, which may be viewed as obscene, violent content isn't subject to the same considerations.[6] Justice Stephen Breyer wrote a dissenting opinion citing studies showing that violent video game content is associated with aggressive behavior. Even though he voted with the majority, Justice Samuel Alito voiced concerns about technology and gear making games more immersive and realistic and soon allowing players to "actually feel the splatting blood from the blown-off head"[7] of a victim.

Whether particular sexual or violent content is obscene can be debated. What's interesting is the difference between how the courts view violence versus sex. The impact of violent content—particularly in video games in which consumers aren't just passive recipients of the content but active participants—has been the subject of multiple studies. Although individual responses vary by gender, baseline psychology, and environmental factors, studies have shown that violent gaming is tied to reduced empathy, reduced moral evaluation of consequence, reduced physiological response to real-life violence, and stronger pro-violence attitudes.[8,9] In sum, the games are linked with desensitization to violence. Studies also show that increased exposure to sexual media content leads to increased acceptance of the sexual practices and attitudes presented and possible increased engagement in risky behaviors—including unprotected sex and, again, lack of moral evaluation of consequence.[10] Thus, media exposure to both sex and violence is associated with problematic sociological impacts.

How we rationalize our differing legal treatment has been questioned by psychologists. As *Psychology Today* columnist Karen Dill put it:

> When it was discovered that one version of Grand Theft Auto contained scenes involving oral sex, the game was removed from shelves. It was not removed because it contained violent scenes that could be argued were equally graphic.... We have to be aware of the double standard in the rules we're playing by: there's such a thing as too sexy for children, but no such thing as too violent for children.[11]

Scalia's argument, in part, rests on the idea that this is how it's always been. Depictions of violence, Justice Scalia added, have never been subject to government regulation. "*Grimm's Fairy Tales*, for example, are grim indeed," he wrote, recounting the gory plots of "Snow White," "Cinderella," and "Hansel and Gretel." High school reading lists and Saturday morning cartoons, too, he said, are riddled with violence.[12]

Precedent certainly provides validity for legal arguments, but it doesn't address the question of how one justifies the view that showing sexual contact between characters in a video game is too obscene for minors, but showing a character killing a hooker to get his money back post-sexual contact—and rewarding the player—in *Grand Theft Auto* is not.

3 Identity Through the Life Stages

In This Part

Eventually, we all grow up. As we mature, the paradigm through which we view ourselves and the environment around us shifts. Despite this, the universal 3Ps (presentation, protection, and preference) are evident across life stages, whether as a teenagers in the throes of adolescent development or as mid-lifers seeking their next chapter. At the same time, the seduction of rationalization and the laws that surround us (learned helplessness, illusion, and recall), provide a labyrinth of external forces that facilitate self-deception, no matter the age or life stage. Though priorities certainly change as one matures, the shared perspective of internal identity and the tempting lure of environmental conditions unite all of us.

9

Teenage Growing Pains

It's difficult to decide whether growing pains
are something teenagers have—or are.

—AUTHOR UNKNOWN

Well, I am having a huge identity crisis. It has been going on for a
while. To be honest, I don't know how to fix it. I don't know who I am
anymore. I am not sure if I am Christian or Atheist, racist or non-
racist, gay or straight. My confidence level has dropped dramatically
in the past years. I'm very unsure of myself and don't even know what
I want to do with my future. I have no idea what to do. How do you
all find yourself?

Those are the lamentations of a teenage boy seeking solace through an online peer forum. Adolescence is that fascinating journey in our lives—the bridge that carries us from vulnerable childhood naïveté to a newly formed adult mindedness. For that reason, the field of child psychology is buttressed by the weight of countless studies exploring how identity is constructed during this essential formative stage. As this helpless teen emotes through his impassioned plea for help, it also marks a critical life stage when we either "find" or "lose" ourselves.

As adults, we can certainly remember those uncertain, often uncomfortable, times. If we suffer selective amnesia, pop culture stands ready to restore the fuzzy memories. Hollywood's arsenal shoots out a seemingly unstoppable blaze of movies, books, magazines, shows, and music aimed at the lucrative teen and tween markets. One such creation came in 2004 with *Mean Girls*. The movie, penned by longtime *Saturday Night Live* cast member and writer Tina Fey, memorably explored the identity crises of teenage girls attempting to survive the metaphorical jungle of high school cliques.

Its uncanny depiction of adolescent strife resonated with millions of teenagers across the globe, contributing to its $129 million in gross receipts at the worldwide box office. In an interview, Fey reflected, "Adults find it funny. They are the ones who are laughing. Young people watch it like a reality television show. It is much too close to their real experiences so they are not exactly guffawing."[1]

In stark contrast to the mass popularity of the movie stood the relatively little-known fact that its premise was based on a book—a nonfiction book, to be exact. In 2002, Rosalind Wiseman's *Queen Bees and Wannabes* offered practical prescriptions to parents and teen girls struggling through the social growing pains of adolescence and ignited the creative spark that inspired *Mean Girls*. In her book, Wiseman identifies seven common roles that girls often play in cliques. Among them, there's the Queen Bee herself, who reigns supreme over all others in the clique, thanks in no small part to a powerful cocktail of looks, money, charisma, and manipulative qualities. Her Side Kick dutifully stands with her, deriving social benefits simply by her association as best friend to the head honcho. The Banker masterfully extracts potentially lucrative information from others in the clique through the unassuming manner by which she collects it, and later shares it. And let's not forget the Target, who often suffers the brunt of social trauma, isolated and excluded from others in the group.[2]

What we find so fascinating about Wiseman's work is that each archetype has a clear identity and an established role that galvanizes the group dynamic. Indeed, it is the typecast tendency that created such relatable and memorable fodder for the book's screenplay adaptation. What was comedic genius for adults was a little too "real" for teens, according to Fey. Indeed, the role confusion portrayed on the big screen by each of the young actresses is something all too familiar to teens struggling to form their identity. Despite the fact that Wiseman's observations are drawn from female cliques, the fluid act by which teens experiment with different roles in an attempt to "find" themselves is a universal characteristic marking this rite of passage to adulthood. The earlier example of a teen boy crying out for help from his peers reflects just how far-reaching the experimentation can be—encompassing religion, sexuality, and tolerance through his self-proclaimed identity crisis.

If adults find the blurring between the physical and virtual worlds dizzying, teens have no notion of two distinct environments in the first place. Today's youth use technology as a means of self-expression and identity formation. Although many adults likely remember the sting of embarrassment from insults traded on bathroom walls, those emotional nicks pale in comparison to the social scars inflicted by texting fingers, opportune camera phones, and pervasive social networking sites. Technology has upped the ante for today's teenager during one of the most critical identity phases of one's life. Its impact on those in its wake is indelible.

The New Status Symbols

Les Parrott, PhD, a professor of psychology, offers several ways in which teens manifest their struggles with identity. He argues that status symbols, including clothing and other possessions, enable teens to express affiliation with specific groups.[3] Today's status symbols have come a long way since the Members Only jackets and parachute pants of the authors' day. Now, in addition to clothing, teens must incorporate the latest *in* devices to gain approval from the *in* crowd. Unfortunately for parents, these devices often carry a heftier price tag and an expectation of service that place a greater strain on the pocketbook than popular clothing brands.

In the case of 16-year-old Bill, one of our study's respondents, having the wrong device can instigate insults, if not outright pity.

> *When you see somebody with a flip phone, like a basic flip phone, like people are gonna be like, "You're still using a flip phone, man? You supposed to upgrade." Since I upgraded my TV and my game system, I should upgrade my phone so I have all upgraded technology.*

Those upgrades come at a price, and teens soon find themselves trapped in a never-ending search for the next technology gizmo to keep up with the Joneses, if not their own insatiable appetite. In 16-year-old Joshua's case, he already knows the familiar twinge of buyer's remorse as he perpetually outgrows devices and is forced to contemplate upgrading or curtailing his needs to fit the capabilities of his latest status symbol:

> *The one thing that annoys me about my iPod is the limited amount of memory you can have and how once you buy a certain iPod, you think, "Oh I won't have more than 8GB" and you're limited to that.*

If peer pressure or device limitations won't provoke an upgrade, perhaps the sheer annoyance of technology that fails will do the trick. Consider the exchange between 13-year-old Robert and 12-year old Frank as they proudly display their new Xbox while narrating why it was purchased in the first place.

> **Frank** *[holding up an Xbox that is not connected]: This was our first Xbox. And it broke and we sent it in. And then when they brought it*

back, we played it for a while and then it broke again. We asked them to fix it again. They gave us back our money and fixed it—gave it to us and it broke. So then we sent it to some other guy and it came back. We started playing it again. It went for a pretty long time. And then it broke. So that's when my mom and dad went out and bought a new one. And then my dad got this one working.

Interviewer: *So what are you going to do with that one [original Xbox] now that it's working?*

Robert: *Sell it.*

Devices reflect status. They are also quite perishable in keeping up with a teen's voracious techno appetite. What is less perishable, and perhaps more important, is the social communities that have become the human status symbols answering the fundamental teen question, "How popular am I?" In the case of some teens, like Bill, one's measure of social status is directly correlated to the number of friends in one's social network. As Bill reflects, teens in his circle are in an unspoken competition to be the one with the most toys—er, friends—on the block.

A lot of my friends have like a 1,000 friends and stuff and I'm only at like 400. It's like "You have 1,000 friends and I only have 400, this is not good." We have a little friendly competition and right now I'm losing. But I'm gonna be up there in a minute. I'll be up there in the thousands.

Bill admits to accepting friend requests from people "who look decent" or from those he *thinks* he knows. It seems almost inconceivable that anyone could personally know 1,000 "friends." Yet, that is the benchmark of the competition in a virtual social world where numbers are easy to compare. In our study, nearly one in five teens admit to frequently sending Friend Requests to connect with new people. The same number confess to frequently accepting Friend Requests from those they don't know well, if at all.

Potential safety issues associated with engaging virtual strangers aside, one may question the psychological impact of this exercise. Adults may criticize the superficiality that now defines *friendship* status. In addition, if the hundreds, if not thousands, of *friends* one aspires to brandish as a mark of social status are nothing more than mere acquaintances (if not strangers), how does that form of illusion affect a teen's identity formation?

According to researchers at the University of Virginia, perception *is* reality. The study determined that teens who perceived themselves to be popular—even if the assessment was not shared by their peers—were increasingly less hostile and more sought out by others. Kathleen Boykin McElhaney, the lead author of the study, states, "Perceiving oneself to be liked may actually be at least as critical in determining future social outcomes for teens as is actually being liked by other teens."[4] The finding suggests that, whether or not the teen is actually as popular as he believes thanks to Facebook's count, the mere perception of likeability is a powerful influence in protecting one's ego and contributing to one's social success.

Unfortunately for parents, the reverse also holds true. According to the same study, adolescents who lacked both a strong sense of their own social acceptance and who were rated by their peers as unpopular were increasingly more hostile, less sought out, and more withdrawn over time.[5] As we cover in a future chapter, the delicate balancing act of protecting one's child online without rendering the teen a social outcast in the process is an unenviable dilemma that today's parents face.

The New Idols

If you are not a teenager, you may not know Amber Portwood. She is one of the breakout stars from MTV's reality series *16 and Pregnant* and its spinoff *Teen Mom*. The former followed the lives of teenage girls as they struggled with being pregnant in high school. The latter continued the chronicles of four original cast members during their first year of motherhood. Each has earned its fair share of popularity. The first season finale of *16 and Pregnant* attracted 2.1 million viewers, the same number of *Teen Mom*'s pilot episode—the highest rated premiere on MTV in more than a year at the time of its debut.[6]

Reality television has been a boon to the entertainment industry. It gives viewers a megadose of raw authenticity that appeals to the inner voyeur, and it does so without breaking the Hollywood bank. Why pay onerous writing and talent fees when the camera can simply roll on the lives of unknown regular people capturing the "real-life" drama that naturally unfolds? In addition, for those participating and watching, there's always an element of wonder about who could be the next breakout star.

Unfortunately, this extreme reality can also have unintended consequences. MTV has come under fire from its critics, who claim that it is glamorizing teen pregnancy. Some reports have gone so far as to suggest that teens looking to attain stardom have premeditated pregnancy just in the hopes of being cast. Although difficult to substantiate, there is evidence that teens are particularly susceptible to role models during this formative identity phase, lending credence to outraged critics that these new reality idols are not exactly what the doctor ordered.

According to Dr. Parrott, celebrities may become models for teens during their experimentation phase. Teens may identify with a known figure, attempt to emulate that person, and lose a sense of their own identity in the process.[7] And, if reality television is not sufficient to seduce the teen's imagination, there is certainly no shortage of "reality" stars in the virtual world, the product of YouTube and other self-expression sites. Look no further than the latest teen sensation Justin Bieber. Had Bieber lived in a time before YouTube, he would have likely been a victim of circumstance, one of millions attempting to capture the attention of a handful of recording insiders who exclusively could have extended him his big break. But, Bieber *did* grow up with YouTube and used the site to promote his talent to legions of fans. An online sensation, Bieber had his pick between two recording Goliaths—Usher and Justin Timberlake—who engaged in a bidding war to sign the young talent with an already growing fan base. In the end, Usher won, and now millions are afflicted with "Bieber Fever."

But, beyond teen moms and YouTube sensations, the virtual world has opened up the possibility for role models much closer to home. Unfortunately, we're not speaking about parental figures in this context. Rather, just as the virtual world unlocked the door to Bieber's fame, teens look for stardom online that can translate to a different variety of "real-world" celebrity. As Bill puts it:

> [My friend] Randall's a Facebook superstar. Like, we went to a fair and like these girls were like screaming his name. One girl was star-struck. She was like, "Oh my gosh, that's Randall."

Combine this want for celebrity with the need for social inclusion, and the stranglehold that social networks appear to have over youth becomes surprisingly understandable. It also helps explain why youth appear seemingly obsessed with their online persona—an extension of their real-world identity—with nearly 25 percent indicating that they frequently spend time updating their social networking page to project the right image of themselves, according to our study. More than half of teens in our study admit to posting updates, comments, or photos about themselves or their families that they later regretted sharing.

The New Villains

In 1971, Stanford University professor Philip Zimbardo embarked on one of the most controversial human experiments of our time. Zimbardo recruited male students to call a mock prison, located in the basement of a campus building, their home for two weeks, during which time the experiment was videotaped. The students were randomly assigned as either guards or prisoners of the facility. Each group wore the prescribed garb for the part—with guards donning uniforms and mirrored sunglasses to avoid eye contact with prisoners and the captives robed in uncomfortable, ill-fitting smocks and stocking caps. On the video, Zimbardo, playing the part of Prison Superintendent, is seen informing the guards of their role in an orientation the day before the experiment's commencement:

> You can create in the prisoners feelings of boredom, a sense of fear to some degree, you can create a notion of arbitrariness that their life is totally controlled by us, by the system, you, me, and they'll have no privacy.... We're going to take away their individuality in various ways. In general what all this leads to is a sense of powerlessness. That is, in this situation we'll have all the power and they'll have none.[8]

To Zimbardo's surprise, it took little time for the subjects to embrace their roles fully. Guards called prisoners by assigned numbers, not their names, to strip them of their identities. They forced the captives to count off repeatedly as a way of learning their new identities and engaged physical punishments—such as protracted exercises—as consequences for counting errors. Guards allowed the physical conditions of the prison to reach unconscionable levels, disallowing prisoners from emptying their sanitation buckets or, worse yet, from urinating or defecating in the first place. Prisoners were left to sleep on cold cement floors or deprived of clothing altogether as additional forms of degradation.

Although the experiment was to last a full two weeks, it was aborted prematurely on the sixth day when Zimbardo's girlfriend (and later wife) visited the facility to observe the experiment. Despite the fact that more than 50 outside persons had witnessed the conditions before her, she was the only one to object to the immorality of the experiment, compelling Zimbardo to bring it to its hasty end.[9]

The Stanford prison experiment has come under fire from critics for obvious humanitarian reasons. However, it has also raised profoundly serious questions about how upstanding students could possibly embrace these horrific roles so completely.

Beyond monetary compensation, there was nothing physically keeping any of the subjects in the environment (in fact, a few abandoned the experiment early because of the intolerable conditions). After all, it wasn't a *real* prison. But that didn't stop the subjects from assuming the identities prescribed to them by their environment.

Although most of us, it is hoped, will never see the inside of a prison cell and therefore may feel comfortable dismissing the experiment as something far removed from our reality, its findings have been linked to something much more common in our daily lives—bullying. The psychology of a bully is an interesting one. David Bernstein, an expert in risk management and a consultant to schools with bullying problems, identifies several characteristics of a typical bully. Among them, bullies need an audience or it's "no fun."[10] In the case of the Stanford prison experiment, the guards egged one another on and *performed* for a camera capturing every move for an invisible audience. Imagine the potential audience of a bully with access to thousands of "friends" online who become unknowing participants in fueling destructive behavior aimed at an innocent target.

Sadly, we don't have to imagine it at all. The stories of the victims are all too real. Thirteen-year-old Ryan Halligan committed *bullycide* after suffering an incessant fury of online harassment. Not seeing any end to the torment perpetuated by an omnipresent virtual world, Ryan quietly and deliberately hanged himself early in the morning hours while his family lay sleeping. He had learned how to fashion the tie of his sister's bathrobe into a noose by researching the topic online. Ryan's online footprint in the days leading up to the tragedy exposed another horror. When Ryan informed a virtual pen pal via an online chat that he was finally ready to take his life, the friend replied, "Phew. It's about f***ing time." Two weeks later, Ryan was dead.[11]

Governments have responded with a swarm of *cyberbullying* legislation aimed at protecting children. This legislation is critical, if for no other reason than to heighten the awareness of the issue for unsuspecting parents and teen bystanders. Recall the Stanford prison experiment once more. There had been more than 50 visitors who had witnessed the deplorable scene in that underground basement. But only one spoke up to stop the abuse. It's even more astonishing when one considers that the experiment was contained to young adults, ostensibly with the mental and emotional maturity to behave in a more humanitarian way. Consider how much more impressionable teens are to their environment. In addition, on a high school campus where crowds hold sway, emotions run high, and peer pressure reigns supreme, the role of "innocent" bystanders in fueling a bully's fury cannot be underestimated. Even worse, in a networked-community age where slander can be spewed and proliferated in seconds, there are far more observing eyes that can instigate the wrath with, unfortunately, far too few speaking up to stop it.

The Technology Conundrum

So, where does all of this leave teens battling to form their identity in a world unbound by physical constraints? In the case of status symbols, one can envision an environment in which devices are purchased for looks and networks provide the functionality. Remember Joshua, our 16-year-old frustrated with the limited memory of his iPod almost immediately after he purchased it? What's his potential solution?

> Maybe if there was a way you could have like buy memory or something or be a way to upgrade or have a huge amount of memory like 300GB. That would be the one thing.

What if that memory could automatically be purchased, on demand, from the network—similar to the way we have become accustomed to purchasing videos on demand? In that case, Joshua's only risk of device obsolescence is in the look of the device itself—not in his insatiable appetite for more horsepower.

In the case of social networks, the guidance isn't quite so clear. First, it is completely natural (and some may argue healthy) for teens to aspire to have fat social networks. The illusion of popularity has been shown to be as effective as popularity itself in shaping a teen's self-esteem and identity. But what is perhaps equally important is the need a teen has for projecting the right image of his forming identity online.

As an aside, we are often asked a question that beleaguers today's service providers: "Why won't today's young adults pay for services?" Many of these service providers are accustomed to offering content, like paid television services or applications, to their market for a price. However, as we see with teens, it is not their access to entertainment, but the presentation of their identity, that is most important to digital natives. In contrast to us older folks, today's youth have only known a life in which content is instantly available and often free. Therefore, service providers accustomed to selling content, like paid television services, often find an audience reluctant to pay. Instead, these younger consumers are likely to turn to the virtual world with alternatives like Hulu and Netflix to fill the entertainment void.

But, if these youth have grown up in a world of ubiquitous content, the same can be said for the pervasive social networks that were completely nonexistent just a few years ago. As such, whereas older generations are more likely to value access to entertainment, younger generations place a higher importance on portraying their image and managing the all-important social network. Accordingly, services that resonate most loudly with these teens incorporate some form of image management, such as one that validates the identity of online *friends*, one of the more popular services we tested among youth in our study.

As we said, technology has upped the ante for teens already perplexed by one of life's most confusing identity stages. The memories of high school last a lifetime—some even argue that high school never ends. Meryl Streep offered this sage advice to university graduates at a commencement address, "You have been told that real life is not like college, and you have been correctly informed. Real life is more like high school."[12] The road we take during our formative adolescent years fundamentally shapes the adults we ultimately become, so much so that Brad Smart, career expert and author, advises top companies looking to recruit top talent to start by asking the interviewee about those significant high school years: "Some interviewers actually like to begin interviewing twenty-five-year veterans with a discussion of high school days. I do. High school days are important developmental years."[13] Indeed, those high school years endure. And, as today's teens know, so too do the growing pains as one seeks to find himself virtually and physically through a life-changing adolescence.

SHIFT SHORT: THE SOCIAL BAROMETER

A study released by the Pew Internet & American Life Project finds that 93 percent of teens are active online and 73 percent are engaged with one or more social networking sites.[14] Some experts, including Dr. Gwenn O'Keefe of the American Academy of Pediatrics, have commented on the impact of technology on teens in today's networked-community age. According to Dr. O'Keeffe, "A large part of this generation's social and emotional development is occurring while on the Internet and on cell phones."[15]

If social media is the engine facilitating teenage relationships, it certainly doesn't stop at this critical life stage. The same Pew report finds that social networking is increasingly attracting older populations. Interestingly, of the 229 Facebook friends estimated by the average Pew respondent, the majority are people the subject knew in high school. Critics quick to dismiss social networking relationships as those lacking meaningful depth should consider the report's other findings, which conclude that Facebook users get more social support than other people, have more close relationships, and are more trusting than others.[16]

For teens, social networking is the new social barometer. A destination like Formspring, a question-and-answer-based social website, has been fashioned into the virtual bathroom wall, where people can anonymously post questions or make comments to humiliate their target. In our study, one-third of teens admit to responding to questions about themselves through this site, which currently claims 25 million among its ranks.[17]

If social networking provides the relationship barometer, counting friends as social badges of honor has now seeped into the pop culture narrative. Consider the episode of *South Park* ("You Have 0 Friends") when Cartman taunts Kyle over who has more friends and Kyle expresses concern for a sad Kip Drodry, who has no friends. As the story continues, Cartman and Kyle masquerade as Stan in an effort to increase Stan's online popularity.

Although the networked-community age in which we now find ourselves has ushered in a new wave of unattractive phenomena, from cyberbullying to Facebook depression to sexting to counting friends, it clearly has also paved the way in reviving dormant relationships, as the Pew report suggests. The dichotomy reflects that social networks are neither good nor bad: Those distinctions are reserved for the people who propel these living networks forward.

Emerging Adulthood: In Search of the Ideal

You're dead if you aim only for kids.
Adults are only kids grown up, anyway.

—WALT DISNEY

Erik Erikson's life reads like a fairy tale. First, there's the essential ingredient of a childhood fraught with challenge and strife. He was the product of an extramarital affair—in itself, a scandalous occurrence in the early twentieth century, but even more sordid when one considers the full backdrop. The affair commenced after Erikson's mother left her husband, who had fled Germany because of allegations of fraud and criminal ties. Born into a broken home and destined never to know the identity of his biological father, Erikson lived most of his childhood as an outsider. At school, he was teased for being Jewish, at synagogue for being blonde and tall.

Next, any good fairy tale protagonist relentlessly chases a dream, despite the odds. Erikson's natural artistic capabilities were denounced by his stepfather, who fancied a distinguished medical career for his adopted son. Instead, Erikson followed his creative pursuits and eventually found himself in Vienna, where a good friend suggested he share his artistic talents by teaching students at a local school. That school happened to be run by Dorothy Burlingham, a close friend of Anna Freud, daughter to famed psychoanalyst Sigmund. The Hietzing School, as it was called, held as its bedrock the psychoanalytic principles espoused by Freud at the time.

Of course, you can't have a notable fairy tale without a quintessential happy ending, with the protagonist conquering the odds and achieving the remarkable. Inspired by Freud's teachings, Erikson began to pursue his own theories of psychological development. Although largely a student of Freud's, Erikson came to disagree with two notable tenets of Freud's ideology. First, Freud postulated that personality and identity are largely formed by the time a child reaches the age of five. In contrast, Erikson earned his indelible mark in psychology by authoring the now-famous stages of psychosocial development. In his theory, Erikson contended that the evolution of one's identity continues through a lifetime of eight stages from infancy to death. At each stage, one is faced with a crisis that, if passed, will ultimately lead to maturation as a healthy adult. Second, although both Freud and Erikson explored the role of the psyche in ego development, Erikson emphasized the importance of society and culture in shaping one's identity. And, these differences in ideology earned Erikson an unmistakable reputation as one of psychology's founding fathers on identity formation—a field that first rejected him because of his lack of pedigree and certification.[1] The artistic youngster grew up to be a medical legend, a feat hardly imaginable even to a headstrong, traditionalist stepfather. Erikson's happy ending is clear. He is the metaphorical phoenix that rises from the ashes to unequivocally silence critics along his journey and earn his rightful place in history books.

As in Erikson's case, the best fairy tales are rich with irony. It is supremely ironic that a man who lived much of his life as an outcast became one of the leading minds in articulating just how profound environmental influences are in determining whom we ultimately become. In fact, Erikson may have been so *right* about society's impact on identity formation that, according to some, his crowning achievement in identifying eight universal life stages may actually be *wrong*.

Erikson coined the eight life stages based on observations of the world around him. In 1950, when he gave the world his masterpiece *Childhood and Society*, there was no way he could have predicted the cultural tsunami that would hit the United States in the next 20 or so years following its release. You see, Erikson lived largely in a time when life stages from childhood to adulthood were fairly distinct, governed by the societal forces he took such care to analyze. After completing multiple phases in childhood (including the tumultuous adolescent phase we recently reviewed), newly formed adults entered the workforce, married, and often started families young and matured through life's remaining crises as they marched onward toward integrity or despair. Society's influence on these stages was well tested. Young adults were expected to leave the home, often to help support the childhood household if not relieve their burden on it. Young women were expected to marry and continue their husband's lineage.

But the liberating decades marked by the sixties and seventies gave rise to a very different worldview. The release of the birth control pill and legalization of abortion enabled young women to postpone pregnancy by a few years, if not indefinitely. A powerful crop of feminists shepherded women's rights that advocated equal pay for equal work, and females entered the workforce in droves. In short, women had choices. Starting a family early was certainly one. But there were multiple other options now in play—from completing college to focusing on career. The institution of marriage suffered a blow partially from the advent of no-fault divorces, which catapulted the divorce rate in America to new heights. Marrying early and starting a family wasn't quite as idealistic or necessary as it had been when Erikson penned his *tour de force*. With women considering and pursuing other options outside the family, men delayed husbandly and fatherly duties in turn.

Undetected by Erikson's social radar at the time of his writing, 20-somethings would emerge to become the next wave of adolescents caught in that unenviable in-between stage. Although reaching physical adulthood, the emotional maturation process would take a bit longer, thanks in no small part to the sweeping cultural reform facilitated by an industrialized nation—environmental factors critically important to one's identity formation, as Erikson theorized. According to a 2010 *New York Times* article, 40 percent of 20-somethings move back home with their parents at least once. On average, they experience seven jobs in 10 years. Two-thirds spend at least some time living with a romantic partner outside marriage, and marriage is a decision increasingly to be put off. In the 1970s, the median age at first marriage was 21 for women and 23 for men; by 2009, it had climbed to 26 for women and 28 for men.[2]

The "Ideal" Life Stage

A new term and life stage, coined *emerging adulthood*, entered the fray in an *American Psychologist* article in 2000. Jeffrey Arnett fathered the phrase to describe that in-between life stage, marked by those aged 18 to about 25, and reflected in industrialized societies, where *adult* decisions, such as career, marriage, and family tend to be more protracted. Critics of Arnett are quick to point out that a developmental life stage must be both universal and essential. In the case of the former, it must apply to all kinds of people from all walks of life. In the case of the latter, to miss the life stage and fail its associated crisis results in long-term maturational and developmental consequences. By Arnett's own admission, emerging adulthood is neither universal nor essential. It is not common in emerging countries or even for individuals in industrialized nations who choose to skip it, either by choice in marrying or starting a career early or by necessity of the same.[3]

Still, it appears that emerging adulthood is not exactly a fad or generational aberration either. Back in those free-wheeling 1960s, Kenneth Keniston, a Yale psychologist, remarked in an article appearing in *The American Scholar* that there was "a growing minority of post-adolescents [who] have not settled the questions whose answers once defined adulthood: questions of relationship to the existing society, questions of vocation, questions of social role and lifestyle."[4] The transition to adulthood, marked by sociologists by five key milestones (completing school, leaving home, becoming financially independent, marrying, and having a child), was and continues to be in a state of flux. In 1960, 77 percent of women and 65 percent of men had reached all five milestones by the time they reached age 30. In 2000, fewer than 50 percent of women and 33 percent of men had done so by the time they reached the critical "age 30 deadline."[5] More scientific evidence is now pouring in to suggest that the delay in emotional maturation may be directly correlated to the physical development of the brain, particularly the prefrontal cortex and cerebellum, those involved in emotional control and cognitive function. Although brain development was once thought to have ceased by age 16, data now suggest that these higher-order regions continue to mature well into one's twenties, supporting a protracted adulthood further encouraged by societal mores.

Among other characteristics, Arnett marks the emerging adulthood phase by what he calls "a sense of possibilities."[6] No longer forced to settle down early and allergic to the notion of the dreaded "daily grind" for a lifetime, emerging adults have more choices than ever. It is not a job they want, but a career. It is not a marriage partner they seek, but a soul mate. The sense of the ideal is still within reach before one fully commits to the rest of one's life. In addition, the pressures confounded by a struggling economy make the temptation to resist commitment even greater. As Bruce, a 22-year-old college student on the brink of graduation, tells our research team:

> Well, it should have been four years [to finish college] but it will be five years for me. I'm applying to law schools now trying to decide where I want to go to law school. I can graduate in two years but that's kind of pushing it. I might take my time like I did in college and enjoy it. Especially with this economy—there's no rush to get out there and work.

Some are quick to criticize young adults like Bruce. He may be branded lazy for wanting to take it a bit easier on his pace to graduate from law school. But that would be a gross and unfair mischaracterization. In Bruce's case, he holds down a full course load at school while tending bar nights. His desire for more is reflective of a life stage marked by uncertainty. Indeed, even among the more "established" young adults who have managed to complete at least a few of the socially acceptable milestones toward adulthood, there is that familiar feeling of not quite being at a definitive station in life. Take Chelsea, a 24-year-old research subject married to her teenage sweetheart and holding down a job while enrolled in nursing school:

> *I'm in nursing school. I've worked at a hair salon for almost five years,*
> *so I'm at the in-between stage of my life.*

Then there are those like Jodi, a 20-something research respondent who recently graduated college and moved to a new area to be with her boyfriend. Her search for the ideal seems to have just started:

> *Currently, I'm employed with a bank. But, I'm still looking for my*
> *ideal job.*

And how does her boyfriend, Craig (another 20-something), describe how he landed his current job with a financial firm?

> *It was a kind of a "can't find anything in my field, gotta find something*
> *now" type thing.*

These young adults are not immune to hard work. They are, however, resistant to settling for anything less than their ideal fill-in-the-blank in a world of possibilities. In a virtual world, those possibilities are all the more endless, making identity maturation all the more complex.

Creeps, Weirdos, and Left-Behinds

In the online world, there is no comparison to Facebook. Among all online social networkers, its heavyweight status is perhaps most understood by emerging adults, those college-aged netizens who once knew Facebook as only their own. Our respondent and recent college graduate Brian and one of his four roommates reflect on when they joined Facebook:

> **Brian:** *He [my friend] started when it was strictly college and then*
> *I started when I entered college. And then I think they opened it up*
> *around 2007 to high school and then all addresses after that. It just*

> *kind of made Facebook explode. But you also get more spam now too. It was kind of cool back in the day because you could see everybody by college.*
>
> **Roommate #1:** *It was a lot less creepy. Because I signed up for it when I came out for orientation. One of the guys was like, "Oh you need to get on Facebook." I was like "Okay." Getting friends even before coming to college wasn't as creepy back then because like it was Facebook and the only people that could be your friends were people from college.*
>
> **Brian:** *And now it's like people can be like, "Oh, I met you last Saturday for like two minutes. Let me add you as a friend."*

Despite the perceived creepiness of Facebook, emerging adults avoid it at their own risk. To not be on Facebook is to be out of the loop—literally. At best, the result is to miss out on the social scene so important in this stage of life. At worst, one risks being labeled for bucking the unavoidable trend. Facebook's origins as a site created by emerging adults for emerging adults help explain its pervasiveness among those in this life stage. Of all the segments we surveyed (including teens), emerging adults are the most likely to engage in a range of social-networking behaviors—from carefully screening the best photos of themselves before posting online, to spending time updating their social networking page to project the right image of themselves, to discussing entertainment interests with others to find similar content.

Facebook is that invisible gravitational force that, in many cases, is impossible to resist. It's not just a matter of being a member; one has to check the site regularly (in many cases, several times a day) or else risk missing out on the latest buzz in the social circle. As another of Brian's roommates admits after being out of the Facebook party line one too many times:

> **Roommate #2:** *You definitely feel like you're missing something if you're not on those things [such as Facebook]. But then you realize how much time you spend on it.*
>
> **Interviewer:** *You said you feel like you're missing something in the moment when you don't have it but when you get back to it, do you still feel like you have missed something? Is it true that you're missing out on something?*
>
> **Roommate #2:** *Yeah. Like on Facebook, when you go to [the Home screen] and you see all the feeds, if you haven't been on them for a week, you feel like you're only seeing the pages you're scrolling down.*

You're never going to scroll to the second or third page to see what
happened in days past. I rely on instant feeds to keep me engaged in
other people's lives.

If a young adult is not on Facebook, well, he or she risks being branded *strange*, to put it politely. When Tara, one of our 18-year-old respondents, describes her brother, who is not on Facebook, she comments that she has to explain to his friends (many of whom are now friends of hers on Facebook, specifically to find a means of reaching him) that he is just "weird." If you're not left-behind or weird, you're part of the Facebook juggernaut, where maintaining one's ideal image becomes increasingly challenging.

Of course, Facebook aficionados are used to the drill. If you want to control how you are perceived by the outside world, you must engage privacy blocks. For some respondents, this involves painstaking attempts to limit the amount of information visible to unknown strangers, casual acquaintances, or intimate friends by establishing unique groups, each with its own permissions as to what is up for grabs in the user's Facebook profile. Among all subjects in our study, emerging adults are the most likely to engage in a range of behaviors to control their privacy settings and manage their relationships. When those privacy settings are changed by Facebook, users must reengage to regain control. As Andrew, one of our 25-year-old respondents, remarks:

I have very strict privacy settings. I have missionary parents and my
friends like to use colorful language and post interesting links. And my
parents are on Facebook and their friends are on Facebook. So I have
all of my privacy settings customized. So whenever Facebook changes a
privacy setting, it's a real pain in the butt for me. Because their default
is to allow more information and I have to go through and make sure
the people that need to be excluded are excluded.

Because Facebook is "open" to the public, beyond the college community it once called home, it now offers recruiters an inside peek of what a job candidate is really like, not just how she presents herself in the all-important interview. For Lorraine, a 20-something college student who aspires to be a teacher one day, the implications are very real:

I want to be a high school teacher and I've heard that I probably
have to delete my Facebook for a little bit because employers do check
on Facebook to see what you're up to and see if you're doing illegal
things—or whatever—if there are pictures of you drunk. If you don't
make it private enough, they can access your profile.

But, in Tara's experience, there really is no way to leave Facebook, or at least no way she has discovered in how to delete her account:

> *I've actually canceled my Facebook before, which is one of the problems I have with Facebook is I don't think there's a way to actually delete yourself. They have an option where you can hide your profile, but if you go back and log on with your email and password, it will replenish it so that everybody else can see it again. So it's either activated or deactivated, it's not deleting it and I don't think that's really fair. I've heard of friends having it be negative of having bad pictures on there and administrative people getting a hold of it and taking disciplinary action because of something they have on Facebook.*

If recruiters aren't enough to worry about, there are those creepers. *Creeping*, as we discovered, is the act of finding information out about someone without him knowing. Think of it as virtual snooping for those with the time, technology prowess, and, most importantly, interest in finding out about their target. For these emerging adults, their online persona is an extension of their real-world identity. With recruiters, creepers, and everyday individuals waiting to take a parting shot at you on sites like Lamebook (a Facebook parody site that allows users to take screen shots of amusing nuggets found on Facebook as fodder for ridicule), there's even more importance in upholding one's ideal image to avoid consequences or embarrassment along the way.

The significance of reflecting one's ideal sense of self overcomes more primal security concerns for Jack, a 24-year-old student. After stumbling on the fact that his address was available for any creeper to find on a site called MyLife, his stunned response offered only one word: "creepy."

> *It bothers me that someone knows my address. I guess they're [MyLife] just trying to get people killed.*

Despite this visceral reaction to the discovery, it doesn't take Jack much time to contemplate if he would rather have his address or a less-than-ideal photo of himself exposed for the world to see:

> **Interviewer:** *Let's say somebody could find out either your more identifying information, like your address that you found on MyLife, or they could find a picture of you getting drunk or a picture of you looking stupid. Which would you rather them find?*
>
> **Jack:** *I'd rather have the first one.*

As discussed in Chapter 7 about the Law of Recall, the potential for Jack's image to be damaged in a world where life plays itself out online is far closer to home (although much more innocuous) than a more serious threat (potentially leading to death in his own mind) that seems so much further removed by comparison. For these emerging adults pursuing their ideal future spouse or career, presenting their ideal sense of self is essential to wooing a potential suitor or recruiter. In short, *finding* their ideal requires *being* their ideal.

Perhaps it comes as no surprise that this life stage craves technology that assists in portraying and managing one's image. One of the more popular features tested among our respondents is analogous to a credit report, but, in this case, it is the subject's image, not bank account, that is monitored. Presenting oneself online is an interesting conundrum. On one hand, it is relatively easy to enhance, if not outright change, the features about oneself that are the most unflattering. By removing the imperfections so common in a real world, the virtual world makes one's ideal image possible. As Tara, our 18-year-old college student says:

> *I think that people go for images on Facebook. I feel like images can be very deceptive. Girls more twist their looks, either with Photoshop or using the lights or using different techniques on the computer to make themselves look prettier … like slight imperfections they're not comfortable with. I use pictures that I think are more attractive of me on Facebook.*

But therein lies the double-edged sword. Although individuals can closely manage their image online to create the desired perception, others can tarnish it with a simple post of an unflattering photo. Control is no longer in the individual's hands. He is literally outnumbered by friends, acquaintances, and random strangers equipped with camera phones waiting to take and share the perfect shot—whether our subject's ideal image is compromised in the process or not. The result is a loss of control and a feeling of uneasiness that accompanies it, as our subject Joel comments:

> *Interviewer: What do you think about that [when someone else tags you in a photo]?*
>
> *Joel: That's one of those weird Facebook things that borders on creepy, I think. And, if you look at it wrong, you're like, "That is creepy, yeah."*

Unfortunately, keeping up with how many times one is tagged is difficult at best. Increasing the challenge, emerging facial recognition technology allows for easy indexing of photos without the need for tagging at all. Subjects keen to protect the image they have taken such care to create need to know of the chinks in their virtual armor. As such, emerging adults, who perhaps are the most tech-savvy and ideal-centric, respond to services that notify them proactively when any photo of themselves—flattering or not, tagged or otherwise—lands in cyberspace.

For these adults, image is central to their in-between life stage, somewhere between immaturity and establishment on the adulthood scale. At the same time, the virtual world enables a seemingly endless buffet of opportunities—career, social, and educational—as they pursue their passions while life gives them time to ponder the possibilities. Critics on the sidelines who simply don't understand or can't relate to this relatively new life stage may question the perpetual delays and false starts these 20-somethings seem to attract. Although Arnett himself would admit that the life stage he coined is neither universal nor essential, some may question the latter point. Recent evidence suggests that those adults who "grow up" faster than others in starting families in their younger years may face greater challenges in educational or workforce advancement as a result, perhaps giving credence to society's increasing tolerance in allowing some time to sow one's oats.[7] As more time and energy are committed to the virtual world, the opportunity to find and create the *ideal* life is more attainable than ever. And, as digital natives come of age in a networked-community era, society may encounter even more seismic cultural changes yet undetected by the brightest prognosticators. Just as Freud inspired Erikson to take psychoanalysis in new directions, Erikson is now the muse to a new crop of psychologists who use his life stage theory as a foundation for their work. If the liberating sixties and seventies could result in a new, although disputed, life stage, what are the chances that the same happens again when more of our future generations live their lives online? Perhaps the virtual world will create life stages yet to be imagined. Like eternal fairy tale heroes, that possibility gives Erikson's legacy timeless endurance.

SHIFT SHORT: PIZZA, RAMEN, AND THE SEARCH FOR THE NEXT BIG IDEA

The search for the next great social network is on. Like Facebook before, many options are coming from the entrepreneurial ranks of emerging adults. One new entrant into the social-networking game is Diaspora*—joindiaspora.com—from four students who met at NYU: Maxwell Salzberg, Ilya Zhitomirskiy, Daniel Grippi, and Raphael Sofaer. They launched their fundraising using efforts on Kickstarter in April 2010, hoping to get $10,000, and after *The New York Times* published an article on them in May 2010, they raised more than $200,000. An NYU media researcher called their effort "a return of the classic geek means of production: pizza and ramen and guys sleeping under the desks because it is something that it is really exciting and challenging."[8]

Emily Nussbaum, of *New York* magazine, sat down to talk with the creators shortly after their initial site launch in September 2010. The driving idea behind Diaspora* is to deliver a "privacy-aware, personally controlled, do-it-all open-source social network."[9] They list a collection of influences from hackers to global thinkers like Clay Shirky to other young programmers like those behind Chatroulette and Linux. The final seed was planted when they saw Columbia law professor Eben Moglen give a lecture, "Freedom in the Cloud," which detailed all the ways consumers have given companies free play with our private information. After listening to the lecture, the four young programmers felt empowered to launch their own social-networking solution with user privacy at its core, not just with the hope of hitting it big like late-nineties tech boom pioneers but with an eye toward solving a very real problem with personal, social, and economic implications.

"On Diaspora itself, there's no money to be made," Zhitomirskiy insists. "But an open platform is good for anybody." He's perched on his windowsill, legs pulled up. "I don't think we want to do ads. Ads are just like ... meh. But that's way down the line, and we're not thinking about that."*[10]

SHIFT SHORT: PIZZA, RAMEN, AND THE SEARCH FOR THE NEXT BIG IDEA (*continued*)

Rafael Sofaer's older brother Mike recalls the four guys' excitement: "There was a feeling like 'we could do anything.'" After months of discussion and consultation, they decided on an approach where user data is decentralized on web hosts, personal servers, or servers of trusted friends. With this approach, their content can be transferred or deleted whenever they wish, data is encrypted, and security measures are put in place to stop outside parties from scraping the data. Moglen, for his part, is a supporter of the endeavor and warns about the risks of computers aggregating all the data we leave behind like the "dandruff of our lives."

Following the launch, the group was overwhelmed with the response from all over the world. In just the first day, the Diaspora* code was translated into seven languages. But the group remains convinced that they can make their mission a success. In a project update on their blog about six months after launching, Salzberg posted new user stats and stats on their connections to the developer community, which is key given their focus on open source code:

Our developer community is growing. Diaspora* has had over 100 unique code contributors and countless others have edited our wiki and updated Diaspora*'s translations in over 51 languages. We have over 4,600 followers and over 840 forks, which means that tons of developers are checking out our code.[11]

Diaspora* hopes to transform how even the most technologically unaware network in the virtual world. "I like the way Ilya described it to me," Salzberg told Nussbaum in 2010. "'We want to move tectonic plates, not kick a rock across the universe.'"[12]

The "Meet" Market

11

What's a nice person like you doing in a place like this?

—CHEESY 1970S PICKUP LINE

A man approached a woman to request a dance, and was refused. He appeared chagrined and left quickly. After a few minutes, he approached a second woman with a similar request. But she did not hear him clearly at first since the music had started at the same moment, and hesitated. He took this hesitation as a second refusal and quickly left the dance entirely. By the time his request has sunk in, the second girl had risen to accept his request. As she stood, she saw him abruptly turn around and leave. Thus standing there embarrassedly, perhaps thinking he had left because he did not like what she looked like at closer range, she sat down again very quickly, red-faced. Another male approached her shortly, and very quickly, without even looking at him at all, she refused him the dance.[1]

The above excerpt is from a journal article published in the late 1970s. At the time, singles dances were a popular, although stigmatized, way to meet others in the dating scene. In his paper, Bernard Berk provides an analysis of the observation and interviews of singles at more than 70 dances. In a time before home computers, mass Internet consumption, or mobile devices, meeting others was largely relegated to physical venues—at work, school, or, in this case, the dreaded singles dance.

Dating. Cohabitation. Marriage. Whatever an individual's end pursuit, there is a pervasive market of exchange that exists among millions of singles looking for a relationship. We prefer the term *mating* as the universal moniker to describe the process whereby an individual seeks a partner, although there are certainly more colorful names woven into the social fabric. For example, the term *meat market* is the culturally embedded colloquialism that captures the similarities of this sociological phenomenon to cold (pun intended), yet simple, economic principles. When one is looking for a mate, he is said to be "in the market." If one has multiple options from which to choose, she is said to have solid "prospects." One's "competitors" are the other singles vying for the opportunity to nab the suitor's target. These aren't just interesting metaphors to describe experiences relatable to most of us. For decades, sociologists have compared the psychological aspects of mate selection with the economic principles found in free markets.

Social exchange theory is a sociological perspective that explains interactions as a series of negotiated exchanges between parties.[2] Rooted in the concept are economic principles we have come to know as consumers in a free market. First, when we purchase a product, we weigh the perceived benefits against the costs. Similarly, relationships involve effort and (it is hoped) yield psychological rewards. It is not simply a matter of rewards exceeding costs that determines whether a relationship will survive. Rather, because we all have different expectations and definitions of satisfaction, our own perceptions determine our cost–benefit tolerance. Marketers understand this principle quite well. It is one of the reasons companies spend billions of dollars each year in advertising to project the appropriate image in the marketplace in an effort to attract the prospect they wish to woo. Finally, there is an element of dependence that factors into the dynamic of the relationship. In the free market, this comes down to *opportunity costs* (a concept we cover in more detail later). For now, let's simply describe it as the investment that an individual must make to leave an unfulfilling relationship. If the individual already has multiple other options from which to choose (such as another admirer waiting in the wings), the decision to move on may be fairly straightforward. In contrast, if he has already established significant equity in the existing relationship through time or other investments, it may prove more difficult to walk away.

In a world dominated by face-to-face interaction, as in Berk's singles dance observation above, the rules of social exchange are dictated by physical constraints. For the male suitor in the opening excerpt, the initial encounter resulted in a rebuff of the dance offer. Upon the second attempt, the perception of the same resulted in an abrupt about-face. The courter in this scenario likely felt an imbalance in the rewards attained to the costs associated with tangible embarrassment. Consider the powerful prose in the narrative as evidence. The reader can see in her mind's eye the vivid imagery of red faces and averted gazes—typical social cues in a physical world to indicate the sting of embarrassment as one's ego suffers an otherwise indiscernible blow. Indeed, back in the 1970s, one's interactions were limited to physical signals in a world where faceless engagements propelled by the Internet had yet to enter the social landscape. In fact, the popular idiom "maintaining face" can be traced back to an article published in the late 1960s in which author Erving Goffman described "face-work" in social interaction and inspired the later writing of Berk in observing the principle in the dating market. In a physical world dominated by personal contact characterized by the dating scene before the turn of the century, one's *face* becomes the tangible most closely associated when initiating a relationship or maintaining a delicate ego.

But how does this change in a virtual world where one's *face*, or image, can be altered, concealed, or revealed in very different ways from those the physical world has allowed? Social exchange theory is not without its critics, including those who admonish its characterization of human intimacy as nothing more than a series of rational choices arising from economic tenets.[3] However, it is a useful paradigm within which to explore how virtual relationships apply in this context. It's no revelation that the Internet has had a profound impact on how consumers and businesses exchange goods and services each day. Applying the same economic principles to how consumers now interact with one another in a networked-community age reflects a vibrant picture of a new *meet market*.

The Laws of Supply and Demand— And Attraction

The laws of supply and demand are an invisible force in our daily lives. More suppliers for a particular good or service creates a more competitive market from which consumers may partake. In contrast, the higher the demand for an item and the fewer suppliers offering it yields the opposite case, with sellers deriving more negotiating power in the exchange. At the heart of this bedrock economic principle are the juxtaposing extremes of choice versus scarcity. The more choices available in the market, the greater is the competitive pressure among suppliers. In contrast, the more scarce a particular service (as is often the case for the hottest gizmo during the peak holiday season) or the suppliers offering it (as reflected in monopolistic or oligopolistic markets), the higher is the price consumers will often face. (Note that we are deliberately ignoring the complexity of markets facing regulation that can reverse the natural tendencies in the supply–demand equation.)

In mating, supply and demand are evident. At its most primal, mating is about reproduction. A species populates to continue its survival. *Evolutionary psychology*, a relatively new discipline, explores how the laws of attraction can be traced back to our primitive urge to reproduce. In addition, we can't explore reproduction without also examining the biological differences that separate males from females.

Our ability to reproduce varies significantly between the sexes. Whereas males have a seemingly endless supply of sperm with which to impregnate females, females are confined to a rhythmic ovulation cycle, in which fertility is confined to specific days of the month. Furthermore, assuming a female is impregnated, she faces a gestation period of nine months, further preventing the option for additional pregnancies during that time. Also, whereas males can father children well into their latter years, a female's abilities become more limited as the biological clock ticks on. In economic terms, the supply of sperm exceeds that of eggs. Because both an egg and sperm are required for reproduction, scarcity enters the mating scene. What results is a difference in how males are attracted to females and vice versa.

Evolutionary psychologists theorize that males tend to be attracted to females who appear more youthful precisely because of the law of supply and demand. In fact, evidence suggests that a male's ability to sense when a woman is ovulating actually heightens this physical attraction and encourages riskier behavior on the part of the man. In one such study, a female student in cahoots with researchers interacted with male subjects. The female was instructed to keep track of her ovulation cycle. During the days of interaction with the male subjects, she was also directed not to wear perfume or makeup or otherwise alter her physical appearance. She was trained to act in a non-flirtatious and consistent manner with each male participant. Of course, none of the male subjects knew the female was part of the study; they were simply informed that she was another subject in the experiment.

The researchers then went to work observing the interesting game of sexual attraction. The female participated along with male respondents in constructing a structure of Lego building blocks. On days the female was ovulating, males tended to mimic her nonverbal cues, an indication of allure supported by other psychological studies that suggest we mirror the behaviors of others we seek to attract. After the exercise, the man was asked to play a computer game of Blackjack with the woman sitting behind him watching his choices. On the days the female was ovulating, the male was more likely to make riskier decisions during the Blackjack simulation.[4]

It comes as no surprise that men are attracted to beauty, but the subtext that this physical inclination is rooted in a more primal survival extinct of propagating a species takes on an interesting nuance. The importance of appearance is evident as a force of attraction for males and a source of deception for females. For thousands of years, females have used cosmetics to enhance physical features. Indeed, social experiments have shown makeup to be successful in attracting males.[5] The virtual world's *makeup* allows for more dramatic altering of one's physical appearance with tools like Photoshop, as discussed in Chapter 10. Or, in more extreme cases, where attractiveness is a scarce resource, some go so far as to steal it. Consider one of the attractive females in our study, Jodi, a 20-something who reminisces on her earlier foreboding experiences with then social-networking pioneer MySpace:

> I started finding other profiles of myself. People would take my pictures and pretend to be me. And there were multiple of them. I'd be different ages. I'd be living in Florida, I lived in Kansas, I lived in New Jersey—all over. They would take pictures of my friends and make profiles of my friends in order to make themselves look more real—more like me.

Jodi's case is not that isolated, considering that nearly 30 percent of those in our study admit to proactively looking for fake social-networking pages set up in their name or using their likeness. Also, the behavior appears to be particularly pronounced among emerging adults, for whom one's presentation becomes all the more important in inviting the right suitor, even if that presentation is a sham.

Continuing with our evolutionary psychology discussion, if males are attracted to the physical, females are attracted to status. The stakes of bearing a child are biologically higher for a female. As such, these costs are powerful inputs to the risk-versus-reward balancing act so important in social exchange theory. For the female, choosing a partner carefully based on long-term potential increases the odds of finding a *dad* as opposed to a *cad* (a playful characterization adopted by scientists to explain the female mating choice).

Regarding the impact of ovulation in attracting a male, it turns out that ovulation has been shown to encourage riskier behavior among females as well. British anthropologists seeking to understand how the birth control pill affects the rules of attraction made an interesting discovery. During a woman's ovulation cycle, the researchers found females to be more attracted to men with masculine characteristics and to those with an immune system genetically different from their own (which some scientists suspect could make for healthier offspring). In contrast, when women were not ovulating, they tended to gravitate toward photos of men with a more feminine look—a subliminal appeal toward men not as susceptible to testosterone and more likely to stick around for the long haul.[6] At a minimum, the study reflects differences in female attraction, depending on if she is ovulating. During times when she is not, she is more likely to be attracted to a man with a perceived ability to provide resources (emotional or otherwise) to sustain the relationship.

In a physical world, status is commanded by material possessions. For example, much to the dismay of everyday working Joes, there is scientific evidence to support the theory that women find men in expensive cars to be more attractive, all else being equal (the same is not the case for men).[7] However, as we discussed in Chapter 9, the virtual world has an entirely different set of status symbols to signify one's success. Among them is how popular one is in attracting attractive mates himself, perhaps explaining the never-ending battle to have the most *friends* online among singles seeking status. According to Jack, our 20-something single male respondent:

> *Jack: I have quite a few friends [on Facebook]. I keep a watch on how many friends I have.*
>
> *Interviewer: Because more Facebook friends means?*
>
> *Jack: I'm popular. The first week I started Facebook, I had like five friends. I was nervous.*

The notion of popularity is not a new concept and certainly not unique to a virtual world. In Berk's paper on singles dances in the 1970s, he noted one of the defense mechanisms used by singles in that social scene:

> *"Coming with a friend," in addition to projecting an image of respectability, can help establish a front of popularity or desirability. The public display of friendship staves off aspersions of unpopularity and attests to the likability of the individual.*[8]

Hence, fronting one's posse as a testament to his likeability is not new. However, in a virtual world where counting friends becomes possible, if not easier, this new measure of status can help separate the attractive from the unattractive in a market thick with choices.

Thus, online individuals have a new scene within which to participate—one in which males can troll for attractive females based on enhanced Photoshop pics and females can count status points like friends more easily. But this sounds like a very depraved depiction (and not entirely fair characterization) of an online dating market that is booming and cultivating happy relationships each day. It is not our intention to pass judgment on how the initial spark of attraction is ignited or how it manifests itself online. Rather, we argue that the virtual world has a dramatic impact on these physical laws. But, for the extreme case of how the laws of supply and demand can apply literally in an online mating environment, consider whatsyourprice.com as the latest social-networking dating site to enter the ring. On whatsyourprice.com, members scan the market for individuals who fit their type. But, rather than go through the normal exchange typical in a virtual world (read: "actually engaging to establish mutual interests before meeting offline"), the site features an online auction of sorts, where suitors and targets can actively negotiate the highest price to secure a date. If you're an Average Joe looking for the Above Average Josephine, send her an offer—say $20, $50, $100, or more—to agree to meet you. If she accepts, you get the date, and whatever happens from there is of no consequence to the site that connected you. If nothing else, whatsyourprice.com will prove to be an interesting sociological experiment. Referring back to social exchange theory, it removes the uncertainty (albeit in a questionable way) of financial costs versus rewards for each party. Of course, social exchange theorists and their critics alike are likely reeling from a site that takes the economic principles of supply and demand in the mating game to an entirely new level.

Endless Opportunities— And Opportunity Costs

In economic theory, an *opportunity cost* is what one gives up to pursue something else. Let's demonstrate with an example. Suppose Amanda has $100 to spend and she is contemplating the choice between a new jacket or pair of shoes. If she selects the shoes, her opportunity cost is the jacket. Depending on how much she really deliberated her decision (in other words, how close the jacket was in contention for her scarce financial resource), the opportunity cost of forgoing the jacket is relatively high. The principle has been used in economics to measure the relationship between scarcity and choice.[9]

In a relevant market confined by physical constraints, one's choices (and therefore opportunity costs) are finite. For example, when considering where to fill up one's gas tank, one likely considers gas stations along an established route or within a specific geographic radius. If I am a New York resident envious of the lower gas prices available in Texas, it would be impossible for me to frequent stations in the Lone Star state. Therefore, although I may desire to save money with cheaper fuel, these Texas stations are not an opportunity cost for me because they were never part of my relevant market in the first place.

Relating this principle back to mating, consider the dating scene before the dawn of the Internet. Finding a potential mate involved a physical meeting of some sort. In the study of attraction, it's referred to as the *propinquity effect*, and it has several attributes.

First, there's the element of *availability*. Just as a New Yorker can't patronize a Texas gas station, singles back in the day were largely confined to physical constraints in meeting someone new. Also, the more frequently the person was encountered, the more likely we were to develop a relationship—whether platonic or romantic. In the dating scene of days gone by, the prospective dater's relevant market was confined to those individuals physically in her life on a regular basis.

Next, there's the notion of *interaction*. The more regular my encounters with a particular individual, the more likely it is that I can anticipate the social interaction that follows. In fact, one begins preparing for these interactions over time. Also, the more preparation that is put forth, the more likely it is that a meaningful relationship will ensue.

Finally, there's the *exposure* effect. Studies suggest that the more we encounter something, the more likely we are to like it. The mere exposure engenders attraction. In Chapter 1, on presentation, we spoke of Lacan's mirror image theory. Recall that the image we see in a mirror is not how others actually see us, but how we perceive ourselves to be. It is also the image that we have grown comfortable seeing every day on a regular basis. Therefore, it comes as no surprise that when offering someone a choice between his mirror image and a photograph taken of him, he is likely to choose the mirror image as the more attractive of the two. The exposure effect would suggest that this has much to do with the familiarity of seeing the mirror image on a regular basis as opposed to an isolated photograph.[10]

What does all this have to do with mating in a virtual world? First, the notion of availability becomes less relevant in a world unconfined by physical boundaries.

Second, interaction shifts as the sequence of communication no longer is bound by physical time constraints (consider the popularity of texting as just one example of asynchronous communication not requiring real-time discourse between two parties). Finally, exposure becomes even more interesting in that it is no longer confined to the physical but also may be enhanced based on how one projects her online persona.

This confluence of factors has one more interesting, and critical, outcome—opportunities for mate selection increase, and, as such, so do the opportunity costs. Psychologist Barry Schwartz forewarns how this tyranny of abundance can negatively affect one's relationship success:

> *People walk starry-eyed looking not into the eyes of their romantic partner but over their romantic partner's shoulder, in case there might be somebody better walking by. This is not the road to successful long-term relationships.*[11]

Perhaps this abundance of choice helps explain the prevalence of Facebook in more and more U.S. divorce proceedings. An innocent exchange between two online friends can quickly progress to a full-fledged emotional affair. In a physical world, the spark would be ignited by a physical encounter—perhaps among coworkers in the same office, where the risks of a tawdry affair being discovered are high among watchful eyes in a work environment. But, with physical boundaries shattered and met by the colliding forces of interaction and exposure in a new networked-community age, Facebook can fuel relationships otherwise impossible to maintain. As Schwartz explains, the proliferation of choice breeds within us the illusion that perfection, or an ideal, exists somewhere in the world, if only we could find it.

If we can't find it, we can always create it. A new site, cloudgirlfriend.com, allows members to design their ideal mate in cyberspace. The fantasy creation then interacts with its creator, even to the extent of posting items on the latter's Facebook wall, as though coming from an actual mate. These are not the interactions designed by faceless bots in the sky. Instead, the site uses real people to engage in fake relationships with those looking to increase their coolness quotient in an attempt to attract others. It's a bit of life imitating art—*Weird Science* meets cyberspace reality—and, as we all know from the popular John Hughes film, the nerdy guys nabbed the beautiful girls in the end simply with the illusion of popularity through their perfectly constructed Glamazon creation.

Caveat Emptor (Let the Buyer Beware)

Carole Markin, a successful entertainment executive active on Match.com (a popular online dating site), found nothing unusual about agreeing to a second date from a potential suitor in May of 2010. After all, she had used Match.com several times before successfully to meet men who fit her needs and already had one date with the man, so why should this be any different? Sure, as Markin acknowledges, people deceive in the online dating world: "People lie about their age or they lie about their weight, but they usually don't lie about having gone to jail." Sadly, for Markin, that's precisely the case that landed her in a dangerous situation with fellow Match.com member—and former sex offender—Alan Paul Wurtzel. Markin alleges that Wurtzel followed her home after dinner and sexually assaulted her.[12]

Of course, the perils of dating are not unique to the online world. But, as we have discussed in other chapters, they are a bit exacerbated when one's natural protection mechanisms are rendered powerless in a market where people are not always as they seem. Markin's lawsuit against the website that matched her with Wurtzel has inspired changes to Match.com's policies, including plans to screen users' names against a sexual predator database. Although certainly noble in its cause, critics are quick to point out the challenges in such an approach. Users may circumvent the system with phony names or other attempts, and well-meaning members may find themselves in a case of mistaken identity if they suffer a common name.

Still, the need for protection is apparent. Beyond the obvious danger of criminals lurking in the online shadows, the temptation to embellish, if not deliberately misrepresent, one's image can present itself in less nefarious, although still concerning, ways. For Julie, the 30-something single soccer mom referenced in Chapter 2 (on protection), there is clearly a need for more sophisticated authentication capabilities to avoid a case of mistaken identity or deliberate fraud. Technology continues to progress at an alarming rate, meaning that we might be able to rely on more unique characteristics about a person in the near future—such as one's voiceprint or fingerprint—to augment today's alternatives of simple name recognition. Remember Julie's comments from earlier to punctuate the need:

> *You know when it's a fake driver's license, right? So, you can't fake this certain person is this age—you know—this information on them. That would be good. Or, even for women—it would say, "Hey, it*

shows on here that he's married, he hasn't gotten a divorce." All that information needs to come out. And it would be their identity—their real *identity.*

Julie's point is even more understood when one considers how skeptical people are of others' intentions online. In our study of more than 5,000 connected U.S. respondents, 77 percent agreed with the statement that others say and do things online that they wouldn't do in the real world, compared with only 21 percent who attributed the statement to themselves. Thus, the gap between perception and reality is magnified in an online world, requiring more sophisticated tools to ameliorate its effects. If Match.com's proposed attempt is convoluted, given the complexities in simply verifying one's name, a more rigorous and foolproof approach using biometric authentication may be the answer. Not surprisingly, this feature is among the top tested in our study.

As in most areas of our lives, the role of technology cannot be overestimated in one of the most important life-changing decisions most of us make—the choice of a mate. Whether we attempt to project the best image of ourselves possible (a presentation attribute), are inundated with limitless choices that can be filtered to our needs (a preference attribute), or aim to avoid precarious situations with unsavory characters (a protection attribute), the role of identity as facilitated by technology becomes more challenging to manage. Still, 17 percent of married couples in the last three years met on an online dating site, and, in the last year, more than twice as many marriages resulted from online dating than from meeting in bars, clubs, and social events combined.[13] Thus, one could argue that the dating scene propelled by a networked-community age may be a bit more complex, but is certainly more effective than the chance meetings at the corner bar or neighborhood hotspot.

Technology is not a substitute for meaningful social interactions, but it certainly can contribute to the same. Consider the exchange between Christine and James, a married couple in their thirties, well past the challenges of the dating scene, but an exchange reflective of the role of technology in projecting our ideal sense of identity all the same:

> *James: I'm at an odd in-between place. My first thing would be to protect my image but I think of that as being mid-twenties, late-twenties, early-thirties—still out there, kind of reckless, whereas now I'm moving into more stable, long-term thinking. So I would say my*

identity would be more important to me now. But I think my initial reaction would be image but as I think about it, it would be identity. I don't know how to phrase it but if technology could have a sense of restraint or propriety.

Christine: *Like protocol or etiquette? Like Technology with a capital "T," like a Being or something? [Laughter]. In a way that it is not manipulated by you but in a way that exists in a certain way?*

Interviewer: *Can you give me an example?*

James [laughing]: *Nobody knows. I take it back. What I'm thinking about can't be learned or acquired by technology but only by people using it.*

James is right. Technology can't stop someone from making poor decisions, particularly in a social scene as complex as dating. However, the opportunity for providers and for daters seeking their ideal match now rests in technology enhancements yet to come. Until then, aspiring daters the world over can at least take solace in being spared the red-faced embarrassment accompanied by rejected advances at those stigmatized singles dances from another era.

SHIFT SHORT: PUCKER UP

The Internet has certainly transformed the dating scene. But it leaves something to be desired in the way of actual physical contact. Nothing quite compares to the human touch, particularly in the realm of romance. Researchers in Japan, however, have devised a new contraption that could allow you to reach out and touch someone—even plant a French kiss on him or her—all from thousands of miles away.

Of course, a *French kiss* in this instance could benefit from definition. The researchers at Tokyo's Kajimoto Laboratory have invented a device that allows a user to waggle his tongue on a plastic straw, thereby making another plastic straw waggle remotely on someone else's tongue.

The "Kiss Transmission Device" resembles a police breathalyzer. Its intention is to support those in long-distance romances who could benefit from a bit of the human touch. In addition, the *kiss* can be recorded and replayed, allowing someone to share in the experience as many times as the heart desires. These recordings may even be of celebrities opting to use the device, bringing raging fans one step closer to their idols (at a price that is yet to be determined).

If a plastic straw doesn't exactly equate to a real smooch, the researchers are clearly not done aspiring to the possibilities. Nobuhiro Takahashi, a graduate student and researcher at The University of Electro-Communications (home to the Kajimoto Laboratory), has this to say: "The elements of a kiss include the sense of taste, the manner of breathing, and the moistness of the tongue. If we can recreate all of those, I think it will be a really powerful device."[14]

Perhaps long-distance romantics have something to look forward to.

The Parent Puzzle

There are two lasting bequests we can give our children.
One is roots. The other is wings.

—HODDING CARTER, JR., NOTED MISSISSIPPI EDITOR

A 1964 *New York Times* article reflects the nostalgia of the time and reminds us how much (and little) has changed for parents of adolescents. The piece, entitled "And Now He (She) Drives," recounts the fiery social debate surrounding teenage driving during the liberating 1960s. To put the timing of the article in context, the 10 years between 1958 and 1968 were marked by unprecedented economic prosperity in the United States, stimulated in part by a federal tax reduction in 1963.[1] Families found themselves the beneficiaries of greater household income and a new level of affluence that accompanied it. Among the more expensive household possessions on the rise? The family automobile.

With automobiles gracing the driveways of an increasing number of households, parents found themselves in an interesting conundrum: how to protect the safety of immature teenage drivers without robbing the adolescents of social freedom in the process. Consider the commentary captured by the 1964 article from concerned parents of the time. "My personal attitude is that I'd be darned before I'd let my teenager drive a car," expressed a passionate father who also happened to be an official of the New York State Department of Motor Vehicles.[2] "If driving licenses were withheld from anyone who hasn't graduated from high school, it would be a strong tool to combat dropouts," hypothesized a concerned high school teacher.[3]

Safety concerns notwithstanding (teenage drivers were and continue to be among the most accident-prone on the road), parents also worried that the car was costing the teen valuable time away from academic and familial pursuits. A booklet prepared by Metropolitan Life Insurance Company and targeted to teens of the day summed it up quite nicely: "Few of us come right out and say it, but the car can also represent escape—from home, from older people who sometimes seem critical and demanding or even escape from oneself, at times when the going's rough and problems seem hard to face." Driving this point home, a study involving 20,000 students in 29 high schools across the United States and Canada commissioned by Allstate Insurance Companies found the following disturbing conclusion about teens and their automobiles in the 1960s: "The first and major point brought out in this study is the detrimental effect of the automobile on teenage grades."[4]

Perhaps the distraction from one's studies had something to do with the new social community the automobile inspired. Cruising and going to drive-ins became popular teenage pastimes. The car was the gravitational pull that coalesced teenagers—whether uniting them at trendy group hangouts or becoming the destination itself for morally reprehensible activities, like sex and underage drinking. The outcries to protect public morality spawned countless anti-cruising laws in communities across America, many of which remain hotly debated to this day. Concerned parental and governmental authorities responded by literally taking back the highways with curfews that could be monitored and enforced. Teenagers across America bemoaned the protest voiced by so many generations before them—*"Parents just don't understand."*

Everything's Different, Nothing's Changed

Does all of this sound strangely familiar? Having the benefit of 20/20 hindsight, we know that the automobile did not create a generation of dropouts. Furthermore, it didn't produce a generation of the morally compromised. Those free-spirited youth of the sixties are now grown-up, contributing members of society. Still, you can't blame concerned parents of the time for worrying about the safety and morality of their children. Although we sit in very different times, the worries of protecting adolescents too young to make mature choices and too old to be coddled persist for today's parents. Only, it's now cruising of a different flavor—adolescents loitering along the seemingly infinite stops of the virtual highway—that captures headlines.

The real/virtual highway analogy has been liberally used in economic conversation, which draws parallels between how the real roadways stimulated growth in metro areas and the virtual highway created similar growth opportunities without geographic discrimination. But consider the equally provocative similarities that compare parental concerns of yesteryear to today using this same analogy. Just as the car created community among teens through cultural pastimes like cruising and going to drive-ins, the virtual world has done the same with social networks that continue to germinate. Just as the automobile enabled a new environment of permissiveness where teens could experiment away from the watchful eye of their parents, the Internet opens virtual doors that expose today's youth to potentially objectionable content. Also, just as parents of the 1960s expressed regrets about losing family time because of the newfound freedom of their children, today's parents long for simpler times when family intimacy remained unchallenged by technology that now competes for the adolescent's attention.

Despite these similarities, the differences are even more profound. Those sixties parents had something quite powerful that would leave today's parents drooling. You see, before the 1960s parents even considered offering a teen the keys to the family car, there was one clear requirement that was non-negotiable: the driver's license. The driver's license reduced ambiguity and familial tensions in several ways. First, there was a minimum age limit, ostensibly created by officials smart enough to know when the mental maturity of the child was sufficient to operate a vehicle. Second, there was a clear test to measure the extent to which the child understood and could effectively execute the rules of the road. Third, there were classes the child could take to acquire the necessary safety prescription for responsible driving and, simply by doing so, could mitigate the risk of accident. That same 1964 article states, "Findings from over 30 studies indicate that trained drivers have only one-third to one-half as many traffic accidents and violations as the untrained during the critical teenage years." [5] Finally, parents had more experience behind the wheel of a car and, as such, had legitimate and persistent expertise that earned them a position of knowledge higher than that of the teen.

For today's parents, the situation could not be more different. There is no virtual driver's license to assess a teen's capabilities. No prescribed safe age when society agrees the youth should be allowed on the virtual highway. No required class to ensure that the child is knowledgeable before entering the virtual world. And, perhaps most importantly, there is no guarantee that the parent is more experienced navigating the virtual highway as a digital immigrant than the child is as a digital native. In fact, the opposite is overwhelmingly more the case, as expressed by Rebecca, a mother of two young children in our study:

> **Rebecca:** *There's no way to stop the technology. I mean, from the time that I was a kid to now, is so vastly different that from the time my kids are now in elementary school to the time when they are in high*

*school will again be so vastly different. Will I be able to keep up with
what kids can do and access?*

Interviewer: *Will you?*

Rebecca: *No.*

Whether considering the parental plight created by the automobile in the 1960s
or the virtual world of today, the same concern prevails: how to balance the inhar-
monious tension created by an adolescent's desire for increasing freedom with the
guardian's primal responsibility of protection. For parents, the role of protection
comes with much higher stakes. Perhaps this dilemma explains why parents in our
study are the most likely to agree that spending a lot of time and money to protect
themselves online means resources well spent.

Social Development: Exposure or Exclusion?

Amanda, a 30-something mother of a preteen boy and one of our study respondents,
reflects on the good ol' days of her youth:

> *I mean, back in the day, what did we do when we were younger? As
> soon as we ate breakfast, we were outside all day long. These kids—
> they seem to want to come in more so they can play the Wii and the
> Xbox, which I don't allow that. Usually, I have to kick them out of
> the house.*

Amanda has responded by limiting her child's access to technological distrac-
tions. He doesn't have a cell phone; no e-mail address; no Facebook account, despite
several of his friends having the same. His time on his gaming devices is limited to
prescribed weekend hours. Also, in an effort to replenish the family's social bank
account, Amanda has recently disconnected service from the one device that, by her
accounts, robbed her family of quality time to the tune of six hours per day—she no
longer subscribes to paid television services.

By the looks of it, Amanda appears to be raising a very well-adjusted, well-man-
nered child. When we ask him what he hopes to see happen with technology in the
future, he responds in a meek voice that carries a powerful message: "Better community." The notion of people helping others using technology as an enabler is a
picture of an altruistic society many of us would endorse. But what if the irony in

this youngster's introspective response rests in his exclusion from the community he so craves?

It's an interesting question and reflective of one of the multiple conflicts parents face in a networked-community age. How permissive should they be with technology in the household? Too much technology, and parents risk raising a disconnected child from the family, or worse yet, according to the worries of at least one of our respondents, an addict. When Susan walked in on her then 10-year-old son a few years ago playing his Nintendo DS in bed way past his bedtime, the result was a young child's cry for help:

> *I caught him playing his Nintendo DS in bed at midnight one time. Right then, he started to cry, "I think I'm addicted to video games." As mad as I was, I didn't get that angry with him because I could tell on his face there was something wrong. I think I've been a little too lenient with the video games and the computer sometimes.*

As Susan shares her story with us, her younger son, Frank (now slightly older than his brother was at the time of the episode), overhears and offers his own unsolicited opinion:

> *I really do think I should stop getting into video games so much. I think I might be getting addicted too. I come home and quickly run to the videogames and then three hours later I'm like, "Oh no, I forgot to do my homework."*

As a response, Susan has limited her sons' access to technology (although not nearly to the same extent as Amanda). They still play videogames and each has a Facebook account. But Susan limits their access to ensure that she doesn't unintentionally raise addicts. The resulting social tension for Frank is evident as we probe his friends' use of Facebook to stay connected:

> *Interviewer: So how do you feel about the fact that you're not on Facebook that often and your friends are?*
>
> *Frank: I don't feel that good. I really should be on there more. Because most of them [my friends] are like, "I told you that we were going to the community center this Friday. Why didn't you go on your Facebook wall?"*
>
> *Interviewer: How does that make you feel when you realize you missed it?*

> *Frank: I feel kind of depressed, angry at myself, frustrated, "Ugh, I just missed a really fun thing."*

Depressed. Angry. Frustrated. Not exactly emotions a parent wants for her child, especially as they pertain to his social development. These types of feelings are now becoming so common among youth like Frank that an April 2011 publication released by the American Academy of Pediatrics dubbed the phenomenon *Facebook depression*. It's a condition that occurs when kids compare such metrics as their number of friends and status updates with those of their peers.[6] Unfortunately for Susan, there is growing evidence to support the idea that technology addiction among youth is also very real, with research finding children more susceptible to an online gaming habit demonstrating higher levels of aggression, desensitization, and anxiety.[7] So, what's a mother to do—raise a socially depressed outcast or a hopeless addict?

To Trust or Protect?

The root of this very complex psychological paradigm for today's parents has not changed much from that of parents in the 1960s. It's an emotional tug-of-war between parents' desire to trust their children and their fundamental requirement to protect them at the same time. On multiple occasions, we heard parents wrestling with this conundrum and wanting to believe the best in their children:

> *Amy (a mother of four young boys): I really struggle with wanting my kid to be honest and not have to rely on the technology to confirm that. And that's one of those lines where I don't know, I don't feel like I need to be Big Brother. I want to raise honest kids. I don't want to have to second-guess what they say to me. Maybe that's idealistic of a mom of an 8 year old and younger kids.*

> *Vickie (a mother of a teenage girl): I don't monitor her texts. I know her. She's really a good kid. She's a good kid. You know your kid.*

> *Bob (a father of three teenage girls): We've raised what for us feels to be very trustworthy children. Of course we have friends who have children who are younger than ours who find out their kids are lying, cheating, stealing, and doing all these crazy things that you're like, "They did what?"*

Rachel (a mother of two adolescents): How much micromanaging should you be doing? I don't know. A lot depends on your kid. If you have a level of trust and that trust hasn't been broken, maybe you don't go that level [of micromanaging].

Susan (our mother of two adolescent boys): I trust them [the kids], which sometimes I question myself if I'm being naive. They're still young and I want to be able to trust them but kids are kids and hide stuff.

The established parent–child trust relationship is multifaceted and challenging. Just as consumers are a bit leery of companies watching their every potential move, we heard the same concern expressed by parents who feared that this perceived intrusion of privacy could lead to long-term damaging consequences to the trust bond with their child, assuming they attempted the same. But, if parents are blinded by an inflated sense of faith that their child is somehow immune to reckless behaviors online given their self-proclaimed "good kid" label, others may step in to fill the guardian role. For example, in a controversial move, the Australian government has proposed a nationwide online "filter" to protect users, particularly children, from inappropriate content. If implemented, it would be the strictest filtering system of any democracy. The move has provoked critics to question how far the proposed filters could go in limiting one's free access to information. Just as U.S. public officials in the 1960s attempted to physically take back the roadways from teens carousing into late hours with their reckless behavior, Australia is proposing to virtually block questionable online destinations that may corrupt youth—and limit today's form of *cruising*.

As one would expect, free-speech critics have vocalized their protests against such proposed legislation. But surely parents would find such controls welcome—the answer to the virtual driver's license dilemma. If the government seeks to protect youth by restricting where they can go online, the difficult parental trust question never enters the conversation. After all, parents would have a clear explanation (and could blame the government) for why the child no longer has access to questionable sites or content. At the same time, they would be reassured that such content would be blocked from curious eyes.

You might think that parents would be relieved by a solution like this. But, as we mentioned in Chapter 5 on learned helplessness, U.S. consumers are doubtful the government can meaningfully control the Internet, and the overwhelming majority place accountability for protecting oneself online on the individual. Parents are not excluded from this belief. Consider Jesse, an ex-military father of two young boys:

> *Interviewer: What about the government—like laws or regulation to police the Internet?*
>
> *Jesse: I think this is where I'm supposed to—because I served in the army for a while—so I think this is where I'm supposed to say "Yes" to the government. But, no, I wouldn't trust the government [with the Internet].*

Analog Parenting in a Digital World

So where does this leave parents raising hyperconnected children? Does one expose or exclude the child from online social activities? Is it more important to trust one's children to make the right choices or protect them from dangerous predators? To address these difficult challenges, parents are resorting to outdated methods that have less relevance in a virtual world. Please don't misunderstand our point. We expect parents to default to wisdom gathered from their own childhood experiences. Unfortunately, these well-intentioned parental techniques, very often the product of recalling how guardians themselves were raised, are ill-equipped and largely irrelevant in a very different digital world. As we mentioned in Chapter 6 on illusion, parents often wrongly correlate truths from the physical world and wrongly assume their veracity in and applicability to a virtual world. These incorrect correlations are expressed in the following three myths that many parents believe.

Myth #1: Boys Are Safer than Girls

The assumption that boys are safer than girls online is just that—an assumption. As we discussed in our Law of Recall chapter (Chapter 7), one of our parents mused that her teenage son, who also happened to be a wrestler, was safer online than her physically weaker teenage daughter by comparison. Although this may be true in a world of sticks and stones, it doesn't apply online. According to a recent McAfee study, "The Secret Online Lives of Teens," girls are more likely to engage in social online behavior, which does place them at higher risk for harassment and bullying. But that isn't to suggest that boys are safer online. Rather than being *safer*, the study found that boys' online behavior and potential risk factors were simply *different*. Boys are more likely to download unauthorized content, particularly unsavory adult material, which places them at different social risks than their female counterparts.[8]

Myth #2: In a Virtual World, Time Matters

Many of us remember growing up in a day when one had to be home before dark. As we grew older, several of us were given curfews. These physical realities still persist for teens in a real world. There's something entirely right about wanting one's child home by a certain hour of the night, when competing alternatives could spell trouble. But there is no protective light of day and no dark shadow of night in the virtual world. Still, parents hold firm to the flawed assumption that somehow children are safer online during bright daytime hours than they are at night:

> *I've caught him [son] with his iTouch at night [on Facebook] so I've taken it away. So now we kind of have a rule that the phone and iTouch need to be upstairs at night and they don't have computers in their room. I just think you're more vulnerable as a young person at night and parents are sleeping or away....*

Myth #3: Home Is a Safe Zone

This is perhaps the most disconcerting myth of all. After all, we're *supposed* to be safe at home. It's our refuge and the place where we are our most real and vulnerable selves. Yet, the proliferation of connected devices literally opens the home environment to external factors—both harmless and downright seedy. Still, this doesn't stop parents from believing that somehow their child is *safe* while in the protected home zone:

> **Interviewer:** *What gives you the reassurance here [home] that even though it could be a weirdo [the children play with online] that nothing could happen?*
>
> **Mom:** *I mean, they're playing a game. I mean it's more removed. It's not like they can give their information in detail.... I mean they're playing their game.*

Really? Tell that to Lisa Grant, mother to 14-year-old son Zach. While chatting on his Xbox, Zach came across a gentleman who had an offer too irresistible to refuse: Microsoft points for Xbox games. All Zach had to offer up in return was his parent's e-mail address and password such that the points could be redeemed. After pressuring a suspicious Zach with a threat, "You have like 20 minutes to get me an e-mail address and password. I'm not a hacker," the youth reluctantly caved. The miscreant wasted no time racking up around $500 in charges to the father's credit card, which was exposed through the exchange.[9] The hacker entered through the virtual door. The home perimeter was violated, and the Grants found themselves the latest victims of identity theft. It all started with an innocent game online.

The Virtual Dashboard

Yesterday's parental techniques are no match for today's parental challenges. Unfortunately for parents, outright restricting a child's access to technology is becoming less feasible, especially as these digital natives explore their own identity and develop social community in a networked-community age. We've talked about trust, protection, exposure, and exclusion. But at the center of it all is the need for control. Parents want to control how and when their children are exposed to content and people that could unduly accelerate or arrest the maturation process. In addition, they want control over how to incorporate such knowledge into a parental style that works in their household (permissive or restrictive) and evolves as the child progresses from adolescence to adulthood.

If there is no such thing as a virtual driver's license for the machine (computer, game console, or mobile device) that the youth knows how to operate better than the parent, then perhaps there is a role for a virtual dashboard. Think of it as a tool that educates and alerts the parent to potentially risky behavior on the part of the child. Many may immediately leap to the conclusion that we already have such tools. After all, parental options for online and television services have existed for some time. But when devices multiply and children mature, maintaining multiple discrete parental controls becomes problematic.

Let's go back to Jesse for an example of how limited these parental controls remain in today's environment. When asked if he would consider putting restrictions on a cell phone he has yet to authorize for his preteen son, he replies:

> I would. That's a tough one because they don't make it where you can
> really lock it down to where you could have say just your "favorite 5"
> [contacts] and your parents. If you give them phone and unlimited
> text, they can go anywhere they want to. You can't lock the phone
> down like you can the Internet. If they could, that would make my

decision [to get my kids a phone] much easier. You hear it on the news all the time. Phones are real big for taking pictures, sending stuff to people that's not supposed to be getting it. You can do a whole lot with the phone.

If Jesse had the means to "lock down" the phone to only authorized contacts, his duties as a responsible parent somehow would become more manageable. Although we encountered multiple parents who already extensively use parental blocks online and on television, most had multiple children in the home. How does one manage multiple blocks that are age-appropriate as children mature? How does this become more complex as each child becomes equipped with multiple devices? Technology has a long way to go to effectively bridge the gap. But, when it does, this version of a dashboard could also go a long way in empowering parents with the appropriate level of control for their household and parenting style. Perhaps this helps explain why this service tested among the most compelling among parents in our study.

Even among those who are not parents but are old enough to remember the dangers they faced online as impressionable children, the virtual dashboard has value. Tara, now a much wiser 18 year old, remembers the unsolicited messages she received as a naive young teen on the rage MySpace. Most of the advances came from much older men. When asked about the value of a control center, or dashboard, that put parents in the driver's seat as it pertains to managing the communications within the household, both she and her 17-year-old boyfriend, Warren, see merit.

> *Interviewer: How would you feel if parents had a control center where they could see what comes in and out of any device in the house, including phones, TVs, computers—that they had the ability to see or receive alerts on that?*
>
> *Warren: Sounds good, because by then, I'll be a parent.*
>
> *Tara: I think it sounds good.... I've heard a lot about phone sex, sexting, where girls take pictures of themselves.*
>
> *Warren: The real problem with that is that it's illegal. You can't send a picture of yourself to someone if you're under 18.*
>
> *Tara: That [virtual control center] would probably have the dad stop that from happening. These girls don't realize these pictures will come back to them down the road.*
>
> *Warren: Not just come back to them, but the fact that it's illegal.*

There's a familiar saying, "The more things change, the more they stay the same." Despite the differences between olden times and today, the delicate balancing act of parental control versus childhood freedom remains a challenge for guardians through the ages. We can look back on the 1960s with reassurance that the automobile did not lead to a degenerate society. Perhaps when we have successfully raised another generation of upstanding citizens, others will look back on this time and reflect on our challenges in parenting the first crops of digital natives.

As we contemplate how technology can serve a higher role in empowering parents and protecting children, consider the aspirations expressed by Julie, our mother of young children, as she blue-skies her ideal future scenario:

> **Interviewer:** *What do you think the future holds for your kids in terms of technology?*
>
> **Julie:** *It's gonna be surrounding them. It already does more than I was growing up. I think it's good for them to be able to learn more and maybe come up with better ideas for the future. But they are gonna have to protect themselves. They're gonna have to have a shield—a web shield. I don't know how it would be done but somebody probably needs to come up with it.*

A "web shield" is a tall order. But practical and transparent tools are within reach and a welcome prescription for today's protective, permissive, and utterly puzzled parents.

SHIFT SHORT: HELICOPTER PARENTS

There is no disputing the fact that parenting may be one of the most difficult jobs in the world. In addition to ensuring the basic survival and protection of a child, an effective parent also takes on the responsibility of ensuring the development of a healthy, well-adjusted person who can successfully navigate an increasingly complicated and interconnected world. Over the course of the past few years, the term *helicopter parent* has firmly established itself as a description of today's over-involved parent. Johnny didn't make the basketball team at school? The helicopter parent demands an explanation from the administration. Susie had an argument with one of her friends? The helicopter parent will jump in to resolve the issue themselves. Even as these children go off to college, programs are being put in place to ground the hovering helicopter parents. The University of Vermont has gone as far as appointing "parent bouncers" to manage these parents, their expectations, and presence.[10]

As technology continues to become an indispensable part of a child's everyday life, many of today's parents find themselves struggling with striking the appropriate balance for their kids. It seems perfectly reasonable to set limits for children when it comes to their technology use—but how far is too far? The input of the ethnographic subjects highlighted throughout this chapter perfectly illustrates this struggle. The pervasiveness of e-mail, texting, gaming, and social networking in the lives of today's kids almost makes one wistful for a simpler time when, moral and/or ethical issues aside, the possibility of sneaking a peek at a child's diary was all a parent needed to do to understand what was really going on in their child's head. It doesn't matter if a parent is considered under-involved, over-involved, or even if they are a helicopter parent. One truth emerges above all others: These parents love their kids, and want to protect them and ensure that they get the most out of life that they can. Learning how to help a child effectively manage his or her desire to participate and fit-in in a networked-community age is just another bullet point on the job description of one of the toughest jobs in the world.

The Midlife Rebirth

Age is an issue of mind over matter. If you don't mind, it doesn't matter.

—Mark Twain, author

He was just shy of his 56th birthday when he first took political office as Governor of California. He was less than a month away from turning 70 when he was inaugurated as the 40th President of the United States, the only one in history to have been divorced and remarried. During his Presidential reelection bid, the old-timer faced a contender 17 years his junior who was determined to make the incumbent's age an issue in the campaign. In the now-famous 1984 debate between then-President Ronald Reagan and opponent Walter Mondale, the "Gipper" (Reagan's nickname based on a role he played during his earlier acting career) quipped, "I will not make age an issue in this campaign. I am not going to exploit for political purposes my opponent's youth and inexperience."[1] Reagan was reelected to four more years in office and remains the oldest person to occupy the highest position in the United States, retiring at the age of 77.

She was 49 years old when her first cookbook, *Mastering the Art of French Cooking*, was published. Her popular television show, *The French Chef*, debuted when she was 50. Eighteen years later, Julia Child founded The American Institute of Wine & Food to "advance the understanding, appreciation and quality of wine and food," fulfilling her lifelong passion.[2]

Grandma Moses began painting at 75. Laura Ingalls Wilder was 65 when she started writing *The Little House on the Prairie* series. Tim Zagat was 44 when he launched the now famous *Zagat Restaurant Guide*. At 70, Golda Meier became the fourth prime minister of Israel. Nelson Mandela became the oldest elected president of South Africa at the age of 74, after surviving a life of imprisonment and apartheid.[3]

These are not simply the extraordinary stories of the chosen few who stumbled upon success later in life, but the reflection of hope that exists as one continues to mature in the later years. You may believe that late bloomers are more the exception than the rule, with all the pop culture references to the so-called midlife crisis. Western cultures, in particular, are taught that midlife is a period to be dreaded. You're "over the hill," devoid of prospects, menopausal if you're a woman, andropausal if you're a man, and generally thought to be slowly deteriorating as you mark time toward your conclusive, inevitable death.

Much as this makes for the fascinating fodder of prime-time sitcoms, big-screen dramas, and stereotypical advertisements, there is evidence to suggest that the midlife crisis is hardly the rule. In fact, as opposed to the gross generalizations that characterize the midlife period of our lives to be fraught with uncertainty and challenge, for the vast majority—in at least one comprehensive research endeavor—it is actually a stabilizing time of harmony and confidence.

The MacArthur project was a series of 11 studies involving approximately 8,000 men and women in the United States ranging in age from 25 to 74. The researchers defined *midlife* as the time stretching from 30 to 70 years of age, with ages 40 to 60 as the core. In one of the studies, nearly all respondents recognized the term *midlife crisis*, yet only 23 percent reported to having experienced one. When researchers dug further, they discovered that only eight percent tied the emotional struggle to the realization that they were aging. The remaining 15 percent reported experiencing a stressful period during their middle-age years but that the crisis was a result of a transition, not aging. "When you look more closely, they are saying this is my crisis that occurred when I was 40 years old rather than what caused it was the fact that I was 40," reports Elaine Wethington, a research team member. Those stressful transitions leading to crisis include divorce, loss of a job, death of a child, serious illness of a close friend or relative, and severe financial problems.[4]

Yes, I Can

Beyond the obvious personal and professional accomplishments of those luminaries referenced at the beginning of this chapter, what is amazing is that these individuals overwhelmingly reached their pinnacle of success long before the seeds of a networked-community age were planted. There was no Internet to further Reagan's campaign. No online bookstores where Julia Child could self-publish and distribute her masterpieces (particularly interesting given that her first cookbook, now a landmark in culinary history, was rejected by its initial publisher). No social media comingled with mobile location–based applications to give Zagat's review guide more wind in its sails. These legends attained success despite the lack of technology, not because it existed. Yet, as we have seen in the other life stages, technology is augmenting the landscape with new possibilities to propel midlifers forward. Also, as respondents in our study reflect, those possibilities are not reserved for the young, but for the young-at-heart.

Although not natives of the networked-community age that pervasively surrounds them, midlifers in our study demonstrate an appetite that makes them increasingly part of this world nonetheless. Their behaviors run the gamut of presentation, protection, and preference categories. More than half spend time updating their social networking page to project the right image of themselves. Nearly 90 percent visit the websites of their favorite brands to find out about the latest coupons and offers. More than half are very or somewhat comfortable sharing information online if it helps them find people or items of interest.

Respondents in our ethnography study paint a vibrant picture of today's midlifer to support the statistical findings from our quantitative phase. Charles, in the midst of midlife as a 50-something, reflects the forever-young attitude we found to be far more pervasive than a woe-is-me mind-set. The online world affords new opportunities for learning, and yesterday's misconceptions as to who is engaging—even hacking— among us are as dated and useful as your grandmother's rotary telephone.

> *I'm very interested in the Android phones and I do a lot of research on that and do a lot of hacking and customizing of it. I just go online and do a lot of research reading different things to try to learn as much as I can about it. [...] I'm like a sponge. Twitter I like because I follow a lot of different types of things and I soak in the information.*

For others like Melinda, our retired empty nester, who may be a bit more cautious of technology, there is still a healthy willingness to learn, if for no other reason than to pass the time productively and generate a newfound sense of accomplishment.

> *I'll take the CDs and discs—I can't be calling them [her sons] to reinstall or redo things if the computer freezes or whatnot so I'll pull different programs that I have to see what I can do on my own. And I feel pretty good. I'll even call the cable company and I'll have people walk me through things. I feel like I'm old enough and I should know*

> *more so I go from that standpoint. And I learn even more now how to walk through and take care of any techno problem I have. Or, I'll go into Fry's or Best Buy and I'll ask questions or stand there by the service desk. I've got a lot of time to kill.*

Melinda's reference to time is an interesting one. For those in midlife, particularly in later midlife as in Melinda's case, fixed incomes are the norm. It would appear obvious, as a result, that Melinda's valuation of her own time is less than that of her finite bank account. At the same time, Melinda is a retiree, therefore the surplus of time by her own measure further exacerbates this point. However, the time-versus-money dilemma is one attribute shared by older and younger generations.

For example, in our own study, we heard from several younger respondents willing to forego traditional services, like paid television services, in favor of online alternatives. Some would argue that this is a case of need. There is no perceived need for paid television services among some when online content is available at a discount; therefore, younger consumers opt to pull the plug on traditional paid television services. There is certainly some truth to this argument. However, along with older respondents, younger cohorts are among the least likely to pay for personalized content available anytime, anywhere. With more time than money on their hands, there is less of an opportunity cost incurred when meticulously searching for these programs on their own.

Indeed, scientific evidence among undergraduate students supports a greater valuation for money over time, given the ambiguous nature of time and its intrinsic flexibility (for example, weekend time is valued differently than workday time).[5] Although significant online behavioral differences between young and old in our study prevail, the commonality of valuing money over time exists, leading to at least one similarity in an aversion to a personalized content service shared by both ends of the age spectrum.

For older respondents in our study, time is not to be wasted. We heard from others like Melinda with an appetite for self-education of the pitfalls and potentials in an online world. One of our more colorful ethnography respondents is Denise, a 50-something remarried widow with an interest in vampires (yes, the bloodsucking variety) and death metal music. Despite her eccentric tastes, Denise comes from a fairly conservative family. When challenged by her sister, who became concerned with the questionable content Denise was posting on her Facebook page, Denise was quick to educate her ignorant sibling as to how the game of social networking is actually played—a topic she had thoroughly researched herself before attempting to navigate uncharted virtual waters.

> *I love vampires—anything vampires I love. Not just because of that show but because I like vampires. My sister's very, very religious and she calls me up and ripped me a new a**hole and said, "Why are you doing this [posting this content on your Facebook page]?" and I said, "Why do you care?" [Sister said] "Well all my friends can read it," and I said, "No, because I did this [established blocks]". Well she didn't believe me. So,* Facebook for Dummies, *I was flying those pages out and highlighting them. Guess who's got the book?*

Denise is a particularly savvy user of Facebook, so much so, in fact, that she has rigged her profile to detect when she and someone else not in her network have at least 10 "friends" in common. Her computer then sends an automated Friend Request to the unknown person on Denise's behalf with an invitation to join her network, given the mutual friends the two strangers have in common. You would expect this to be more typical behavior of a 20-something digital native, not a 50-something digital immigrant. Although Denise is an outlier in her demographic with respect to this carefree approach to social networking, what she does share in common with her cohort is a zeal for equipping herself with technology knowledge. Whereas Denise chooses to use this knowledge to reveal herself to others who share her peculiar tastes in death metal music and vampires, other midlifers self-educate to protect themselves from those with questionable intentions. But don't picture this as digital cocooning. Although it is true that midlifers don't enthusiastically practice as many online behaviors as frequently as their younger counterparts, they won't be left behind entirely. They are simply more likely to be armored or calculated when they do engage online, to mitigate the invisible risks that may be lying in wait.

No, You Can't

As one ages, there is more time to acquire wealth and establish a reputation. As such, there is also more to lose as one matures in life. To win the elusive trust of a midlifer, companies must first break through the walls of skepticism that have had some time to harden over the years, established and reinforced through personal experiences and those of others. Emma, our unemployed former health worker, opines about the price of information in a networked-community age:

> To me, I don't trust any of those companies that say, "Well, we promise we won't sell your information" or "We'll keep it private." I don't trust any company like that. I'm sure there's some price that somebody's willing to pay that they would accept it. It's about money. That's just my opinion. It's about money.

There are many ugly stereotypes propagated by Western cultures about aging. One stereotype shattered by our study is the notion that older individuals are more susceptible to being too trusting—and are easy prey for the duping. Emma is representative of her demographic. She is far more likely to exercise caution precisely to avoid the consequences of more reckless (some may say trusting) behaviors. Older respondents are far less likely to shop online using a public Wi-Fi hotspot, ignore a browser warning of a security threat, or use recommendation engines to discover goods and services in alignment with their unique preferences. To this latter point, one could question if the use of these tools is resisted precisely because of Emma's concern above (everyone's information is available at a price, thereby increasing the risk factor of exposing one's preferences to potentially unscrupulous companies) or if today's engines simply misfire on the preference filter. Consider her observation about Amazon [Emma takes us to her Amazon.com personal page]:

> **Researcher:** If you go back to the main page of Amazon, do you ever scroll down below that [to the Recommendations area] or do you always just go right to what you're looking for?
>
> **Emma:** I usually just go right to what I'm looking for.
>
> **Researcher:** So what happens when you scroll down there [to the Recommendations section]? What do you find?
>
> **Emma:** Just things that I'm actually not looking for. [Laughs]

Although some may ridicule older respondents for what may be considered overly cautious behavior, the social dividends appear to be paying off. These respondents also admit to being far less likely to post an update about themselves or their families that they later regret sharing, correct offensive posts about themselves online, or ignore a Friend Request because they didn't want the person to see their posts.

At the same time, contrary to the gross generalization that mischaracterizes older individuals as being naive and easy targets for criminals, these respondents are no more likely to have been victimized by online fraudsters than younger consumers. Perhaps this goes to a key difference in how these older respondents psychologically identify themselves vis-à-vis those younger whippersnappers. Older respondents are more likely to self-identify as being private and careful—closely managing how and where they are and what they are doing online with others. Consider the sage advice offered by Bob, a midlife father of three teenage girls, as he counsels them on the potential perils awaiting the naive online:

> Well, there was a story within the last few weeks or so, of a girl who wrote on her Facebook and she wrote something like, "John and I are going to the concert to see such-and-such play," or whatever. So another person looked up where that concert was, called the bar and said, "What time is the concert?" and so now knew the house would be empty between these hours of the concert, went to the house and robbed the house while they were at the concert.

As a result, Bob exercises caution with what he and his family reveal about their household online. He carefully controls what is posted and, more importantly, what is not (such as sensitive address information that could potentially endanger his family or belongings). This need for control is a commonality shared by respondents across our study and corroborated by the above-referenced MacArthur project. Although researchers involved in this series of studies dispelled many myths about midlife, most notably that most of us are destined to face a crisis simply through the realization of our own mortality, one finding was universal. As Americans, we strive to be in control of our lives. Although many would assume that, as we get older, we feel more distressed because of a lack of control (ostensibly resulting in or arising from the popularized midlife crisis), the MacArthur researchers discovered quite the opposite to be true. Among the respondents tested, the sense of control over work, finances, and marriage increased in the late forties and early fifties and continued rising into old age.[6] Control is valued in a networked-community age. More than 80 percent of midlifers in our study say they are very or somewhat comfortable sharing information about themselves if they have control over who sees it.

Technology has a role to play in offering respondents more control in a virtual world, especially as one has more to protect in his later years. Perhaps this helps explain why services that most move the needle among this cohort are those that allow the respondent to "trust but verify" (popular advice espoused by none other than Ronald Reagan) that those lurking online are who they say they are. Rather than seeking a new cop on the beat to protect them, these older respondents are wary. Only three percent believe that the government can be effective in policing the Internet; more than 75 percent believe that security online is a matter of personal responsibility.

We started the chapter with some well-known folks who left their indelible mark in history as they peaked in midlife. Consider the lives of the ordinary who attained their own extraordinary feats during a dreaded life stage assumed to derail the masses. Verta Tucker, a former bus driver driven by a passion to inspire youth, enrolled in college after 40 years of being out of school. She ultimately graduated with a teaching degree and renewed aspirations to pursue a Master's degree in her chosen field.[7]

There's also Frank Chandler, former investment manager who suddenly found himself unemployed in his forties. But, rather than retreat, Chandler chose rebirth. An event that would send many into a tailspin allowed him to pursue one of his life-long passions in forming and organizing a music festival. His inspirational story was fodder for local press, who asked him his age at the time of executing his dream. He coyly replied, "Forty-eight, a perfect age for a middle-age crisis."[8] Some crisis.

Evidence suggests that midlife is more often a time of rebirth, not crisis. It's more often accompanied by confidence, not insecurity. It's more often associated with deeper relationships, not loneliness. And it is marked by an assurance of finally knowing who one is and not apologizing for it (perhaps explaining one of the largest differences between what older and younger respondents value in a service, with the latter paying a premium for those designed to protect image and the former gravitating toward services designed to protect self). Although the virtual world is new to all of us, it is embraced by older individuals through a different lens of identity—one characterized by a true sense of who one is. Consider the exchange between Denise and our researcher:

> **Researcher:** *Do you feel you have a pretty consistent personality across all relationships and aspects of life?*
>
> **Denise:** *Now I am. I don't feel like I was like that when I was younger because who had time? I don't want to say you were phony but you were just like, "Hi, Bye, Nice to see you," get the kids and go. You didn't have that time to have a deeper relationship or that deeper feeling about each other.… Those types of [shallow] relationships are not in my life anymore. I want more value.*

More value is possible in a world without boundaries. We don't yet know who the next Julia Child, Nelson Mandela, or Grandma Moses will be in their respective fields. But, for those in the precious midlife years, there is hope in knowing that one doesn't simply retreat because of a chronological number. That's not to suggest that one does not meet different crises, such as career or personal transitions, that must be overcome. As Erikson discovered, there are multiple life stages at which unique trials must be addressed, and midlife is no different. But, despite its standing as one of the most popular life-stage crises, the midlife period represents so much more than the one-dimensional view of failure and strife that remains the tasty ingredient for pop culture fodder. Indeed, this period of life also presents the opportunity to fully transform into the self that has been in the making since birth.

SHIFT SHORT: THE NEW POPULATION MIGRATION

Americans reaching midlife are on the move. In a reversal of trends with younger age cohorts and the generations that came before them, more and more midlifers are heading into rural America for retirement. According to projections from the U.S. Department of Agriculture, the number of 55–75 year olds in rural and small towns will increase 65 percent—from 8.6 million to 14.2 million—between 2000 and 2020.[9]

Why?

Rich Karlgaard, publisher of *Forbes* magazine, outlines this trend toward "living larger lives in smaller places" in his book, *Life 2.0: How People Across America Are Transforming Their Lives by Finding the Where of Their Happiness*.[10] The #1 factor in Karlgaard's book is technology, which has "made it possible to perform sophisticated white collar work in small towns." Workers can stay connected to urban-based companies and customers. Technology has also made the culture gap between city and country much smaller but with cheaper home prices and fewer "status competitions" that are an income drain.

In the past, the classic response to a midlife crisis was new toys—new cars, new boats—but harsh economic realities are changing how people view their lifestyles. Now, midlifers are looking for smaller, more manageable homes and for careers that may not make them the same amount of money, but that offer more fulfillment and the ability to sustain work past traditional retirement age.

SHIFT SHORT: THE NEW POPULATION MIGRATION (continued)

As they move to the countryside, midlifers are expected to have a positive impact on the local economies, raising income and employment rates, even as the areas may need to make additional investments in infrastructure. Where that meant schools in the past to attract younger couples and families, that now means healthcare to attract this new, older set. The rural migration is highest in the early retirement years, before health issues result in limited mobility and physical activity that may require being closer to larger cities with more resources.

Not all rural areas are expected to attract this new population. Financial planning publications and websites like *Forbes*, *U.S. News and World Report*, and *Money* magazine often list smaller cities as the top places to retire if they offer stable employment and housing markets, top-notch healthcare facilities, proximity to colleges and universities for lifelong learning and recreation opportunities, and attractive taxation policies that allow people to draw more favorably on retirement income.

Who Are We Becoming?

And remember, no matter where you go, there you are.

—CONFUCIUS

As a senior in college, Andrew had a problem. He found himself growing apart from his friends. There was a new game on the street, *World of Warcraft*, that had captured the imagination (and time) of his comrades. He recalls his first reaction to a pal who encouraged him to get with the new program:

> I remember when my friend and I walked to Target. He said, "We got this great new game called World of Warcraft that we're all playing. You should buy it." And I looked at it and it was like $40 for the game and then he told me there was a monthly subscription and I was like, "I don't think there's any way I'm going to get my money out of this."

But, putting money into the game was exactly what Andrew had to do—if he wanted to continue to hang out with his friends, that is. According to Andrew, they had "disappeared" into a world that he was not part of. He had to rectify the situation. He purchased the game he was confident would not yield a return on investment. But he found that it actually delivered more than he bargained for.

> Pretty soon, I was putting in more time in the game than I was in school. But, it was a lot of fun. It's a very social game, so it just kind of became a new way to hang out with my friends. And, make new friends, too.

World of Warcraft opened new doors for Andrew's relationships. It also introduced a new problem. Andrew's passion for the game left little time for school, or much else.

He repeated his senior year of college, wiser for the experience and with reinforced and emerging friendships to boot.

We've discussed several psychological theories in the pages of this book and related them to how technology can play a part in helping or hindering how we see ourselves and the world around us. But, as in Andrew's case, the virtual world brings with it opportunities to try on new identities, if not explore aspects of our own self that are more difficult to express in a physical realm. Gamers like Andrew know the fulfillment of a world unbound by physics, time, or space; a world that allows us to pursue certain dreams and possibilities more readily and easily; and one with an influence in shaping who we are ultimately becoming.

We Want to Get Away

The online world offers a means of escapism. For some, this translates to having fingertip access to news, entertainment, or relationships—in essence, being free from the limitations of the physical space surrounding us. For others, escapism goes much further. Virtuality, adorned with its whimsy and possibility, can offer a distorted lens through which to view the world—one that is oddly more attractive than reality itself. As Colleen, another gamer, reflects upon exploring a virtual wasteland within a first-person shooter game:

> *While you're playing this game, you're looking for stuff that's going to kill you. So, you don't typically look up. But then, recently I accidentally hit the thing [remote controller] and it went up during nighttime [in the game environment]. I was like, "Oh my gosh, the constellations are up there." It looked exactly like when you look out the window. They [the game developer] didn't change it. So, they put in a lot of details on the sky. It was like, "Hmmm, I never noticed that before." It's quite eerie—like you see that everything is quite fine in the sky, but when you look down, it's all this horribleness. I love this game.*

Although the game is clearly fantasy, it offers those who explore it a megadose of reality, even in the minutest details of a sky that many will likely never discover. In fact, for another subject, Tara, the virtual world can be so real that she fears for society's ability to distinguish between reality and fantasy. She should know. As a digital native and the girlfriend of a gamer who, by his own admission, was recently spending as much as nine hours per day in *World of Warcraft*, she can attest firsthand to the seduction of a fantasy land:

> *I think what to be most scared about are people not being able to dif-*
> *ferentiate reality and the virtual world and just creating a sense of*
> *difference on that space.*

In fact, the blurring of fantasy and reality is a natural effect in a networked-community age. Our lives are no longer exclusively played out in the real or virtual worlds. Increasingly, the identity we construct across both planes is an integrated composite of who we are or want to be. Escapism allows us to retreat to a virtual world without physics. But, given how intertwined this world is in our daily lives, some express a desire, if not impossibility, to escape its grasp:

> ***James** [a 20-something recent college graduate]: I don't really wish*
> *that I could disconnect but when I do disconnect, I definitely like it.... I*
> *don't disconnect when I'm home but when I go somewhere that doesn't*
> *have access to the Internet or other electronics, I like it a lot.*
> ***Beth** [a 30-something wife]: We [husband] went to a resort with no*
> *cell phones, no TV, no Internet, no nothing. It was detox. Seriously.*
> *Like I'd have a thought and I'd be like, "Let me check Google. Oh my*
> *gosh, there's no Google here." Being disconnected like that just totally*
> *changed our lives.... Having it [technology] taken away was stressful*
> *at first, but then it was just delightful.*
> ***Zack** [a 30-something professional]: Technology is fun and good but*
> *it's nice to get away from it too though, to just be quiet. People that are*
> *on like every day, all day long. It's funny, you're reading Facebook and*
> *they're posting all day long. People that Twitter all day long. That's*
> *not a necessity of mine.*

There are polar extremes to any debate, and the intersection of self with technology is no different. Whereas some struggle to escape the virtual world that frees them, others find it equally difficult to return to the simplicity of an unplugged life, even if only for a few moments. Perhaps Tara is right to be concerned on this point. After all, for most of us, there really is no separation between real and virtual worlds. Each is an extension of the other. As real and online planes increasingly collide, the role of technology in helping us better manage our lives, if not fulfill an idealized sense of ourselves, becomes more essential.

We Want More

As we've discussed, the virtual world unlocks billions of possibilities, available at the click of a mouse or stroke of a key. A world that knows no time of day will not be constrained by the same. We are becoming more productive, able to squeeze more hours into an otherwise finite day. We do this by hypertasking or hyperconnecting. In the case of the former, most of us have learned to divide our attention across multiple incoming stimuli, such as when watching television while also surfing online, thereby allowing us to squeeze more entertainment or productivity into an interval of time. In the case of the latter, the technology that increasingly connects us also allows us to fundamentally change the way in which we communicate.

Before the days of technology, remote communication was asynchronous. If you wanted to communicate with someone outside of physical practicalities, you could do so by good old-fashioned snail mail. Send a letter and wait for a response. When the telephone reached ubiquity, remote communication became synchronous, mirroring that of face-to-face communication. Individuals were no longer relegated to the write-me-back approach. Simply by pressing a few buttons or turning a dial on a rotary phone, we could speak real-time with friends or loved ones in remote locations. Communication became a real-time, two-way street, thanks to the technology that bound us.

But times have changed once again, and the technology that affords us real-time access to distant friends, family, and coworkers now increasingly offers us even more possibilities through asynchronous communications. Unlike the discrete snail mail approach of years gone by, this new breed of hyperconnected communications allows for multiple conversations simultaneously—in essence, giving us more time back in our otherwise limited day. Consider Andrew, our gamer:

> *I have rolling conversations with about six people every day and sometimes that will have about a total of six lines of chat. At 4:20 on Monday was the last time he [my friend] talked to me and he talked to me again at 11:04 this morning. And then I responded. And it's now 1:00 and he hasn't responded.... We realized that conversations don't need to be continuous. You don't need to let someone know if "I'm going away from my computer. I'll be back in 5 minutes." So, eventually, we started having these rolling conversations.*

Particularly among digital natives, this relatively new way of texting is definitely preferred over the seemingly passé alternative of phoning someone real-time. Take Chelsea and Joel, both 20-something and recently married:

> **Joel:** *It's easy to text versus calling. I've never liked talking on the phone. Texting allows you to say whatever you need to say in a single block message and they don't have to respond.*
> **Chelsea:** *And he can text all six of his siblings at the same time. He can do a mass text and they'll all get it.*
> **Joel:** *It's more convenient. You can do it in school. They frown upon you talking in school. But, it's a lot easier to hide a text.*

In a world dominated by Facebook and Twitter, where one's musings leave a lasting impression in cyberspace, the need to distribute a message quickly, yet also effectively, becomes more obvious. Talking requires one to immediately react. Texting and social-networking updates do not. As Lisa, another digital native and current college student, puts it:

> *I like texting, then Internet, then talking on the phone. I don't like talking on the phone because you don't know their facial reactions and you don't know how they really feel about things but you still have to respond right away. When you're texting, you can think about what you want to say.*

Some are critical of this new world of status updates that seem to supplant the need for meaningful relationships. As Jack, another of our digital natives in the study, one who has admitted to having weaned himself from the two to three hours per day he used to spend on social-networking sites, reflects:

> *[Social networking] is kind of making socialization cheaper. It becomes a commodity to have friends. It makes it cheaper to have friends.... I read this one book that said that social networking is to friends as reality TV is to reality itself. It cheapens life.*

This was stated another way by Juan, a 20-something Brazilian amused by the rabid appetite Americans have for technology:

> *I think technology increases the amount of relationships but decreases the depth.*

Despite this craving for asynchronous communication on one's own timetable, technology may prove to shift the way we communicate yet again in the very near future. Avatars, which are digital representations of ourselves in the virtual world, are not relegated to a niche market. Half a billion of us worldwide wear an avatar at least 20 hours per week to represent ourselves.[1] Controlling those avatars no longer requires extensive time investment in complex gaming controllers, with image recognition devices now proliferating in households. The *Guinness Book of World Records* recently awarded the fastest-selling consumer device of all time—Microsoft's Kinect, which uses image recognition to allow a person to virtually control an avatar in a game without the use of a controller.[2] Microsoft recently unlocked this image recognition code for millions of developers worldwide, providing the opportunity to create a new category of consumer applications that use sensor recognition technology.[3]

Researchers at Stanford University are already imagining a world where avatars are so much more than the commonly associated image of gaming characters. In fact, avatars could fundamentally transform the way we communicate with others and the companies that serve us. Among other things, one item notably absent from today's text-based, asynchronous communication modes is the ability to respond to the wealth of nonverbal cues inherent in face-to-face communication. Even something as basic as mirroring the body language of the person opposite us—a concept known as *mimicry* in psychology—can have a profound influence in changing attitudes and perceptions. Research conducted at Stanford University paints a picture of how far a new virtual world, comprised of avatars with contextual emotions, can take us. Students in a control group were shown a 3-D (three-dimensional) avatar with a message requiring them to wear student identification at all times while on campus. Students in the experimental group were shown the exact same avatar with the same message, with just one notable difference. The avatar was programmed to detect the slight head movements of the respondent (each respondent was wearing headgear that projected the 3-D avatar) and repeat those movements four seconds later. Those in the experimental group rated the avatar more credible, intelligent, and trustworthy than those whose avatar did not mimic their body language.[4]

Although we may not envision a world where we walk around with 3-D headsets in the near future, we are already living in one with gesture recognition technology entering the households of everyday consumers, through devices like Microsoft's

Kinect and Nintendo's Wii. Consider the implications of a virtual world where full sensory context can be experienced, where companies can program customer-service agent "bots" to mimic the nonverbal cues of their consumers, and where all of this technology happens simplistically and intuitively. Given the multiple challenges discussed in this book of subjects craving more precision in reading and authenticating the faceless person at the end of the connection, this new wave of immersive communications may usher in the next Facebook juggernaut. Also, if trust is the currency in a networked-community age, this new era may also prove fruitful to companies seeking a more meaningful relationship with their consumers.

Until that day comes, we can already revel in an age when technology affords the best of both worlds—the ability to contemplate how one presents oneself through asynchronous communication with the efficiency of distributing said message to multiple parties simultaneously. In essence, today's networked-community age breaks down the barriers of both space and time. It allows us to get more of both. As such, it is fundamentally changing the way we engage with one another. What some are quick to label superficial communications relegated to a block of text limited by so many characters, others paint as the most efficient means to engage with more people than ever before.

We Want to Be ...

Technology will never define us, but it certainly allows us to express who we are. For some, the physical world may not always accommodate the "trying on" of different personas, if not the exploration of deeper aspects of one's personality. A virtual world without time or space also comes without gravity—that which may otherwise hold us back from being more than we are. It allows so many to follow professional interests, less available in a physical world, as we personally encountered:

- An IT professional by day who spends his evenings selling doodles on greeting cards by night. The online business allows him to pursue his creative passions, something not afforded in his daily 9-to-5 grind.
- A single mother who runs an online business as a personal shopper with a talent for scavenging the latest deals at thrift stores and compiling them into one-of-a-kind ensembles.

- A consultant to the military who found a side career of culinary pursuit, thanks to the tasty dishes she would prepare for her live-in boyfriend to take to work. His friends were so impressed by the treats that they offered to pay her for the same. A few months later, an online business was in the making.
- A retiree who avidly watches cooking shows and then adapts the recipe to her liking. She is looking to publish said recipes online in her own cookbook creation.

If trying on a new professional hat isn't the goal, the virtual world also allows us to explore what we wish we could be in the physical sense. As Warren, a 17 year old, tells our research team of a fellow gamer online:

> He has a very deep voice. He's 24 years old and he looks younger than me. He looks like he's 13 or 14 years old. He's been kicked out of his school for anger management. All these things he told me made me think he's so big and scary. And, he talks with this very deep voice online, but I know it's not his real voice. I can tell just by looking at him.

Perhaps the individual in question is wrestling with an identity crisis. Perhaps he enjoys being something he can't be in the physical world. Or, perhaps he is content just *being*. Whatever the case, he is certainly not alone. The virtual masks we wear online can be far apart from who we really are, an extension of ourselves or an aspiration of who we want to be. Although technology does not influence which of these realities may actually be the case, it enables us to explore our options in the first place.

Technology is neither good nor evil. It does not have an identity. It cannot substitute for sound judgment. Only humans are capable of all of the above. But technology has helped create a world foreign to our natural senses. This book does not provide prescriptions for the cure of identity crises yet to emerge as a result of worlds colliding. Unfortunately (or fortunately), we as human beings are a bit too complex to be relieved by a one-size-fits-all technology panacea. That said, technology providers attempting to win the consumer's heart, mind, or wallet must first put the user in control of presenting how she wants to be seen, being protected from unintended blind spots, and navigating countless choices targeted to her preferences. All the while, consumers must recognize that technology and those who provide it will never be a match for one's own capacity to become deceived, helpless, or susceptible to hype. Regulators must understand that a world without boundaries is also too overwhelming to attempt to control, as the vast majority in our study believe.

As society continues to evolve, and technology along with it, this will be a topic debated in the halls of research and court of public opinion for some time. While experts search for new theories to describe what is happening as our identities form in a networked-community age, consumers will continue to wrestle with the challenge of finding and representing who they are as real and virtual worlds intersect. As Andrew poignantly reflects:

> I've been kind of making a conscious effort—because it is just so easy to slide in and out of these personas online—to be a lot more honest and open with people and consolidate the way that I behave around everybody, so that I don't feel like I have these split personalities.

There are millions like Andrew struggling with the same issue. A company that empowers, without exploiting, netizens may potentially discover or reinforce its own identity along the way—one that truly "gets" the complexity of the consumers it serves. Providers that answer the call stand to inherit the most valuable currency consumers have to offer—their trust.

Many spend a lifetime in search of the self. Challenges present opportunities to persevere or moments to fail. That's just par for the course in an analog world, let alone one mired with new trials brought forth in a networked-community age. Despite the complexities, one thing remains clear. Although technology alone does not define us, it frees us to explore ambitions, relationships, and passions as we simultaneously discover who we are. For that reason, it also plays a part in helping us fulfill whom we ultimately become.

SHIFT SHORT: JAPANESE IDOL

Aimi Eguchi is the ideal pop star. Young, fresh-faced, beautiful, and talented, Aimi seemed the perfect fit for the immensely popular Japanese girl group AKB48. Shortly after she joined the group as a trainee, the talented 16-year-old quickly amassed her own fan base that was eager to learn more about this up-and-coming talent. Her profile page on the AKB48 website said that she was athletic and loved to compete in track and field in her home prefecture of Saitama on the island of Honshu. As a testament to her popularity, Aimi was even selected to appear along with some of AKB48's more veteran members in a candy commercial— an unheard of honor for a trainee. This is where the story of Aimi Eguchi

SHIFT SHORT: JAPANESE IDOL *(continued)*

starts to unravel. Some of Aimi's most devoted fans began to notice several uncanny coincidences. Not unlike the clever viral marketing campaigns that accompany some of Hollywood's biggest movies and television shows, there seemed to be some strange connections between Aimi and Ezaki Gilco, the candy company she was now representing. Aimi's online profile stated that her birthday was February 11 and that her favorite track and field event was the 300 meters. Ezaki Gilco was founded on February 11 and their company slogan is "Hitotsubu 300 meter." Fans began to demand answers to the point that AKB48 producers felt the need to reassure fans that Aimi was real. Only with the release of a "making of" video was the truth finally revealed. Aimi was actually a computer-generated composite of features of six other members of the group. Her voice? It was the product of auto-tuned recordings of a seventh group member. What's astounding here is not that the technology exists to create an artificial image and companion voice, but rather that the image and voice are so realistic that Aimi only raised suspicion through the linkages in her online profile to the candy company. If consumers are already confounded by the collision of physical and virtual worlds, just imagine the potential pitfalls, opportunities, and complexities that can arise when "Aimi Eguchi" and the technology behind her become more than just a clever way to sell music and candy.

Through the Lens of Research

Research is to see what everybody else has seen, and to think what nobody else has thought.

—ALBERT SZENT-GYÖRGYI, SCIENTIST

Identity is a topic rich with nuance. A research approach attempting to study it requires the same nuance. Our journey began with in-depth interviews among experts in the fields of security, privacy, and image as viewed from a technology or behavioral vantage point. After probing the professionals, we studied the average consumer—more than 60 of them across 30 households, to be exact. We cohabitated for hours with these subjects, watching them live their lives and asking questions to ground the enormity of the topic at hand. We wanted to know how these individuals see themselves in a networked-community age and the role of technology in influencing the same. Our subjects freely exposed their concerns, aspirations, and questions during this process, providing rich fodder for the quantitative phase that followed. This latter phase explored the attitudes and behaviors among more than 5,000 connected consumers in the United States. Because identity is hardly a topic that is black or white, we forced these respondents to make tough choices about the types of services and policy decisions that could potentially ameliorate the ambiguity so common in today's networked-community age, while mitigating the downsides inherent in any given approach.

The evidence acquired through this year-long process provided the framework for this manuscript. In particular, those who so openly shared their lives with us equipped the research and book that were to follow with the nuance this complex topic deserves. Their verbatim responses have littered the pages of this book, giving context and emotion to the thorny issues at hand. Because these individuals are as rich with substance as the responses they provided, following are their unique stories. Of course, all names have been changed to protect their true identities in the process.

Amanda is a 30-something military wife and mother of a preteen boy. The family is accustomed to the military lifestyle and is often forced to relocate every four years or so. Amanda restricts her son's access to technology. He has no cell phone, Facebook account, or e-mail address. She disconnected paid television services in an attempt to gain back more family time. She also restricts his usage of gaming devices, confining his play time to weekend hours. She is conscious of the effect that technology has had in stealing precious moments away from the family, indicating that it is common for her to spend as much as 90 minutes per day on Facebook, sometimes even during sacred family meals. As such, although she recognizes the benefits of Facebook in enriching long-distance relationships (an occupational hazard due to her husband's job), she limits the number of friends she maintains to about 50 because, "When you accept tons of people, you have to see their mumbo jumbo." She is particularly concerned about identity theft but finds herself overwhelmed by the complexity of technology, often relying on her husband as the tech-savvy head of household. In the future, she aspires for technology to be simpler, especially on the device front. Hardly a technophile at heart, she believes that every new device is more difficult to figure out, causing some to reject gadgets because of intimidation. In leaning on her husband as a technology crutch, she acknowledges it may prove more difficult for her to jump in with new technology in the future, essentially as her technology muscle begins to atrophy.

Amy is a 30-something wife and mother of four sons under the age of 10. She and her husband are both professionals concerned with maintaining the appropriate image as work and personal lives collide. She admits irritation when others post unauthorized pictures of her or her children. Her husband indicates feeling the same when a colleague used him as a reference without his consent (he only found out about the occurrence when Googling himself and promptly asked the person to remove the post). Amy struggles with how to effectively empower her children while protecting them from the dangers of technology. She limits their gaming usage, has defined kid-friendly bookmarks online, and has instituted parental blocks on unsavory television programming. Still, she can't help but wonder when being able to trust her kids will be a given, without having to rely on technology as a snooping mechanism. As such, she resonates with services that alert her to potentially harmful content without requiring her to consistently spy for the same. She relies extensively on technology for her work life, enjoying the freedom it provides her to telecommute up to a day a week without anyone realizing she is not in the office. She manages a team, some of whom she has never met in person. At the same time, she remains uninterested in enhanced video chatting capabilities, preferring instead to maintain the visual anonymity she currently enjoys with today's phone, text, and e-mail options. She is not as concerned with identity theft, storing her passwords in a simple memo application on her phone, unable to imagine how such passwords in the wrong hands could be harmful because she doesn't believe the culprit would "have enough info to know what to do with them."

Andrew is a 20-something college student and self-described "nerd." An avid gamer, Andrew maintains accounts in *World of Warcraft* and *League of Legends*. After being convinced by friends to join the former, he soon found himself dedicating more time to the game than to his studies, forcing him to give school a rest. In hindsight, he suggests that his lack of interest in his studies was to blame, leading him to pursue gaming as an escape. Since then, he has changed course at school and now finds his new curriculum path engaging. As such, he has lessened his dependence on games and balanced his time. He wrestles with having multiple personas online and off. The son of missionary parents, he is reserved and quiet among close family. Among friends, he is more boisterous and outgoing. Even in the gaming world, he straddles the line between outright aggressive in *League of Legends* to a more "Care Bear" cooperative profile in *World of Warcraft*. He yearns for the day when his multiple personas can be blended and more reflective of the complex person living within. When asked to blue-sky his future, this technophile imagines a world when mental thoughts control the machines around him—a type of human/machine connection that has historically been the product of sci-fi imagination.

Beth and **John** are an affluent married couple in their thirties with no children. Both are avid users of Facebook. For Beth, social networking has allowed her to maintain relationships with her 100+ first cousins. For John, Facebook has replaced Google as the one-stop-shop for recruitment efforts, as John calls the former the "de facto identity place on the Internet." They take caution when shopping online, frequenting only "big name" stores, where security issues presumably have been addressed. Still, they resist using debit cards online, opting instead for credit cards such that they "aren't on the hook" for potentially fraudulent charges. Long-time users of feature phones, they have only recently upgraded to smartphones because not having the latter was "totally screwing up their social life." They ascribe trust to companies who reciprocate, noting that Netflix, in particular, regularly extends the benefit of the doubt to customers (such as by exchanging damaged discs with no questions asked).

Bill is 16-year-old son to 33-year-old single mother **Caroline**. Television is at the center of this working-class household. As Caroline admits, the television is on all the time, even as a babysitter for the dogs while mom and son are away. When first moving to their current home, the family went without television service for a few days. That didn't stop them from turning on their TVs and longing for programming to replace the blue screens staring back at them. Caroline is an aspiring entrepreneur in the clothing business. She finds herself at an interesting crossroads with technology. On one hand, she requires the latest technology to support her business endeavors. On the other, she actively looks for alternatives to prune her expenses, and communications is no exception. Bill's mobile phone is compliments of a friend's mother, who bought the youth the device so that Bill can keep in contact with her son. Caroline's laptop is broken, thus she is currently borrowing one to avoid an upfront purchase. She prides herself on establishing her own website, though simple in its representation. At the same time, she struggles with projecting the right business image of herself as a budding entrepreneur on the site when relatives are inclined to post pictures that are in conflict with that image ("I may not want my clients to see me with alcohol"). She readily admits she will only buy from established brick-and-mortar locations online, leading her to question her own credibility in attracting clients as a fledgling business. Mom and son have a very close relationship and seem to be the center of their respective social networks. Still, as his mother, Caroline is not allowed to be friends with Bill on Facebook. As he protests, "None of my friends do!"

Bob is a 40-something husband and father to three teenage daughters. He is a small-business entrepreneur managing the performance aspirations of his daughters. To this latter point, he actively works to promote his daughters' talents while seeking to protect their safety. He uses caution to ensure that no physical address is associated with their website. The three girls are forced to share one Facebook account with strict rules, including the requirement that posts pertain only to past activities, not future alerts of where the girls will be. He sagely advises his girls that "anything" they do can be videotaped and posted online, so the pressure to watch what they say and do is constant. He values face-to-face communication and worries that teens' use of texting can be problematic and antisocial. As such, he refuses to pay for texting plans for his daughters, leading two of the three to save enough money to purchase iPod Touch devices, where free texting is possible. Although he also maintains a site for his construction business, much of Bob's energy is directed at his daughters. He is accustomed to not being the center of attention in his household and is forlorn, yet matter-of-fact, when he claims that a Google search on his daughters renders all sorts of news clips, photos, and the like, whereas he comes across as a "nobody."

Brenda is a 40-something wife, kindergarten teacher, and mother to two teenage sons, including 16-year-old **Joshua**. Brenda offers a tour of her well-manicured home, including the "man cave" dwelling of her husband, a tech-savvy white-collar professional pursuing a side business online. At the same time, other areas of the home are dedicated to shared spaces for technology, such as the family computer, where Mom feels more comfortable that she can watch her teenage sons online (despite both having access to smartphone devices 24/7). She is friends with her children on Facebook and even has their passwords to check their accounts for suspicious or salacious activity. She laments that the family has lost quality face-to-face time with the advent of technology and nostalgically reminisces of a time when a snowstorm blacked out all communications, forcing the family to reconnect with "old-school" favorites like board games.

Brian is a 20-something recent college graduate living with four roommates. Each roommate contributes to the needs of the household, including technology, as they regularly troll craigslist for good deals. The living room is a sort of *feng shui* homage to technology, as the television is in perfect view from the kitchen while cooking, dining room while eating, or couches while lounging. In contrast, the adjacent room is a technology-free zone, serving as a throwback to popular board games to be played while one admires the scenic panoramic view. Brian is also an avid user of LivingSocial and, when describing the service, uses an interesting choice of words to acknowledge his affiliation ("I am part of LivingSocial.") Each roommate uses Facebook regularly to check social updates. Before Facebook, there was MySpace. Before that, there was Instant Messenger. In fact, these college graduates cannot recall a time when information about their friends was not available at their fingertips. As such, if they had to "unplug" for any length of time, they fear it would result in their "missing something."

Bruce is a 20-something college student and bartender. His late hours at the bar translate to late hours of slumber in the morning—often until noon on some days.

Bruce's room is painted black to shut out the morning light. Despite this, his cell phone sits beside his bed (and not in silent mode) so that he can receive calls and texts in the morning while drifting in and out of sleep. He uses Facebook to keep in touch with others but admits he isn't very active. He claims to know "girls who are always looking at people's profiles and stuff," but he doesn't do so. Instead, he uses Facebook Places to check into work each day because he finds it funny that he is seen to frequent the same bar consistently. Furthermore, he remarks that technology loses some of the tone that is rich in face-to-face interactions. Even with an emoticon or "LOL" at the end of a text, he thinks that sometimes meaning can be lost or confusing. For this reason, he finds it funny to watch "older" people on Facebook, who don't seem to "get the concept" as far as he can tell. For example, when a friend of his joked that Bruce was "married" to his girlfriend, his friends easily caught the sarcasm, whereas his relatives were upset about not having been invited to the wedding. He is not selective about categorizing friends in Facebook, with the exception of his *Mafia Wars* buddy list, a group of people who share his passion for the game but are restricted from seeing anything else on his profile as they are "foreign" to him.

Chelsea and **Joel** are a newly married couple in their twenties. Both are at an "in-between" stage of their lives, holding down jobs while preparing for their careers (she in nursing, he in music). Neither shares much through online accounts, nor has either ever made changes to the default privacy settings in Facebook. According to Joel's view, the Internet and Facebook are intended to be "open." As such, he links his multiple social networking profiles—MySpace, Facebook, and Twitter—for easy access by others. In a family with seven siblings spanning in age from 14 to 31, Joel acknowledges the digital divide between the oldest and youngest. The youngest has grown up with technology, so "it is easier for her." In contrast, the oldest is the most "out of the loop." They have noticed the youngest sibling's tendency to emulate one of her older sisters in her style online but don't worry about her exposing anything inappropriate or potentially dangerous about herself. Self-described "Mac people," Chelsea and Joel easily paint popular brands with particular personalities. Google is "smart," Yahoo! is "Google's little brother," and Netflix "follows through on their promises." Joel is a PlayStation gamer, choosing to play live with others online, although not belonging to a particular guild or set "team" of other players. He regularly chats with friends while playing, not about game strategy but, rather, as a way of "connecting" about other mutual interests.

Christine and **James** are a middle-income couple in their thirties. Christine is a teacher, James a bartender. Rabid television watchers and self-professed "HD snobs" (that is, they actively choose what content to watch based on availability in HD), Christine indicates that she alone watches four hours of television a day and prefers not to multitask during that time. James takes the lead when it comes to technology purchases for the household, recently buying an iPhone for Christine, much to her protest. It didn't take long for her to fall in love with the device because James now jokingly refers to it as her "mistress." An Apple enthusiast, James aspires to an iPhone someday but would prefer to wait until he can afford the entire Apple setup (including laptop). He asks for Apple gift cards on every special occasion to get him closer to his dream configuration. A cost-conscious couple, Christine and James watch finances closely. He proudly admits that he bought his first car with cash. Christine is careful when online shopping to use only one credit card designated for such. Although they are both on Facebook, they admit to watching more than posting. For Christine, in particular, the fuzzy relationship between teacher and student is blurring and difficult to manage. As such, she will not befriend students on Facebook and is careful about maintaining the appropriate online image.

Colleen is an active 19-year-old gamer living in a household of the same (her mother and her mother's live-in boyfriend **Zack**). Colleen's social network is not dictated by Facebook but, rather, Second Life. Much of her time on Second Life is spent building things—a creative outlet and interesting parallel for this aspiring welder and mechanical engineer. She met her current boyfriend through Second Life and had just returned from a trip to visit him out of the country. She admitted to loaning him $100 to purchase a new motherboard so that he could stay active in the game. In a house full of gamers, technology reigns supreme. The family has just about every gaming system ever made (including an Atari on the plasma television) and a universal remote controller that seamlessly shifts from one console system to another and rotates the television for easy viewing from any vantage point in the living room. As the family admits, "It's lazy, but awesome!"

Craig and **Jodi** are recent college graduates in their twenties, employed although still searching for their ideal careers. Craig makes the technology decisions for the household and takes pride in having connected the multiple devices (TVs, DVRs, computers) to interoperate seamlessly himself. They are avid entertainment watchers, wishing their DVR could record more multiple shows simultaneously to reduce conflict in the household. Any show not watched live or via DVR is viewed online via Hulu or other sites. They view online and offline personas as synonymous, although they acknowledge that they manage different online profiles for different purposes (LinkedIn for professional pursuits, Facebook for personal relationships). Keenly aware of the potential hazards of having inappropriate content about their image online, each admits to Googling themselves, particularly when job-seeking. Craig admits he can't live without his computer; for Jodi, the essential item is her cell phone. They rely heavily on e-mail and texting to remain in contact during the day. For Jodi, in particular, texting is indispensable. She recalls an auto accident that left her on an ambulance gurney texting her family and Craig to alert them of the situation, and the response from the paramedic on duty, who could only muster a sigh at the habits of "youth" these days.

Denise is a remarried widow and retired chef in her fifties. For her, technology is about releasing her creativity. She is in the process of compiling an original cookbook based on her unique twist to recipes found online. She and her husband have relied on computer-aided design to redecorate their home, despite not having the financial means of higher-income households. Denise credits Facebook with changing her life and views it as her preferred mode of communication ("E-mail is where I get my bad news" and "Phone calls are too time-consuming"). She uses it to connect with others who share her unique pursuits, including vampires and death metal music. She has never met many of her 1,000+ friends in person, although she feels close to them nonetheless. She yearns for a capability to more readily search for others who share her interests, such that she can possibly find women in her age range with her unique interests. Until then, she happily settles for the mixed bag of friends of all ages she has found through Facebook. Denise expresses a need for technology to revolutionize other industries, particularly healthcare, because her husband struggles with Lupus. She vents, "I wish I could staple his health records to the doctor's forehead," as she criticizes those in the healthcare field for not reviewing his full medical history to accelerate treatment. She is particularly interested in the "chip" that will carry one's entire healthcare record, although she can't help but wonder if this will truly improve the level of care her husband is accustomed to receiving.

Emma is an unemployed healthcare worker in her fifties and a self-described introvert. She has only recently discovered her penchant for art in the past few years and proudly displays her creations throughout her home. She has been forced to cut back on expenses because of her situation. She no longer subscribes to cable but has a robust library of DVD movies to supplement her online watching through YouTube and other sites. As a former healthcare worker who has seen the impact of chronic disease on her family (her immediate relatives suffered from breast cancer, whereas Emma struggles with diabetes), she is most interested in technology solutions that accelerate healthcare improvements. Facebook is her social outlet, particularly as a transplanted woman away from her hometown friends. AOL is her "home base," and she relies on the service to keep her PC clean of viruses. She readily dismisses Norton anti-virus pop-ups while we observe her, indicating that she doesn't need another virus program. Although she acknowledges the scan from AOL in qualifying her computer as clean, she could do without this extra layer of notification, because the alerts are "annoying."

Jack is a college student in his mid-twenties living with a family friend. In exchange for low rent, Jack offers babysitting services for the friend's children. He currently holds down two jobs and therefore appreciates the ability to take all of his classes online. He admits to using the Internet to cheat on exams, although he acknowledges being caught and receiving a failing grade recently. Given the household's budget cutbacks on cable television, Jack streams most of his entertainment from sites like Hulu and LimeWire. He is also a self-described gamer who lights up when our interviewers watch him play a game on the Adult Swim website. He has an interesting love/hate relationship with Facebook. Early in the interview, he criticizes Facebook for "cheapening relationships by making them too easy." However, he later acknowledges his struggle from being "sucked into" the site, admitting that he was regularly spending several hours per day on the site at the expense of school, work, and other activities. He measures popularity by his number of friends, using one friend in particular as his social barometer. As long as he has more friends than she does, he is content. Otherwise, the race for more friends is on, despite his admission that his "opponent" hardly knows that such a competition is even in play. He is extremely concerned about image, not wanting to come across as "boring," "narcissistic," or "crazy." He is careful about what images appear about him online, not wanting to be seen with unattractive people who could put him in an unfavorable light.

Jesse is a 40-something husband and father to two tween sons. The kids are active gamers, and Mom imposes rules about how much gaming is allowed in the household, setting thresholds on grades as one allowance. Jesse's 10-year-old son reflected on how games can sometimes be a distraction that leads to lower grades. At the same time, he recalled at least one time when games actually served him in attaining higher grades in school, in this case when his class studied medieval warfare, something he had personally experienced through a video game. Like other parents in our study, Jesse struggles with protecting his children without becoming overbearing. He warns of the dangers in relying too much on technology to monitor one's children, as a friend recently "lost" his child when the latter's cell phone battery drained, leaving him inaccessible. He and his wife have contemplated "chipping" their children to monitor their whereabouts in the physical world—a thought that is bittersweet to his 10-year-old son, who can see the safety advantages but worries that his parents may use it to micromanage him. When Jesse offers that such tracking capabilities would be best served by the local police department (thereby eliminating the potential trust breach perceived by his son), both father and son agree such an advancement would be worthwhile. Jesse is particularly fascinated by how much children know about technology, recalling a recent experience whereby he learned how to replace a defective Blackberry screen via a video of a child doing the same on YouTube. He saved $50 in the process and is now fixing the screens of two other friends, "all because of a 7-year-old kid on YouTube."

Juan is a 20-something Brazilian holding down three jobs and living with his mother. Juan pays the rent for the household. He enthusiastically seeks new ways to expand his knowledge, subscribing to Audible.com, which he uses to listen to audio books while tending to his jobs. He has a passion for music but avoids iTunes because of its restrictive format. Instead, he uses the peer-to-peer site Soulseek for most of his selection. He listens to Pandora but pans its recent addition of advertisements that "totally wreck the mood." He is quite inhibited by his slow computer and hopes to buy a laptop. Until then, he is very aware of finding software that is "light" versus "bulky." He deeply values face-to-face relationships and admits to losing several friends because of their addiction to online gaming. He possess an Xbox but rarely uses it for gaming; instead, it is his entertainment hub to stream online video (Netflix) and music. He is less worried about privacy online, attributing the concern to an American culture, less pronounced among Brazilians. Regarding the future of the Internet, he is concerned about governments or entities that might attempt to control it, because he feels that this would be a major breach of "freedom of information." At the same time, he thinks that things that are illegal offline (stealing) should be illegal online—interesting, perhaps, as some may classify his music-sharing habits as just that.

Julie is a 30-something self-described "soccer mom" to an 11-year-old son and seven-year-old daughter. She chose the apartment the family lives in based on the reputation of the school system, citing high-tech updates as one of the key benefits. She is reluctant to interconnect too much of her technology (such as connecting the PlayStation, computer, and television in a streamlined fashion) because she doesn't want to feel too "settled" in the apartment and potentially procrastinate in achieving her ultimate desire to own a home. Although she admits to wanting to monitor her children's activities online, she worries that she may come across as "controlling." She offers a specific guideline that the Internet is a tool for researching information but has a difficult time sticking to this principle herself, because she admits to being consumed by social networking. Her biggest worries for her children revolve around her preteen son being exposed to objectionable content. She indicates that children his age are already sexually active and blames the occurrence on "naive" or "absent" parenting. Over the weekend, her son had landed his first girlfriend via text messaging, leading her to exclaim, "Now, everything happens so fast!"

Lisa and **Lorraine** are college roommates in their twenties sharing a coed dorm with eight other students. The men live downstairs; the women are upstairs. There is no cable or satellite subscription service in the dorm. Instead, the young adults stream all content from sites like Hulu and Megavideo. Lisa points out that she is unafraid of what others may find out about her online because she has "nothing to hide." At the same time, she becomes uneasy when contemplating the safety of an electronic health record, indicating that "some things should just stay on paper." All of the roommates are active on Facebook, but Lisa indicates that she is careful about what she posts so as not to be the subject of ridicule on sites like Lamebook. Both Lisa and Lorraine prefer texting over face-to-face or phone conversation because the mode gives them time to think of an acceptable response. The young adults pass the time playing games on a vintage Nintendo game system because they say it reminds them of their youth. Although hyperconnected, the two acknowledge that they have interests outside the online world and worry that today's younger generation may be too digitally connected and may lose interest in other pursuits like reading. As the two contemplate what the future of technology may hold, neither is keen to make a bold prediction, although they are certain of one thing, "It will continue to evolve faster than we can even imagine."

Melinda is a 53-year-old empty nester with a chronically ill husband. She attempts to keep in touch with her three adult sons but repeatedly points out, "They are always so busy, you know." The primary form of communication between them is e-mail and cell phone, the latter of which is paid for by her sons for both Melinda and her husband (a gift she greatly appreciates). In an attempt to save money, Melinda recently downgraded to dial-up, thinking "things must have improved since the old dial-up." Her experiment was short-lived (less than a week), reflecting how indispensable broadband is in her household. She is extremely resourceful in determining how to navigate or troubleshoot technology, often relying on customer service agents at her service provider or local big-box retailer to fill the knowledge void created when her sons left the household. She appreciates ads on Facebook because they are a welcome distraction when contemplating what to post. As a retired teacher, she is particularly aware of the potential damage done by one's social-networking page and exercises extreme caution as a result.

Rachel is a 40-something wife and mother to two sons (16 and nine years old) and a 13-year-old daughter. She points out two artifacts that are less relevant to today's generation—cursive writing and clocks—lamenting that she must often read birthday cards sent by older relatives to her daughter, who has a difficult time comprehending cursive, and that some of her daughters' friends cannot read the analog clock found in most classrooms. Each of the children has their own computer, with one rule: The door must never be shut when the child is on the computer because, "Why should they close the door?" The daughter has her own mobile phone with limited voice minutes and unlimited text. If the children want data on their cell phones, they must pay for it themselves, something unnecessary for the daughter, who currently spends most of her time texting. The landline phone system in the household is used as a retrofitted intercom system so that family members do not have to yell for each other between rooms. When Rachel contemplates eliminating the landline and/or cutting back on cable service, to her daughter's protest, she simply responds, "These are the choices you have to make!" Rachel's daughter spends about an hour a day on Facebook, but she is not allowed to post any pictures of herself, leading to ridicule by others who speculate that she must be "really ugly." Although seemingly unbothered by such hateful comments, Rachel acknowledges that there will come a time when her daughter can post pictures, just not yet. Rachel's older son is an avid gamer, with restrictions on his Xbox that he may only play on the weekend to avoid the risk of addiction. He often comes home from school on Friday afternoon and plays straight through Sunday evening to get his fix before the system is off-limits throughout the week. He is jealous of friends who have more permissive gaming privileges, even admiring those who are able to skip school the day following a major game release to play it.

Rebecca is a 40-something wife, fitness instructor, and mother to two young children. A clear *road warrior*, she relies extensively on her iPhone to keep her engaged with friends and colleagues while shuttling her children between activities and herself between the multiple gyms she frequents. Her preferred mode of communication is Facebook. She is not as concerned about online security as she claims her husband is. For her children, her concerns do not surround physical security but in their potentially careless clicks that could lead to viruses. She admits to using her iPhone "all the time" while driving and craves a larger-screen iPad that offers a better image while on-the-go. She consults YouTube for workout inspiration and uses Shazam regularly to identify music suitable for the same.

Samantha is a tech-savvy 27 year old living in an urban market. An aspiring entrepreneur with a food service business, she is also an event planner at a consultant for the military. A self-professed Mac person, she admits to using it three to four hours per night as a "resource for everything." She has an Android device but longs for the application storefront of the iPhone. Her boyfriend has an outdated Nintendo system, which is a frustration because Samantha would prefer an upgraded model that would allow her to stream Netflix (she currently uses the mail-in option of the service). She admits to not worrying about identity theft. However, she is a bit more careful about shopping online after having been duped by a company that pulled a bait-and-switch on her. After asking for her money back and getting no response, she relied on her bank to settle the dispute.

Susan is a 40-something wife, homemaker, and mother to 13-year-old **Robert**, 12-year old **Frank**, and a four-year-old daughter. She and her family have lived in the same house in rural America for 15 years, and she admits to rarely, if ever, locking her doors. Susan struggles with the balance between careful parenting and overactive monitoring of her children. Both Robert and Frank are active Xbox gamers. Robert has saved sufficient money to purchase an account to play *Call of Duty* with others online. Frank has not been able to do likewise and therefore shares his brother's online account or plays offline. Frank recently invested his money to purchase the latest *Halo* game, which he appreciates for the building, not fighting, aspects of the game. Robert can immediately check the status of his friends online and will often text to see who is interested in playing. Susan fears that this type of engagement is a poor substitute for "real" social interaction. She is keenly interested in a technology "control center" for the household and can imagine paying $10 to $15 per month for such a service. As she laments about budget, she indicates that technology purchases are now a significant line-item category in her household's purchases.

Tara is an 18-year-old college freshman living with 17-year-old high-school sweetheart **Warren**. Tara comes from a divorced household on a meager income and has been self-sufficient in paying for her technology needs (laptop, cell phone) for some time. Warren's parents are still married and live in an affluent home, where Tara spends most of her time sharing a room with Warren. Both are Netflix enthusiasts, streaming as much as eight to nine hours per day over a two-week period to quickly catch up on an entire season of a television program. They claim to never use the mail-in feature of Netflix and wish for a larger library of on-demand streaming videos to satiate their viewing appetite. Warren is a hard-core gamer, and both he and Tara agree that most gamers are "nerds," with Warren believing he is likely the coolest gamer out there. Tara does not understand how individuals, particularly gamers, can completely lose themselves in a virtual world and lack a "real" life as a consequence. Warren admits that his previous eight to nine hours per day gaming habit was unhealthy before he met Tara. He still admits to gaming, although not as significantly and during hours (for example, late night) that do not impose on his social time with Tara. Warren's desire for a completely virtualized, avatar experience stands in stark contrast to Tara's concern of people losing touch through a fantasy world. Tara claims to have at least 15 Gmail addresses, simply disposing of existing addresses when spam becomes overwhelming and opening a new account. Warren acknowledges using e-mail for one-way communication only, such as to receive information on subscriptions or orders from companies.

Todd is an unemployed 25 year old living with his brother, sister, mother, and 50-something father, **Charles**. A landscaper by trade and volunteer worker in his spare time, Todd views his identity as consistent across online and offline worlds. The family's home is superwired for entertainment—there are no less than four DVRs, three computers, and two gaming systems. Todd primarily uses a laptop but has a desktop in his room (a refurbished basement) "just in case." Charles's office computer serves as the family's primary outlet for streaming music, an activity witnessed by researchers while in the home. For a relatively younger subject in our study, Todd is less concerned about image and more wary about identity theft. Having been a victim of an e-mail account breach, he expresses concern over the security of his correspondence and wishes for a comparable security indicator, such as the popular security lock common on many e-commerce sites, to indicate that his e-mail is safe from potential snoopers or advertisers. Although interested in technology, Todd is not as knowledgeable about how things work and speculates that his family's avid use of technology, particularly smartphones, may be exposing them to miscreants sniffing the "airwaves" in an attempt to do harm. Although not believing he would be a direct target of such an attack, the mere possibility gives him pause. Despite this concern, texting is his preferred mode of communication, as he estimates he receives 100 to 200 texts per day from his girlfriend alone. In contrast, Charles is a self-proclaimed "gadget geek" of his Android phone, hacking it to provide new capabilities, such as providing wireless for his laptop and streaming media from his desktop. An avid follower of technology topics himself, Charles is aware of the ongoing *net neutrality* debate and believes that service providers should be allowed to charge more for higher data usage, just as he would expect to pay higher car insurance for a Ferrari.

Vickie is a 40-something wife and mother to three tween girls living in a low-income household in rural America. Her extended, large family is remote, and she relies heavily on technology to stay in contact. Her oldest daughter (age 12) regularly texts with friends and cousins, and her amount of texting has become a point of dissension in the household. Vickie has taken measures to attempt to restrict her daughter's texting behavior. After removing the unlimited texting option from her account, Vickie faced $200 in texting charges for one month, despite her daughter's claim to curtail her usage. Vickie has also established "girls' out days" in which technology is forbidden, yet still finds that she and her daughters are seduced by mobile technology on those outings. Vickie and her husband have established security controls on the devices in the household, including limiting Internet usage from the PC and mobile phones. Vickie's primary concern is keeping her daughters safe. She is less worried about the perceived intrusion on privacy that may result. She reminds her children that she is their parent, not their friend because, "There is plenty of time to be friends once they are over 18."

Prologue: Who Are You?

[1]"Jim Henson," Muppet Wiki. http://muppet.wikia.com/wiki/Jim_Henson.

[2] "(It's Not That Easy) Bein' Green" (from 'Sesame Street'), NIEHS Kids' Pages. http://kids.niehs.nih.gov/games/songs/movies/greenmid.htm.

[3]Ibid.

Chapter 1: Presentation: The Mirror Image

[1]Sean Homer, *Jacques Lacan* (London: Routledge, 2005), 24–25. Questia, Web, 4 February 2011.

[2]Ibid.

[3]Bernadette Casey, Neil Casey, Ben Calvert, Liam French, and Justin Lewis, *Television Studies: The Key Concepts* (London: Routledge, 2002), 183. Questia, Web, 4 February 2011.

[4]Philippe Rochat, "Five Levels of Self-Awareness as They Unfold Early in Life," *Consciousness and Cognition: An International Journal* 12 (2003): 717–731. www.psychology.emory.edu/cognition/rochat/lab/PDF/Fivelevelsofselfawarenessastheyunfoldearlyinlife.pdf.

[5]M.R. Montgomery, *Saying Goodbye: A Memoir for Two Fathers* (New York: Knopf, 1989), quoted in Note 4, page 718.

[6]Frank Reed, "42% of Americans Have Googled Themselves; None Have Gone Blind." (29 January 2010). www.marketingpilgrim.com/?s=Americans+Have+Googled+Themselves.

[7]Ibid.

[8]Scott Barry Kaufmann, "How to Spot a Narcissist," *Psychology Today*, (5 July 2011). www.psychologytoday.com/articles/201106/how-spot-narcissist.

[9]"Heather Is a Total Babe" (30 June 2011). http://thedirty.com/2011/06/heather-is-a-total-babe/.

[10]"Dirt, Lies and The Internet," *The Dr. Phil Show*. (Original air date 11 November 2010).

Chapter 2: Protection: Exposing the Blind Spots

[1]Emily Sohn, "The No-Fear Woman (And What Her Brain Reveals)," *Discovery News* (16 December 2010). http://news.discovery.com/human/fear-fearless-brain-emotion.html.

[2]Ibid.

[3]Larry K. Brendtro and James E. Longhurst, "The Resilient Brain," *Reclaiming Children and Youth* 14, Issue 1 (2005).

[4]Ibid.

[5]Lucian Constantin, "Half of Phishing Victims Expose Their Credentials Within the First Hour" (3 December 2010). http://news.softpedia.com/news/Half-of-Phishing-Victims-Expose-Their-Credentials-Within-the-First-Hour-170526.shtml.

[6]Matt Richtel and Verne G. Kopytoff, "E-Mail Fraud Hides Behind Friendly Face," *The New York Times* (2 June 2011).

Chapter 3: Preference: The (Un)Conscious Filter of (In)Finite Choice

[1]Antonio Damasio, *Descartes' Error: Emotion, Reason, and the Human Brain* (New York: Penguin Books, 2005), p. 50.

[2]Ibid., p. 51.

[3]Tilmann Betsch, "Preference Theory: An Affect-Based Approach to Recurrent Decision Making," *The Routines of Decision Making*, ed. Tilmann Betsch and Susan Haberstroh (Hillsdale, NJ: Lawrence Erlbaum Associates, 2005).

[4]Paul Slovic, Melissa L. Finucane, Ellen Peters, and Donald G. MacGregor, "Risk as Analysis and Risk as Feelings: Some Thoughts about Affect, Reason, Risk, and Rationality," *Risk Analysis* 24, no. 2 (2004): 311–322).

[5]Rik Pieters, Luk Warlop, and Michel Wedel, "Breaking through the Clutter: Benefits of Advertisement Originality and Familiarity for Brand Attention and Memory," *Management Science* 48, No. 6 (June 2002): 765–781).

[6]http://staff.washington.edu/gray/misc/which-half.html.

[7] "Television: Sex and Suffering in the Afternoon," *TIME* (12 January 1976). www.time.com/time/magazine/article/0,9171,913850,00.html#ixzz1QriVUkUX.

[8]Sam Schechner, "Soap Opera Fans Rally to Save Their Shows," *The Wall Street Journal* (18 June 2011).

[9]See Note 7.

[10]Sam Ford, "In the Wake of ABC Soap Opera Cancellation, Is the Death of Soap Opera an Inevitability?" *Fast Company* (15 April 2011). www.fastcompany .com/1747516/in-the-wake-of-abc-soap-opera-cancellation-is-the-death-of-soap-opera-an-inevitability.

[11]See Note 8.

[12]See Note 8.

Chapter 4: Trust: Meeting at the Crossroads of Identity

[1]David Gelles and Gillian Tett, "From behind Bars, Madoff Spins His Story," *Financial Times* (8 April 2011).

[2]H. Rudolph Schaeffer, Anna Greenwood, and Meyer H. Parry, "The Onset of Wariness," *Child Development* 43, No. 1 (March 1972): 165–175.

[3]Ibid.

[4]Robert C. Solomon and Fernando Flores, *Building Trust: In Business, Politics, Relationships, and Life* (New York: Oxford University Press, 2001).

[5]Ian Sherr and Nick Wingfield, "Play by Play: Sony's Struggles on Breach," *Wall Street Journal* (7 May 2011).

[6]Juro Osawa, "As Sony Counts Hacking Costs, Analysts See Billion-Dollar Repair Bill," *Wall Street Journal* (6 May 2011).

[7]Jeffrey V. Butler, Paola Guiliano, and Luigi Guiso, "To Trust or Not to Trust: The Answer Lies Somewhere in the Middle," *Vox* (8 October 2009). www.voxeu.org/ index.php?q=node/4067.

[8]David Hancock, "Sony PS3 Data Breach Highlights What a Loser I Am," *CBSNEWS TechTalk* (27 April 2011). www.cbsnews.com/8301-501465_162-20057996-501465.html.

[9]Jon Stewart, "Anthony and Cleopenis," *The Daily Show* (1 June 2011). www.the-dailyshow.com/watch/wed-june-1-2011/anthony-and-cleopenis.

[10]Jami Floyd, "Where Weiner Went Wrong," *It's a Free Blog* (17 June 2011). www.wnyc.org/blogs/its-free-blog/2011/jun/17/where-weiner-went-wrong/.

Chapter 5: The Law of Learned Helplessness: Failure Is the Only Option

[1] "Jaycee Dugard: Her First Interview," *ABC News Special* (10 July 2011). http://abc.go.com/watch/abc-news-specials/SH559036/VD55134353/jaycee-dugard-her-first-interview.

[2] Wikipedia.org, "Learned Helplessness." http://en.wikipedia.org/wiki/learned_helplessness.

[3] John S. Watson and Craig T. Ramey, "Reactions to Response-Contingent Stimulation in Early Infancy," revision of paper presented at the biennial meeting of the Society for Research in Child Development, Santa Monica, California (March 1969).

[4] D.S. Hiroto and M.E.P. Seligman, "Generality of Learned Helplessness in Man," *Journal of Personality and Social Psychology* 31 (1975): 311–327.

[5] Michael McDonald, "Voter Turnout," *United States Election Project*. http://elections.gmu.edu/voter_turnout.htm.

[6] Guy Winch, "Will American Voters Succumb to 'Complaining Learned Helplessness' in 2010?" The Squeaky Wheel, *Psychology Today* (26 October 2010). psychologytoday.com.

[7] Stefanie Hoffman, "Norton Study: 65 Percent of Internet Users Are Cybercrime Victims," *CRN* (8 September 2010). www.crn.com/news/security/227300377/norton-study-65-percent-of-internet-users-are-cybercrime-victims.htm.

[8] Wikipedia.org, "Learned Helplessness." http://en.wikipedia.org/wiki/learned_helplessness.

[9] Christopher Peterson, Steven F. Maier, and Martin E.P. Seligman, *Learned Helplessness: A Theory for the Age of Personal Control* (New York: Oxford University Press, 1995).

Chapter 6: The Law of Illusion: Lie to Me

[1] Alan Schwarz, "Suicide Reveals Signs of Disease Seen in NFL," *The New York Times* (13 September 2010).

[2] Ursula Reutin, "New Football Helmets Give a False Sense of Security," KIRO Radio (28 March 2011).

[3] A.M. Dowell III and D.C. Hendershot, "No Good Deed Goes Unpunished: Case Studies of Incidents and Potential Incidents Caused by Protective Systems," *Process Safety Progress* 16, No. 3 (Fall 1997).

[4] "Outdoor Lighting and Crime: Is there a Connection?" *Selene* (April 2004). www.selene-ny.org.

[5] Rita Rubin, "Driving Study Deals Blow to Hands-Free Phones," *USA Today* (10 March 2008).

[6] Kendra Cherry, "What Is An Illusory Correlation?" *About.com.* http://psychology.about.com/od/iindex/g/illusory-correlation.htm.

[7] See Note 3.

[8] Maia Szalavitz, "10 Ways We Get the Odds Wrong," *Psychology Today* (1 January 2008). www.psychologytoday.com/articles/200712/10-ways-we-get-the-odds-wrong.

[9] Susan Phillips, "False Alarms Lull Residents into a False Sense of Security," *Newsworks* (4 March 2011).

[10] "Expert: TSA Screening Is Security Theater," *CBS News* (31 July 2009). www.cbsnews.com/stories/2008/12/18/60minutes/main4675524.shtml.

[11] Jeff Wise, "Security and Terrorism Expert Bruce Schneier: TSA Scans 'Won't Catch Anybody,'" *Popular Mechanics* (10 November 2010). www.popularmechanics.com/technology/military/news/tsa-scans-security-theater-interview.

[12] "Airport Body Scanners 'Unlikely' to Foil al-QaedaMP," *BBC News* (4 January 2010). http://news.bbc.co.uk/2/hi/uk_news/8439285.stm.

Chapter 7: The Law of Recall: Taking It from the Top

[1] "Boy Mauled by Shark Still Faces Difficulties," *St. Petersburg Times* (6 July 2004).

[2] Wikipedia.org, "Summer of the Shark." http://en.wikipedia.org/wiki/summer_of_the_shark.

[3] Ibid.

[4] Jeordan Legon, "Survey: 'Shark Summer' Bred Fear, Not Facts," *CNN* (14 March 2003).

[5] Raymond S. Nickerson, *Cognition and Chance: The Psychology of Probabilistic Reasoning* (Hillsdale, NJ: Lawrence Erlbaum Associates, 2004), p. 371. www.questia.com/PM.qst?a=o&d=105969568.

[6] Amos Tversky and Daniel Kahneman, "Judgment under Uncertainty: Heuristics and Biases," *Science* 185 (1974): 1124–1131.

[7] Amir Efrati, Scott Thurm, and Dionne Searcey, "Mobile-App Makers Face US Privacy Investigation," *The Wall Street Journal* (5 April 2011).

[8]Tomi Ahonen, "Everything You Ever Wanted to Know about Mobile but Were Afraid to Ask," *Communities Dominate Brands* blog. http://communities-dominate .blogs.com/brands/1010/05/everything-you-ever-wanted-to-know-about-mobile- but-were-afraid-to-ask.html.

[9]Tara Parker-Pope and Felicity Barringer, "Cellphone Radiation May Cause Cancer, Advisory Panel Says," *The New York Times* (1 July 2011).

[10]Michael Murray, "Study Finds Cellphones May Cause Cancer, but Brain Cancers Have Not Spiked," *ABC News* (1 June 2011). http://abcnews.go.com/US/cellphones- cancer-brain-cancers-spiked/story?id=13737320.

[11]See Note 8.

[12]See Note 8.

Chapter 8: Rationalization: Finding Harmony in the Discord

[1]"Chicago Saved by 'Reprieve' Claims Savant," *Lodi News-Sentinel* (22 December 1954).

[2]Wikipedia.org, ("When Prophecy Fails"). http://en.wikipedia.org/wiki/ when_prophecy_fails.

[3]LaPiereFirmin, Michael W., "Commentary: The Seminal Contribution of Richard LaPiere's Attitudes vs. Actions (1934) Research Study", International Journal of Epidemiology, Volume 39, Issue 1, pp 18-20, First published online January 2010.

[4]S.M. Corey, "Professed Attitudes and Actual Behavior," *Journal of Educational Psychology* 28 (1937): 271–280.

[5]"Calmly Await the End," *Tri-City Herald* (21 December 1954): 2.

[6]Adam Liptak, "Justices Reject Ban on Violent Video Games for Children," *The New York Times* (27 June 2011). www.nytimes.com/2011/06/28/us/28scotus .html?pagewanted=all.

[7]Ibid.

[8]Nicholas L. Carnagey, Craig A. Anderson, and Brad J. Bushman, "The Effect of Video Game Violence on Physiological Desensitization to Real-Life Violence," *Journal of Experimental Social Psychology* 43 (2007): 489–496. www.psychology.iastate.edu/ faculty/caa/abstracts/2005-2009/07CAB.pdf.

[9]Jeanne Funk, Heidi Bechtoldt Baldacci, Tracie Pasold, and Jennifer Baumgardner, "Violence Exposure in Real-Life, Video Games, Television, Movies, and the Internet: Is There Desensitization?" *Journal of Adolescence* 27 (2004): 23–39. http://videogames .procon.org/sourcefiles/Empathy.pdf.

[10]Stacy L. Smith, Emily Moyer-Gusé, and Edward Donnerstein, "Media Violence and Sex: What Are the Concerns, Issues and Effects?" *The SAGE Handbook of Media Studies*, ed. John D.H. Downing et al. (Thousand Oaks, CA: SAGE Publications, 2004), 541–568. www.sagepub.com/mcquail6/PDF/Chapter%2026%20-%20The%20SAGE%20Handbook%20of%20Media%20Studies.pdf.

[11]Karen Dill, "How Fantasy Becomes Reality," *Psychology Today* blog (27 June 2011). www.psychologytoday.com/blog/how-fantasy-becomes-reality/201106/sex-is-too-obscene-kids-violence-isnt-brown-v-entertainment-.

[12]See Note 6.

Chapter 9: Teenage Growing Pains

[1]Wikipedia.org, "Mean Girls." http://en.wikipedia.org/wiki/mean_girls.

[2]Rosalind Wiseman, "Girls' Cliques: What Role Does Your Daughter Play?" *iVillage* (17 May 2002). www.ivillage.com/girls-cliques-what-role-does-your-daughter-play/6-a-144522.

[3]Amy Bellows, "Your Teen's Search for Identity," *Psych Central* (2007). http://psychcentral.com/lib/2007/your-teens-search-for-identity/.

[4]Rick Nauert, "Teens' Perception of Popularity Is Important," *Psych Central* (19 May 2008). http://psychcentral.com/news/2008/05/19/teens-perception-of-popularity-is-important/2312.html.

[5]Ibid.

[6]Wikipedia.org, "16 and Pregnant." http://en.wikipedia.org/wiki/16_and_pregnant.

[7]See Note 3.

[8]Wikipedia.org, "Stanford Prison Experiment." http://en.wikipedia.org/wiki/stanford_prison_experiment.

[9]Ibid.

[10]Anthony Karge, "Expert: Parents Need to Help End Bullying," *WestportPatch* (30 March 2011). http://westport.patch.com/articles/expert-parents-need-to-help-end-bullying.

[11]Wikipedia.org, "Suicide of Ryan Halligan." http://wikipedia.org/wiki/ryan_halligan.

[12] "More Quotes from Women," *The River*. www.river.org/~dhawk/qwomen.html.

[13]Bradford D. Smart, *Topgrading: How Leading Companies Win by Hiring, Coaching and Keeping the Best People* (New York: Penguin, 2005).

[14]Keith Hampton, Lauren Sessions Goulet, Lee Rainie, and Kristen Purcell, "Social Networking Sites and Our Lives," *PewInternet* (16 June 2011). http://pewinternet .org/Reports/2011/Technology-and-social-networks.aspx.

[15]Sean Banville, "Do You Suffer from Facebook Depression?" *Breaking News English* (1 April 2011). www.breakingnewsenglish.com/1104/110401-facebook_ depression.html.

[16]See Note 14.

[17]Tom Cheredar, "Q&A Social Network Formspring.me Reaches 25M Users," *SocialBeat* (28 June 2011). http://venturebeat.com/2011/06/28/formspring-me-reaches-25m-users-infographic/.

Chapter 10: Emerging Adulthood: In Search of the Ideal

[1]"Erik Erikson," *NNDB*. www.nndb.com/people/151/000097857.

[2]Robin Marantz Henig, "What Is It about 20-Somethings?" *The New York Times* (18 August 2010).

[3]Ibid.

[4]Ibid.

[5]Ibid.

[6]Ibid.

[7]Stephanie Cosner Berzin and Allison C. De Marco, "Understanding the Impact of Poverty on Critical Events in Emerging Adulthood," *Youth & Society* (23 November 2009). http://yas.sagepub.com/content/42/2/278.abstract.

[8]Jim Dwyer, "Four Nerds and a Cry to Arms against Facebook," *The New York Times* (11 May 2010). www.nytimes.com/2010/05/12/nyregion/12about.html.

[9]Emily Nussbaum, "Defacebook," *New York Magazine* (26 September 2010). http://nymag.com/news/features/establishments/68512/.

[10]Ibid.

[11]Maxwell Salzberg, *Diaspora* blog entry (1 June 2011). http://blog.joindiaspora .com/2011/06/01/graphs-graphs-graphs.html.

[12]See Note 9.

Chapter 11: The "Meet" Market

[1]Bernard Berk, "Face-Saving at the Singles Dance," *Social Problems* 24, no. 5 (June 1977): 530–544. www.jstor.org/stable/800123.

[2]Wikipedia.org, "Social Exchange Theory." http://en.wikipedia.org/wiki/social_exchange_theory.

[3]Ibid.

[4]Douglas Kenrick, "Do Women's Pheromones Trigger Economic Riskiness in Men?" *Psychology Today* (28 February 2011).

[5]Nicolas Gueguen, "Brief Report: The Effects of Women's Cosmetics on Men's Approach: An Evaluation in a Bar," *North American Journal of Psychology* (March 2008).

[6]Linda Carroll, "The Pill Makes Women Pick 'Dad' over the 'Cad'," *MSNBC* (8 October 2009). www.msnbc.msn.com/id/33199927/ns/health-womens_health/t/pill-makes-women-pick-dad-over-cad/.

[7]Matt Withers, "Men Who Drive Flash Cars Really ARE More Attractive to Women, Say Welsh Academics," WalesOnline.co.uk (24 March 2009). www.walesonline.co.uk/news/wales-news/2009/03/24/men-who-drive-flash-cars-really-are-more-attractive-to-women-say-welsh-academics-91466-23217419/.

[8]See Note 1.

[9]Wikipedia.org, "Opportunity Cost." http://en.wikipedia.org/wiki/opportunity_cost.

[10]John Galt, "Understanding Mental Health: What Is Propinquity?" *Yahoo!* (20 February 2008).

[11]Hara Estroff Marano, "The Expectations Trap: Why We're Conditioned to Blame Our Partners for Our Unhappiness," *Psychology Today* (1 March 2010).

[12]Andrew Springer and Alex Stone, "Woman Suing Match.com over Alleged Assault Comes Forward," *ABC News* (19 April 2011). http://abcnews.go.com/US/woman-suing-match-alleged-assault-forward/story?id=13407806.

[13]"Match.com Study: 17% of Married Couples Met on a Dating Site," *Online Personals Watch* (20 April 2010). www.onlinepersonalswatch.com/news/2010/04/matchcom-study-17-of-married-couples-met-on-a-dating-site.html.

[14]Doug Gross, "Japanese Lab Invents Internet Kissing Machine," *CNN* (5 May 2011). http://articles.cnn.com/2011-05-05/tech/computer.kiss.device_1_kiss-device-tongue?_s=PM:TECH.

Chapter 12: The Parent Puzzle

[1]Paul Monaco, *The Sixties, 1960–1969* (Berkeley, CA: University of California Press, 2003).

[2]Barbara Lang, "And Now He (She) Drives," *The New York Times* (8 November 1964).

[3]Ibid.

[4]Ibid.

[5]Ibid.

[6]Robert David Jafee, " 'Facebook Depression': Do You Have It?" *Huffington Post* (30 March 2011). www.huffingtonpost.com/robert-david-jaffee/facebook-depression_b_841794.html.

[7]Dorthe Flauer, "Avoiding Video Game Addiction," *Sherwood Park News* (March 2011). www.sherwoodparknews.com/ArticleDisplay .aspx?archive=true&e=3048279.

[8] "The Secret Online Lives of Teens," *McAfee.com* (2010). http://us.mcafee.com/ en-us/local/docs/lives_of_teens.pdf.

[9] "Family Becomes Victim of Identity Theft through Son's Xbox," *WCNC* (29 March 2011). wcnc.com/news/local/Mom-becomes-victim-of-identity-theft-through-sons-Xbox-118833304.html.

[10]Lori Gottlieb, "How to Land Your Kid in Therapy," *The Atlantic* (25 August 2011). www.theatlantic.com/magazine/archive/2011/07/how-to-land-your-kid-in-therapy/8555/.

Chapter 13: The Midlife Rebirth

[1]"Debating Our Destiny: The Second 1984 Presidential Debate, October 28, 1984." http://www.pbs.org/newshour/debatingourdestiny/84debates/2prez2.html.

[2]Wikipedia.org, "Julia Child." http://en.wikipedia.org/wiki/julia_child.

[3]ToKnowInfo [anonymous blogger], "Success StoriesNever Too Old, Never Too Late: Late Bloomers' Dreams and Achievements," *HubPages.* http://hubpages.com/ hub/Success-Stories-Never-Too-Old-Never-Too-Late-Late-Bloomers-Dreams-and-Achievements.

[4]Sally Squires, "Midlife without a Crisis," *Washington Post* (19 April 1999), p. Z20.

[5]Erica Mina Okada and Stephen J. Hoch, "Spending Time versus Spending Money," *The Journal of Consumer Research* 31, no. 2 (September 2004): 313–323.

[6]See Note 4.

[7] "Commencement Student Speaker Finds Success Later in Life," *EMCC News* (3 May 2011). http://news.estrellamountain.edu/2011/05/03/verta-tucker.

[8]Richard Duckett, "A Dream Job at Midlife; Worcester Native Mixes Love of Music and Family to Form Nateva Festival," *Worcester Telegram & Gazette* (25 June 2010).

[9]John Cromartie and Peter Nelson, "Baby Boom Migration and Its Impact on Rural America," *U.S. Department of Agriculture Economic Research Report* Number 79 (August 2009). www.ers.usda.gov/Publications/ERR79/ERR79.pdf.

[10]Rich Karlgaard, *Life 2.0: How People Across America Are Transforming Their Lives by Finding the Where of Their Happiness* (New York: Three Rivers Press, 2004).

Epilogue: Who Are We Becoming?

[1]Jeremy N. Bailenson and Jim Blascovich, "Virtual Reality and Social Networks Will Be a Powerful Combination," *IEEE Spectrum* (June 2011). http://spectrum.ieee.org/telecom/internet/virtual-reality-and-social-networks-will-be-a-powerful-combination.

[2]Peter Cohen, "Guinness Awards 'Fastest Selling Device' Moniker to Kinect, Not iPad," *The Loop* (10 March 2011). www.loopinsight.com/2011/03/10/guinness-awards-fastest-selling-device-moniker-to-kinect-not-ipad/.

[3]Andrei Dobra, "Kinect Developers Are Now Unlocking Full Sensor Potential, Microsoft Says," *Softpedia* (24 June 2011). http://news.softpedia.com/news/Kinect-Developers-Are-Now-Unlocking-Full-Sensor-Potential-Microsoft-Says-207878.shtml.

[4]See Note 1.

INDEX